CONDEMNED TO DIE

Condemned to Die is a book about life under sentence of death in American prisons. The great majority of condemned prisoners are confined on death rows before they are executed. Death rows typically feature solitary confinement, a harsh regimen that is closely examined in this book. Death rows that feature solitary confinement are most common in states that execute prisoners with regularity, which is to say, where there is a realistic threat that condemned prisoners will be put to death. Less restrictive confinement conditions for condemned prisoners can be found in states where executions are rare. Confinement conditions matter, especially to prisoners, but a central contention of this book is that *no* regimen of confinement under sentence of death offers its inmates a round of activity that might in *any* way prepare them for the ordeal they must face in the execution chamber, when they are put to death. In a basic and profound sense, *all* condemned prisoners are warehoused for death in the shadow of the executioner. Human warehousing, seen most clearly on solitary confinement death rows, violates every tenet of just punishment; no legal or philosophical justification for capital punishment demands or even permits warehousing of prisoners under sentence of death. The punishment is death. There is neither a mandate nor a justification for harsh and dehumanizing confinement before the prisoner is put to death. Yet warehousing for death, of an empty and sometimes brutal nature, is the universal fate of condemned prisoners. The enormous suffering and injustice caused by this human warehousing, rendered in the words of the prisoners themselves, is the subject of this book.

Robert Johnson is a professor of justice, law and criminology at American University, editor and publisher at BleakHouse Publishing, and an award-winning author of books and articles on crime and punishment, including works of social science, law, poetry, and fiction. He has written four social science books, including *Condemned to Die: Life Under Sentence of Death* and *Death Work: A Study of the Modern Execution Process*, which received the Outstanding Book Award of the Academy of Criminal Justice Sciences. Johnson has edited six social science books, including *Life Without Parole: Living and Dying in Prison Today* and *A Woman Doing Life: Notes from a Prison for Women*. Johnson has published extensively in professional journals, including law reviews, and has testified or provided expert affidavits on capital and other cases before U.S. state and federal courts, the U.S. Congress, and the European Commission of Human Rights. Johnson's scholarship also features creative writing on crime and punishment. He is the author of one novel, *Miller's Revenge*; four collections of original poems, most recently, *A Zoo Near You*; and one anthology of fiction, *Lethal Rejection: Stories on Crime and Punishment*. Johnson's fiction has appeared in literary and fine arts publications. His short story, "The Practice of Killing," won a national fiction contest sponsored by *Wild Violet* magazine. Another short story, "Cell Buddy," was adapted for the stage and read at the Kennedy Center in Washington, DC. Johnson's independent literary press, BleakHouse Publishing, features creative writing, art, and photography on matters relating to social justice, showcasing the work of a wide range of writers and artists, among which are included current and former American University students as well as current and former state and federal prisoners. He is a Distinguished Alumnus of the School of Criminal Justice, Nelson A. Rockefeller College of Public Affairs and Policy, University at Albany, State University of New York.

Johnson's study is widely acknowledged to be the closest anyone can come to an inside view of capital punishment, and the report of his study exemplifies the best any of us could hope to achieve in trying to convey the depth and import of significant human experiences, and in both capacities this book has been, and remains, a classic.

Hans Toch, Emeritus Distinguished Professor of Criminal Justice
University at Albany, State University of New York
Author of Living in Prison: The Ecology of Survival

If more people in our society understood the true nature of the death-sentencing process in our society—how it actually operates and what it necessarily entails—and came to terms with, as Camus said, what the death penalty "really is," as opposed to the "padded words," myth, and misinformation with which it is typically depicted, then the practice would have ended a long time ago. Robert Johnson's extraordinary book brings us much closer to that enlightened understanding.

Craig Haney, Distinguished Professor of Psychology, University of
California Presidential Chair, 2015–2018

Perhaps the most cruel and unusual aspect about capital punishment in the United States is what Robert Johnson, in this second edition of his classic, *Condemned to Die*, characterizes as the "living death" of life under sentence of death. This book is an essential resource for anyone seeking a full understanding of the death penalty in America today.

Robert Bohm, Emeritus Professor of Criminal Justice
University of Central Florida
Author of DeathQuest: An Introduction to the Theory and Practice of
Capital Punishment in the United States

Prisoners, especially those on death row, are subject to a huge amount of abuse. Their abusers require two things be in place to get away with torture: The prisoners they abuse must be viewed by the larger society as less than human, as animals even; and the abuse must be secret, invisible to the general public. Robert Johnson exposes and undermines both prerequisites for abuse by letting prisoners on death row tell their stories, very human stories filled with multiple traumas; and by unblinkingly presenting the harsh reality of life on "the row." *Condemned to Die* is a very well researched and poignant book, and absolutely a must-read for all those who oppose torture and value freedom.

Terry A. Kupers, M.D., M.S.P. The Wright Institute
Author of Solitary: The Inside Story of Supermax Isolation and How We Can Abolish It

Once again, Robert Johnson has given a voice to broken men who the state wishes to obliterate. He challenges us to recognize the inherent dignity of death row residents by making us privy to their fears, hopes and daily troubles. This project of rehumanization is vitally important if the cruelty and toxicity of capital punishment are to be laid bare. It is to be hoped that *Condemned to Die* will add momentum to the drive to eradicate an abhorrent—and increasingly anachronistic—practice.

Ian O'Donnell, Professor of Criminology, University College Dublin.
Author of Prisoners, Solitude, and Time

This new edition of Robert Johnson's *Condemned to Die* takes the reader deep into the world of Alabama's death row in 1978, while bridging the gap between now and then with critical insight and humane sensitivity. An invaluable resource for anyone who wants to understand the death penalty in America.

Lisa Guenther, Queen's National Scholar in Political Philosophy and Critical Prison Studies at Queen's University, Canada Author of Solitary Confinement: Social Death and Its Afterlives

Professor Robert Johnson's exploration of life on death row simultaneously condemns as torture solitary confinement and capital punishment. Beautifully written, compellingly argued and researched, this is the essential study of how human rights should be enlisted in the legal reform of our most onerous punishments: death row and execution.

Fred Cohen, Professor Emeritus, SUNY@Albany, School of Criminal Justice

The view from death row narrated by Robert Johnson in *Condemned to Die*, largely through the voices of those who experience it, is a compelling but difficult read. Puncturing some of the myths about the individuals consigned to a "living death," Johnson shines a light into the very deepest corners of the American penal system, exposing both its horrors and the resourcefulness and dignity of the human beings who endure extreme confinement. The exquisitely cruel journey from conviction to execution—or in some cases, simply interminable years of languishing in conditions of social and material deprivation—that Johnson subtly guides us through, rightly interrogates a punishment that serves no proportionate penological purpose. Powerful and affecting, this book will leave a lasting impression.

Yvonne Jewkes, Professor of Criminology, University of Bath

Condemned to Die is an exceptionally powerful and important book. By building a detailed, first-hand account of the everyday and existential anguish of being a death row prisoner, Johnson makes a compelling case for the abolition of capital punishment, while providing exceptional insight into the nature of humanity and tragedy, survival and deterioration, and hope and despair.

Ben Crewe, Deputy Director of the Prisons Research Centre, University of Cambridge

In this classic, groundbreaking work, Johnson exposes the agony and cruelty of what passes for life on death row—as Johnson calls it, a "grave for the living." As demonstrated in this revised edition, this "psychological nightmare" has only gotten worse in recent decades as the agonizing wait for death has grown even longer for most prisoners. As difficult as it is to contemplate these horrors, *Condemned to Die* should be read by all those who oppose the death penalty or students who want to understand it better. Yet, more importantly, it should be required reading for death penalty supporters. Few could maintain such views in light of this powerful research.

Shadd Maruna, author of Making Good: How Ex-Convicts Reform and Rebuild Their Lives

Robert Johnson's *Condemned to Die* is a beautiful if devastating deep excavation of the lives buried behind the multiple concrete walls and steel locks of America's death rows. The book is compelling, uncovering vivid life stories and horrific traumas, told often in the voices of the prisoners and the condemned themselves. With careful integration of social theory, contextual statistics, and other studies of prison conditions and death row experiences, however, Johnson avoids the sensationalism of reality television or true crime novels. A must-read for those who care about criminal justice policy, those who want to understand the experience of the deepest end of incarceration, and those who are interested in re-thinking the meaning of cruel and unusual punishment.

Keramet Reiter, Associate Professor, University of California, Irvine

CONDEMNED TO DIE

Life Under Sentence of Death

Second Edition

Robert Johnson

Routledge
Taylor & Francis Group

NEW YORK AND LONDON

Second edition published 2019
by Routledge
52 Vanderbilt Avenue, New York, NY 10017

and by Routledge
2 Park Square, Milton Park, Abingdon, Oxon, OX14 4RN

Routledge is an imprint of the Taylor & Francis Group, an informa business

© 2019 Taylor & Francis

[First edition published by Elsevier Science Ltd 1981]

Library of Congress Cataloging-in-Publication Data
Names: Johnson, Robert, 1948– author.
Title: Condemned to die : life under sentence of death / Robert Johnson.
Description: 2 Edition. | New York : Routledge, [2019] |
    Revised edition of the author's Condemned to die, c1981. |
    Includes index.
Identifiers: LCCN 2018038991 (print) | LCCN 2018041230 (ebook) |
    ISBN 9781351112390 (Ebook) | ISBN 9780815362333 (hardback) |
    ISBN 9780815362395 (pbk.) | ISBN 9781351112390 (ebk)
Subjects: LCSH: Death row inmates—United States.
Classification: LCC HV8699.U5 (ebook) | LCC HV8699.U5 J64 2019
    (print) | DDC 364.660973—dc23
LC record available at https://lccn.loc.gov/2018038991

ISBN: 978-0-8153-6233-3 (hbk)
ISBN: 978-0-8153-6239-5 (pbk)
ISBN: 978-1-351-11239-0 (ebk)

Typeset in Bembo
by Swales & Willis Ltd, Exeter, Devon, UK

To the newest members of our family, Aya and Aaron, our first grandchildren. May we all be treasured by our loved ones.

To our sons, Brian and Patrick, now proud fathers.

To our daughters-in-law, Kyoko and Alison, now proud mothers.

To my remarkable wife, Deirdra McLaughlin, whose love and support give meaning to my life.

CONTENTS

ACKNOWLEDGMENTS

I am grateful to several dedicated and talented students in the Department of Justice, Law and Criminology at American University, my academic home. Most notable among these remarkable scholars are Casey Chiappetta, who reviewed this book in its entirely and provided a raft of helpful comments about style and insightful comments about substance; Gabe Whitbread, who offered thoughtful remarks on research and theory in relation to the various pathways leading to death row and the corollary issues relating to culpability; and Jacqueline Lantsman and Alyssa Purdy, whose research on death row blogs and confinement conditions, respectively, provided a valuable context for understanding some of the patterns examined in this book. I thank Robert Bohm (Foreword) and Craig Haney (Afterword), noted authorities on the death penalty, for taking time out of their busy schedules to write thoughtful and evocative essays for the book, to my edification and that of my students and readers. I also thank fellow scholars who reviewed the book closely and provided generous appraisals: Terry Kupers, Yvonne Jewkes, Ian O'Donnell, Fred Cohen, Shadd Maruna, Lisa Guenther, Keramet Reiter, Thomas Zeitzoff, and Hans Toch. I owe a special thanks to my mentor, Hans Toch, whose work and sensibility has always been an inspiration to me.

THE SMELL CAME

On August 28, 1987, there was the sound of a generator kicking on and then hissing and popping, and the lights in the hall outside my cell flickered on and off. And then through the night, the smell came. It's hard to explain what death smells like, but it burned my nose and stung my throat and made my eyes water and my stomach turn over. I spent the next day dry heaving, my stomach retching and twisting. All up and down the row, you could hear men blowing their noses, trying to get the smell away. There was no real ventilation or air circulation, so the smell of death—like a mixture of shit and rotting waste and vomit all mixed up in a thick smoke of putrid air that you couldn't escape—seemed to settle into my hair and in my throat and mouth. I rubbed at my eyes until they were red and gritty. I heard one of the guys complain to the guard about the smell.

"You'll get used to it." The guard laughed. "Next year or one of these days, somebody's going to be smelling you just the same. What do you think you gonna smell like to everyone? Not too good."

Anthony Ray Hinton
Former Alabama death row inmate, 1987–2015
Exonerated April 3, 2015

FOREWORD

The degree of civilization in a society can be judged by entering its prisons.

(Fydor Dostoevsky, 1862)

The mood and temper of the public in regard to the treatment of crime and criminals is one of the most unfailing tests of the civilization of any country.

(Winston Churchill, 1910)

It is said that no one truly knows a nation until one has been inside its jails. A nation should not be judged by how it treats its highest citizens, but its lowest ones.

(Nelson Mandela, 2002)

Perhaps the most cruel and unusual aspect about capital punishment in the United States—more so than execution itself—and one that receives little attention, is the death row experience, or, what Robert Johnson, in this second edition of his classic, *Condemned to Die*, characterizes as a "living death." For Johnson, death row is where condemned prisoners are "warehoused for death" and further "dehumanized." Currently, death row inmates average more than 15 years on death row before execution. Some inmates have spent nearly four decades on death row. Until the late 1950s, by contrast, death row inmates were often executed within a matter of months. The problem—among many other problems—is that more than 90 percent of death rows (so-called "solitary-cell death rows," such as those in the major executing states of Texas, Florida, Virginia, Alabama, and Oklahoma) were never intended to house inmates for long periods of time. They were not designed and built with long-term incarceration in mind. They were intended as relatively short-term holding facilities for prisoners awaiting execution. As a consequence, death row inmates today experience physical and psychological trauma, or what has been called the "death row phenomenon" and the "death row syndrome," which was largely unknown to former inmates who were executed following much shorter death row stays.[1]

Until recently, little was known about the death row experience beyond anecdotal stories that conveyed the uniformly terrible, and, as has been argued here and there, unconstitutional conditions in which inmates await their executions. So far, the U.S. Supreme Court has not upheld challenges to long stays on death row, the execution of elderly and infirm death row inmates, or death row conditions. Few systematic studies of death row conditions exist. A notable exception is described in this book—first published in 1981, reissued with changes in 1989, and now reissued and updated for a third time for a new generation. Johnson's pioneering and compelling exposition of life on Alabama's death row during the late 1970s remains one of the best accounts of death row conditions, *as experienced by death row inmates themselves.*

Part of the fascination with Johnson's research is his face-to-face interviews with 35 of the 37 inmates then on Alabama's death row. As anyone who has attempted to conduct research in prisons or in the inner sanctum of prisons—death rows—knows, they are difficult research settings to penetrate. Corrections officials do not like or want the public and especially researchers prying into their domains. That is why so little empirical research is conducted in those venues and with those populations. Johnson's good luck was that he had conducted research on the psychology of solitary confinement (uncommon, at that time) and was referred to one of the attorneys in an Alabama case challenging death row conditions (serendipity strikes again!). The attorney hired him to conduct the court-ordered interviews and write a report. At the time, Johnson was a young assistant professor with an academic interest in prisons and the death penalty, who was given the plum but terrifying assignment of meeting face-to-face with presumably the "worst of the worst" inmates in Alabama's prison system. As it turned out, he would meet alone with the inmates in a locked room with a window looking into the execution chamber and "Yellow Mama"—Alabama's electric chair. Trepidation aside, Johnson carefully plotted a strategy that involved gaining rapport with his subjects by smoking cigarettes with them and giving them cigarettes—the standard currency in prisons at that time (remember it was 1978!)—to keep. Most of the interviews, it appears, were conducted in a cloud of smoke. Despite the challenges, Johnson was able to gather candid and thoughtful responses to his many open-ended questions, as the direct quotes in this book attest. In this edition, Johnson extends his narrative by evaluating his main findings in the context of subsequent research on the subject, as sparse as it is. Newer studies, we learn, corroborate his earlier work.

Such corroboration is helpful. A problem with generalizing the results of Johnson's research to the contemporary situation is that the inmates interviewed by Johnson had served relatively short periods of time on Alabama's death row, in comparison to today's death row inmates. Johnson conducted his research at the end of the most momentous decade in death penalty annals—the 1970s. In 1972, following a series of challenges to various aspects of capital punishment, the U.S. Supreme Court (the "Court") decided in *Furman v. Georgia* that the death penalty, as then administered, violated the U.S. Constitution's Eighth (cruel and unusual punishment) and Fourteenth (due process) Amendments, mostly because it was applied arbitrarily. Thus, for the first and only time in U.S. history the death penalty had been abolished, albeit for only four short years. A direct consequence of the *Furman* decision was that Alabama's death row, like all death rows in the United States, was emptied of inmates, who either had their death sentences commuted to a term of years, were given new sentencing hearings, or were paroled. A second consequence of the *Furman* decision was that the Alabama legislature, like most of the other state legislatures that had their death penalty laws invalidated, passed a new death penalty law designed to meet the new requirements set forth by the Court, and Alabama state courts, like most other state courts in death penalty states, began sentencing offenders to death based on the new statute. In 1976, the Court heard challenges to the new death penalty statutes and decided, in *Gregg v. Georgia* and companion cases, that some of the statutes—those that guided judges (at the time) and jurors in their sentencing decision— were acceptable because, the majority believed (without any evidence to support their belief), that the guidelines would reduce arbitrariness in death sentencing to a constitutionally acceptable level. (On the same day the Court decided *Gregg*, it rejected statutes that mandated the death penalty upon conviction of a capital offense.) Thus, with *Gregg*, the Court reinstated the death penalty. Alabama quickly passed its new death penalty statute in 1976, and executed its first death row inmate based on the new statute in 1983. When Johnson conducted his interviews with Alabama death row inmates (September 1978), none had been executed, and the longest an inmate had spent on death row was approximately three years—much shorter than the average of 15 years today. Consequently, the death row experience of Johnson's death row inmates may not have been representative of the experience of today's death row inmates, whose experience on death row most likely is much worse.

If the death row experience today is more severe than when Johnson conducted his interviews—it certainly is longer—then his narrative is even more alarming. The "living death," by which he characterizes life on most death rows, is, according to him, rooted in three main factors: (1) powerlessness, (2) fear, and (3) emotional emptiness or emotional death. "Powerlessness" refers to the feeling that a person cannot "influence significant aspects of the living environment or fight back and gain autonomy." The result is a sense of helplessness and defeat. "Fear" is the inability of a person "to defend himself against danger, or to ignore perceived threats or occasions of danger." Fear elicits a sense of vulnerability. "Emotional emptiness" or "emotional death" occurs when a person "is beyond the reach and support of significant others and has been abandoned or forgotten by them and the free community in general." With emotional emptiness or emotional death, inmates experience loneliness, a deadening of feelings for self and others, and a decrease in mental and physical acuity, which, in turn, causes apathy, passivity, and decay. All three factors combine to produce the "death row phenomenon" or the "death row syndrome." Based on my own research and experience; especially my recent visit to Florida State Prison's death row, I, too, can corroborate much of Johnson's account, at least as it applies to the many older death rows still in use. On those death rows, conditions have not changed much during the past four decades.

In the updated last chapter of his book, Johnson reluctantly offers reforms that he believes would make life on death row less cruel and damaging to the inmates. Among his suggestions are: (1) classification of death row inmates and their assignment to different, more humane living arrangements; (2) special work or study programs to reduce loneliness and boredom; (3) visits, including contact visits, to sustain emotional ties with family and friends; (4) expanded recreational opportunities with supervised small group activities; and (5) self-help activities and programs to help manage stress. The reason Johnson made his recommendations reluctantly (perhaps his publisher requested them) is that he believes that reforming death rows is like "putting lipstick on a pig." My analogy, not his! Pigs (death rows) can be made prettier (more hospitable) with lipstick, but they are still pigs (death rows).

An alternative to solitary-cell death rows, which to some extent are the death rows of Johnson's reforms, is "congregate-solitary death rows." In these death rows, such as those in North Carolina and Utah, inmates remain isolated from the larger prison population but are allowed to leave their cells during the day, sometimes for many hours, and gather in small groups in dayrooms on the pod or tier in which they are housed. The major problem with congregate-solitary death rows is that research shows they are not much better than solitary-cell death rows. As Johnson states, "Death rows . . . even the best of them, are human warehouses that impose . . . [a] regime of confinement that amounts to torture"— the hallmark of which is dehumanization. "Congregate solitary confinement," maintains Johnson, "is a psychological nightmare that very few survive." For Johnson, then, death rows, in whatever form, are inherently cruel and torturous places and, thus, in violation of the Eighth Amendment's prohibition of cruel and, yes, unusual punishment.

Another alternative to both solitary-cell and congregate-solitary death rows is an institution modeled after Missouri's maximum-security Potosi Correctional Institution (PCI), which "mainstreams" or fully integrates most death-sentenced inmates with non–death-sentenced inmates in the general prison population. Since 1989, PCI has housed only three types of inmates: (1) those who have been sentenced to death, (2) those who have been sentenced to life imprisonment without parole (LWOP) for first-degree murder, and (3) those who have been sentenced to a parole-eligible term, usually of at least 50 years. Research shows that integrating these inmates does not appear to cause inflated security problems. According to an important study by Mark Cunningham, Thomas Reidy, and Jon Sorensen, over an 11-year period (1989–2002), none of the death-sentenced inmates at PCI killed or attempted to kill another inmate or staff member. Furthermore, the rates of major and minor assaults of death-sentenced inmates were no higher than the rates of LWOP inmates and were 20 to 25 percent lower than the rates of inmates serving parole-eligible terms. The researchers also found that the PCI "mainstreaming" model, compared to maintaining a separate solitary-cell death row, provided the state long-term cost savings of about 50 percent. Despite the apparent advantages of the PCI model, Johnson finds it wanting. He notes that the PCI model, like death rows, does nothing to meaningfully prepare inmates for the threat of execution. He points out that the psychological effects of this type of confinement have not been studied, so how death row inmates experience being mainstreamed into the general prison population is unknown. Finally, he argues that most maximum-security prisons, though less repressive and dehumanizing than death rows, are still human warehouses. Thus, for Johnson, there likely is no humane way to house inmates awaiting execution.

On the surface, then, one can think of *Condemned to Die* as a fascinating history of Alabama's death row 40 years ago. If it were just that, the book would be an invaluable historical resource about an institution most people can only imagine. However, the book has much more to offer. For example, in his second chapter entitled "Pathways to Death Row," Johnson uses his interviewee's demographic data and life experiences, as well as previous research, to present an empirically based analysis of who death row inmates are and how they ended up on death row. He begins the chapter with a discussion of the media's role (and the role of some academics) in dehumanizing ("monsterizing") capital offenders and in deceiving the public about who they really are. He points out that the inhabitants of death row are not a monolithic group, though they share some common attributes. Johnson describes:

> Almost without exception, men on death row share a history of deprivation, neglect, and abuse rooted in dysfunctional families and often augmented by harsh punishments meted out in juvenile confinement settings. Severe deficits in socialization and development, often including neurological impairment, are common expressions of the traumas that mark and mar their lives. It appears that the greater the deprivation in terms of abuse and neglect, which in turn is associated with greater neurological impairment, the more heinous the capital crime.

Johnson concludes the chapter with this observation about death row inmates: "There are here no monsters or mutants, no creatures beyond human comprehension, as the media would have it. There are, instead, human violence and human indifference—both on the part of the offenders and the society." His point: Society shares with the capital offender culpability for capital crime. Too many people are blind to this nexus and attribute capital crime to the capital offender alone ("complete culpability"), thereby relieving themselves and society of any responsibility. For Johnson, to condemn the capital offender is to condemn those aspects of society that helped to create that person. Too many people continue to believe the myth that executing a capital offender will somehow significantly reduce the problem of capital (or other) crime. Evidence indicates that it will not. On the other hand, if the conditions that helped produce the capital offender are left unaddressed, then the most likely outcome is more misery for victims, offenders, and the rest of society.

A principal insight of Johnson's research is that not much has changed on death rows in four decades or on the amount of scholarship devoted to the topic. For the most part, death row and the death row experience remains an unexplored feature of the U.S. criminal justice system and that is too bad because, on another level, the way a government treats its presumably worst offenders reflects the fundamental values by which a government and a society operates, as the quotations at the beginning of this Foreword suggest. All three quotations emphasize the deeper meaning of Johnson's scholarship on death rows, and that is: A society cannot claim to be civilized or humane without a thorough understanding of how death rows operate, and their effect on the inmates they confine. Only then can U.S. citizens have an informed debate about whether death rows and, more generally, capital punishment, should exist at all. Johnson's research, insights, and commentary about death row inmates and the death row experience are an essential resource for anyone seeking a full understanding of the death penalty in America today.

Robert M. Bohm
Professor Emeritus
University of Central Florida
May 19, 2018

Note

1 States, in turn, have had to bear the costs and related issues of dealing with an increasingly traumatized death row population. One of the related issues is the question of whether an inmate is "fit" to be executed. Presumably because of the trauma experienced by today's death row inmates, some of them become flagrantly mentally ill and are deemed "unfit" to be executed. To execute them, they must be rehabilitated, which extends their stays on death row even longer, sometimes much longer. An example of this problem is Gary Alvord, who resided on Florida's death row from 1974, until his death from brain cancer in 2013 (39 years!).

PART I

The Death Sentence and the Condemned

Only the ritual of an execution makes it possible to endure. Without it, the condemned could not give the expected measure of cooperation to the etiquette of dying. Without it, we who must preside at their deaths could not face the morning of each new execution day.

Nor could you.

No matter how you think you feel about capital punishment, no matter how you imagine you would face the legal giving or taking of life, you would meet the reality of it by holding tightly to the crutch of ritual.

(Byron Eshelmann, former death row chaplain, San Quentin Prison)

Power, Simone Weil observed, is the capacity to transform a living person into a corpse—that is, into a thing. Through our laws and our electric chairs, we are taking upon ourselves that power. But even if we do so, we cannot forget that as long as they are alive, these condemned men are human. It would be nice if we could get rid of evil by defining it out of the human species, declaring that anyone who does these horrible things is not human. But it will not work. The capacity of man to do evil, no less than good, is what defines us as human.

(Stephen Gettinger, Sentenced to Die, *1979)*

You can't threaten to kill someone every day year after year and not harm them, not traumatize them, not break them in ways that are really profound.

(Bryan Stevenson, Equal Justice Initiative)

1

MAN AGAINST HIMSELF

Studying the Human Dimensions of Capital Punishment

Most Americans support the death penalty. Their reasons vary, but no justification for capital punishment, other than raw vengeance, demands or even permits warehousing of prisoners under sentence of death. The punishment is death. There is neither a mandate nor a justification for harsh and dehumanizing confinement before the prisoner is put to death. Yet warehousing for death, of an empty and sometimes brutal nature, is the universal fate of condemned prisoners. The enormous suffering caused by this human warehousing, rendered in the words of the prisoners themselves, is the subject of this book.

The portrait of life under sentence of death presented in this book is drawn primarily from Alabama's death row, a reasonably representative solitary confinement death row. Most death rows feature solitary confinement in which prisoners are kept in single cells for 22 or more hours a day. Solitary confinement death rows are in fact the standard regime found in active death penalty states, which is to say, states in which executions occur with regularity and in which death row confinement is seen by prisoners and staff alike as "confinement in preparation for execution."[1] In states in which executions are infrequent or even rare, more relaxed death row regimes typically emerge as the expression of reform efforts, often class action suits. These reformed regimes offer what I call congregate solitary confinement, as distinct from the standard individual solitary confinement. In congregate solitary confinement, prisoners are out of their cells for much of the day and thus have more freedom of association, but the group is isolated on death row, away from the main prison population. If solitary confinement death rows are barren warehouses, these reformed death rows are marginally more congenial and accommodating warehouses (though sometimes posing unique problems for staff and inmates alike). Be that as it may, solitary confinement is imposed on *all* condemned prisoners during the death watch, which takes place in the final days and hours before an execution. Thus, it can be said with confidence that "it is *universally* the case that condemned prisoners on the threshold of execution live under conditions of close and restrictive solitary confinement, conditions that have changed little, if at all, from years past."[2]

Like most death rows, then, particularly in states in which executions occur with regularity, Alabama's offers condemned prisoners a regimen of solitary confinement. Alabama prisoners typically spend 22 or more hours a day in their cells; they receive few services and even fewer amenities.[3] The psychological experience is grim, featuring powerlessness, fear, loneliness, and the ever-present threat of decay. "We were all dying from our own fear," observed Hinton, reflecting on his 30 years on death row in Alabama before he was exonerated in 2015, "our minds killing us quicker than the State of Alabama ever could."[4] The Alabama prisoners I interviewed, in words later echoed by Hinton, describe death row as a "living death" that serves as a prelude to death by execution. Prisoners on many other death rows—again, particularly on solitary confinement death rows in states in which executions occur with regularity—share this grim perception.[5]

Some death rows have been reformed since 1981, when the first edition of this book was published. Typical reforms have been modest. Most often, condemned prisoners have been allowed out of their cells for a few hours each day, primarily to socialize with one another in day rooms or recreation cages, or to visit the prison's law library.[6] Personal visits, too, may be made more readily available than in 1981. In limited instances, prisoners and their loved ones may be allowed to have physical contact with one another—to hug and kiss, usually at the beginning and end of a visit, or simply to hold hands. Alabama's death row has been reformed in these ways, though chronic staff shortages regularly undermine these reforms. In the words of a former Alabama death row prisoner, exonerated in 2015 after 30 years on death row: "Holman was always short staffed, and the row was no different . . . It was easier for them to keep us in our cages where we couldn't get into trouble rather than let us out."[7] The resulting daily death row regime is, in practice, something closer to unadulterated solitary confinement, much as existed during the original research undertaken for this book and that exists today on many death rows in other states, most notably Texas' death row, home to the highest execution rate in the nation.[8]

Reforms of death row, even imperfect and unevenly implemented reforms, are laudable on purely humanitarian grounds. I will suggest reforms in the closing pages of this book. But it is doubtful that reforms will substantially improve the quality of life under sentence of death. I will show that death rows may differ in the details of their administration, but no death row—reformed or otherwise—offers its inmates a round of activity that might in *any* way prepare them for the ordeal they must face in the death house.[9] In a basic and profound sense, condemned prisoners are indeed warehoused for death. They languish on death rows, whether they are confined to cells and regimens of confinement that are barren or, by prison standards, gilded. Accordingly, this book is perhaps best understood as a study in the bare essentials of life under sentence of death, written in the hope that it will reveal the essential realities of capital punishment as experienced by condemned prisoners on today's death rows.

Some 2,900 prisoners live under sentence of death in the United States today, most of them confined on death rows that impose a regimen of solitary confinement. The vast majority of condemned prisoners, 98 percent, are men. Since the return of the modern death penalty with the execution of Gary Gilmore in 1976, over 1,476 prisoners have lived and died on America's death rows. Capital punishment is thus an active feature of American justice, and one that disproportionately affects men, though annual rates of capital convictions and executions have been dropping in recent years.[10] Because almost all death row prisoners are men, and all the subjects interviewed for this book are men, this book focuses exclusively on the experiences of men on death row and in the death house.

The ordeal of persons relegated to death row has not been a major concern in the study of the modern death penalty. Prior to the first edition of this book, it was difficult to find systematic descriptions of the death row experience. For the same reason, the impact and consequences of death row confinement were largely unexplored. Even today, the experience of death row confinement has only recently come to figure in some legal considerations of the capital sanction and in discussions of the correctional management of the death row inmate. The courts and legislatures remain primarily concerned with fairness and impartiality in the use of death sentences. Prison officials, for their part, have been constrained to maintain close control of the condemned, which limits the possibility of reforms to death row living environments, and to participate dutifully in the impersonal ritual of execution.[11]

Capital punishment, however, does not only involve handing down sentences and then carrying them out. Death row confinement occurs during the legal appeals process, which can last for years and even decades.[12] The average wait time from sentence to execution today (according to the latest official record) is 15 years and 6 months.[13] This extended period of confinement is a critical time in the lives of condemned men and of growing concern to legal scholars, who have come to understand that death row confinement constitutes a distinctive species of cruelty. This cruelty, I contend, raises Eight Amendment issues that arguably undermine the very legality of this sanction. Information concerning the impact of the death row experience is also relevant to persons involved in writing and implementing capital sentences, as well as to the general public. Legislators, judges, and jurors must fully understand the consequences of their decisions regarding the capital sanction. Correctional managers need such information because they must take responsibility for the care and handling of condemned men. The general public, which sometimes expresses strong feelings on the death penalty and whose views influence policy, may also benefit from a more complete description of the capital punishment process.[14]

Death Row Confinement: Background

Death row is barren and uninviting. The name itself—death row—brings to mind "foreboding imagery: adjoining cells made of bars of cold steel, ensconced deep within prison walls, inhabited by an assemblage of doomed offenders who mark the relentless passage of time that alone separates them from death by execution."[15] The setting is well named: The typical death row inmate must contend with a segregated environment marked by immobility, reduced stimulation, a pervasive sense of vulnerability, and the prospect of daily tensions and conflicts with impersonal, and sometimes hostile staff, all experienced in the shadow of the executioner.[16] There is also the risk that visits from loved ones will become increasingly rare, as the man who is "civilly dead" is often abandoned by the living.[17] The condemned prisoner's ordeal is usually a lonely one that must be met largely through his own resources. The uncertainties of his case—pending appeals, unanswered bids for commutation, possible changes in the law—may complicate his adjustment. A continuing and pressing concern is whether one will join the minority who obtain a reprieve or will, instead, be counted among the to-be-dead. Uncertainty may make the dilemma of the death row inmate more complicated than simply maintaining hope or surrendering to despair. The condemned can afford neither alternative, but instead must nurture both a desire to live and an acceptance of imminent death. The death row inmate must achieve this equilibrium with little support or encouragement from others, fellow prisoners, or staff. In the process, he must somehow maintain his dignity and integrity.

Few man-made environments offer stress surpassing that produced by confinement under sentence of death. French penal colonies, like that in French Guinea in South America, which were open until 1953, would qualify.[18] Geographically and culturally far removed from the civilian life of their captives, the radical transition from free world to penal colony proved too much for some prisoners, who died at the outset of their confinement. For others, extended terms of hard labor made their confinement tantamount to a death sentence.[19] The French penal colony at French Guinea, combining a shockingly abrupt transition from freedom to captivity along with grueling labor, registered a stunning death rate of 75 percent.[20] Russian forced labor camps, too, have been said to comprise a world wholly apart from regular civilian life, an extended "archipelago" in which injury and death from exhaustion, exposure, or physical abuse are regular events.[21] Prisoner-of-war (POW) camps have been notoriously harsh settings. The high mortality rates in some Japanese POW camps during World War II, for example, stand as monuments to brutality.[22] Nazi death camps, of course, have no parallel in the technology of human destruction.[23]

Yet even in some of the worst confinement settings, the term of incarceration was generally limited and could be endured with the aid of luck, work, and companionship. Penal colonies, labor camps, and POW camps sometimes left room for hope. Confinement did not inevitably close off the possibility of recapturing and rebuilding one's life. Death row, in contrast, may all too often seem to be indefinite, empty, friendless confinement, which is often and aptly perceived as a "living death."

For a few men, death row is paradoxically a context for growth. Caryl Chessman is perhaps the prototype of this response to death row. For Chessman, almost 12 years of solitary confinement inspired introspection and resulted in the discovery of meaning in the experience and in his life. More recently, Hinton, an Alabama death row exoneree, found freedom in the extreme captivity to which he was exposed, which produced enormous suffering but also a renewed faith in his fellow man. His struggle was palpable: "I was afraid every single day on death row. And I also found a way to find joy every single day." In the end, he concluded that, "We want our lives and our stories and the choices we make to matter. Death row taught me that it all matters."[24] For remarkable men like Chessman and Hinton, both outspoken advocates against the death penalty, death row may be an affirmation of life.[25]

Most men, though, find the experience demoralizing. To be sure, there are a few who seem oblivious to their fate. They indicate no remorse over their crimes, show no fear regarding the prospect of execution, and seem untouched by the stressful features of their environment. For many men, however, death row confinement spawns ineffectual coping, resignation, and defeat. Suicide rates are high. Depression is widespread. Apathy and deterioration commonly occur, followed by execution or a reprieve, which normally entails a life sentence in prison, often amounting to a harsh existence shadowed by residual trauma.[26]

The broad outlines of coping and failing to cope on death row were inferred from the sparse research literature on the subject at the time of the first edition. The usefulness of that research was limited, however, by a number of unresolved methodological problems. Differences in measurement instruments, characteristics of the populations under study, the extent and nature of social organization within the death row setting, and the perceived probability of death by execution all affected the quality and generalizability of this body of work. When interviews were used to embellish and organize research results, they rarely furnished insights regarding psychological survival and breakdown on death row.

A 1962 study by Bluestone and McGahee, for example, used projective tests to assess the reactions of prisoners under sentence of death covered a period when executions were comparatively commonplace.[27] The researchers described marked deterioration among many of their subjects, a reaction that was aggravated by destructive peer interactions on death row. Some 10 years later, Gallemore and

Panton used a personality inventory to survey the adaptations of condemned prisoners during a period of declining executions.[28] Although the prisoners expressed fears concerning possible execution, there were no executions immediately before, during, or after the study. This lack of executions may have been a source of optimism for the prisoners; their social world appeared oriented primarily toward alleviation of discomforts resulting from a closed environment. Stress symptoms, though quite prevalent, were keyed to situational pressures and appeared generally less disabling than those revealed in earlier research, when executions occurred with regularity. These findings appear to be replicated on death rows today in states that have had few executions; on several death rows today, executions are years or even decades apart, and the death row conditions are comparatively relaxed.[29]

At the time of the original study reported in this book, conducted in 1978, there were some indications that inmates facing a death sentence operated under the assumption that executions were unlikely. At this juncture, the wave of executions in the 1980s and 1990s had yet to materialize. As a consequence, some condemned prisoners viewed death row confinement as a temporary phase of their prison careers. Florida's condemned in the 1970s, for example, have been characterized in this fashion.[30] Some Texas death row prisoners during the 1970s reported similar perceptions of their situation in an interview survey.[31]

Other Texas prisoners at that time were less optimistic, seemingly bracing themselves for impending executions. (This was also true for the Alabama prisoners I interviewed, as will become apparent as this book unfolds). A few Texas death row prisoners spoke eloquently about the helplessness they felt as a pervasive feature of their lives on death row; the constricted movements and sterile routines they suffered; the impersonal, even Kafkaesque, justice system that had apprehended, sentenced, and confined them; the bleak and uncertain futures they faced. They spoke also of the challenge of having to adjust to the insular world of death row, which was marked by tension and the potential for violence; the pain of separation from loved ones, which included both loneliness and the inability to help or protect those left behind in the free world; their abandonment by the prison, which provided minimal care, and by society, which seemed oblivious or indifferent to the pain of condemned prisoners.

As a general matter, Texas death row prisoners in the late 1970s vividly portrayed the humdrum minutiae of life in the close quarters of death row.[32] (Their guards, incidentally, portrayed a similar picture of the death row prisoners' mundane existence.) Yet many of the personal traumas of life under sentence of death were not broached in the interviews with these prisoners. The inmates' fear was not examined; their anger was noted but not explored for its significance in their adjustment and psychological survival. Neither deterioration nor personal breakdown was considered in any detail. They did, however, record the occasional observations made by prisoners about their apparent premature aging. The interviewees, for the most part, were effective copers, or at least portrayed themselves as such. Many told stories about *other* men who panicked, broke down, or regressed. The inside story of stress and crisis was untold, however, because the victims themselves were never heard from.

Psychiatric research conducted before the original study reported in this book revealed some common features of adaptation to death row among prisoners who were facing (or who believed they were facing) a realistic prospect of execution. At least at the outset, these men appeared unable to accept and explore the implications of their situation. They often employed denial as an extreme measure of ego defense. The shock of receiving a capital sentence and the subsequent admission to the insular world of death row appeared to create a climate for introspection that most prisoners struggled to resist.

For example, the condemned commonly showed nonchalance and proclaimed immunity from anxiety, depression, or fear. This attitude may have been reinforced by a belief that commutation or successful appeal was imminent. Alternatively, shock was cushioned by a feverish concern for day-to-day matters of existence or by excessive preoccupation with appeals, religion, or intellectual pursuits. For a few prisoners, denial of feelings became so acute that they retreated into a private psychotic world in which they believed themselves free men, exempt from execution.[33]

Another line of adaptation among these prisoners entailed projection of feelings of anger and fear onto others in the environment.[34] Projection, like denial, is a rearguard method of ego defense. Men who opt for projection were characterized as suspicious, resentful, and hostile. Full-blown persecutory delusions sometimes developed, particularly after extended periods of confinement. These men attributed responsibility and blame to the environment, which, as they saw it, caused their problems. Some emerged transformed from "dissolute criminals into martyrs," perhaps adding a dimension of meaning and dignity to their lives.[35]

The body of psychiatric research on death row prisoners available at the time of the original study portrayed the concerns of condemned men as reflections of mental defenses (such as denial or projection) rather than as accurate responses to the world in which they lived. Making the case that denial is an ego defense to a death sentence is comparatively easy. A death sentence carries a clear risk (death) and the inability to accurately perceive this risk suggests that distortion or patterned inattention are being used to protect the person from confronting an objectively ugly circumstance. The case for projection as an ego defense in this context is harder to make. The argument is that some condemned prisoners attribute their anger and fear to others in the external world and thereby "create" in their minds the dangerous world on death row that justifies the anger and fear they felt in the first place. If they are martyrs, then, their suffering is self-inflicted. The world is shaped, through projection, to fit their needs.

The anger and fear experienced by condemned prisoners, as we shall see, are often the product of realistic perceptions of their vulnerability. Death row confinement is frustrating and dangerous, and the condemned have ample reason to worry about their safety. They also have a reasonable basis for anger over their sentences since many similar offenders were spared the death penalty. They may still project their feelings, of course, and this may add to their sense of vulnerability. Anger and fear may be commonly attributed to others (in other words, projected) because recognition of these feelings in oneself may be too threatening and painful. A self-fulfilling prophecy may then be set in motion. Violence-suffused perceptions augment an objectively violent world; a dangerous environment read with fear provides added cause for alarm. If adjustment falters, private perceptions can dominate a person's thinking and can lead, in some instances, to delusions. Generally, however, condemned prisoners characterized in some research as having employed projection as an adaptive strategy may have simply (and correctly) located the source of their feelings in the external world.

Research available at the time of the original study suggested that the adaptations of condemned prisoners were likely to be similar to those employed by terminal patients and others exposed to objectively life-threatening situations.[36] Elizabeth Kubler-Ross described five stages of adjustment that frequently appear as reactions of persons facing a terminal illness.[37] The first two stages—shocked denial followed by anger and fear in response to a world that inflicts premature death on some but not others—have been observed in the research on death row inmates. The remaining stages are bargaining, depression, and acceptance. In the bargaining stage, the person attempts to postpone death. This reaction involves partial denial ("Yes, I'm dying but . . ."), and a plea for an extension of life contingent upon promised good behavior. The object of bargaining may be the doctor, God, or in the case of condemned prisoners, perhaps the governor or appeals court. There may be a magical or mystical quality to such bargains. Persons may attribute their respective conditions to past failures or inadequacies and assume that a willingness to suffer and play by the applicable rules is the key to cure or reprieve. As good patients, good souls, and possibly good prisoners or litigants, they may acknowledge their dilemma but hope to negotiate a more acceptable outcome.

The fourth and fifth stages of adaptation usually coincide in the terminally ill patient, as they may in the condemned prisoner. The stage of depression encompasses both reactive and preparatory grief. This includes sadness over opportunities that have been missed in life, as well as those that, due to one's impending death, will never materialize. Persons who have reached the final stage, acceptance, are "neither depressed nor angry" over their fate. "It is almost a void of feelings. It is as if the struggle is over, and there comes a time for 'the final rest before the long journey.'"[38]

The various stages of adaptation do not occur in an ironclad, discrete sequence, nor do they adequately characterize the reactions of all persons. For example, denial often recurs throughout the person's adjustment to stressful situations; it operates as a buffer or cushion that allows the person time to rest, regroup, and mobilize more constructive defenses. Some persons do not experience all of the adjustment stages; they may become frozen in a defensive posture or may become chronically depressed. Others may experience reactions that are simply not captured by Kubler-Ross' model of adjustment stages, such as grief experienced as a kind of temporary madness. Finally, the social environment can play a critical role in determining the nature and outcome of coping efforts, influencing the pattern in which adjustment stages occur as well as shaping their content and relative impact.

Research available at the time of the original study suggested that hospitals and prisons were particularly uncongenial settings for persons facing impending death. Dying patients and condemned prisoners are marginal clients of their institutions. Medical technology is powerless to help terminally ill patients and correction (a presumptive goal in correctional institutions) is deemed irrelevant for inmates under sentence of death. At best, the normal schedules and activities of hospitals and prisons may be unable to meet the human needs of these persons. At worst, the institutions may directly undermine adjustment efforts. For example, while the person in these institutional settings should be encouraged to face and acknowledge threats to his life, he may instead be rewarded for playing the role of the uncomplaining, stoical patient, or of the manly, self-sufficient convict. Desperate anger and resentment directed at staff, at those who are living and who are making the person uncomfortable, may often be deflected back to their source—the now "ungrateful" patient or "problem" inmate—rather than absorbed or treated. When the strained hope underlying bargains for time and for life deserves to be tempered, pleas may be discounted, considered affronts to professional competence, or counted as indices of malingering or mental illness. When grief should be expressed and losses mourned, the person may be sufficiently isolated and ignored that staff will not have to relinquish their protective professional roles and be forced to relate to a person in crisis. Finally, when the individual approaching death reaches out for quiet comfort and support, the division of labor in hospitals and prisons may provide few persons equipped to play this basic human role.

In spite of the confining hospital environment, we knew at the time of the original study that many terminally ill patients were able to adjust to their fate. They did so with the aid of family and other community-based resources. The comparative flexibility that can be incorporated into hospital procedures gives patients a limited sense of control over their life and also adjustment to their situation.[39] At the same time, it seemed apparent that condemned prisoners were not as fortunate. Family support and assistance are seldom present for these men,[40] and the death row environment is, by design, rigid and unresponsive. The resignation of condemned prisoners may stem not only from the inability of the institution to meet their fluctuating and diverse needs, but also from the absence of the social support and personal autonomy needed to give meaning to their experience. It is tragic that persons so deprived may ultimately succumb to the impersonal forces of the prison. For condemned prisoners, then, the plausible expectation at the time of the study was that the prospect of impending death in the barren death row environment would regularly yield defeat seen in varying degrees of regression and decay.

In sum, at the time of the first edition of this book in 1981, comparatively little was known about the psychological impact of death row confinement. Some clues about the nature of stress and coping on death row were revealed by prior research, but, never having been posed in a systematic manner, a range of critical questions remained unanswered. What pressures impinge, intimately and uniquely, on condemned men? The objective characteristics of the death row environment were known, but little was understood of the human environment of death row—the environment as it was perceived and experienced by the prisoners themselves. Even less was known of the avenues of adaptation open to condemned prisoners, how and when various adaptations were employed, and with what consequences. The general orientations assumed by men on death row, conceptualized in the psychiatric literature as mechanisms of defense, had been studied. The relevance of defense mechanisms in explaining adjustment to death row, however, was not always clear. Moreover, defense mechanisms are broad categories of response within which important variations may occur. Portraits of terminally ill patients suggested that the sequence of adaptation described for death row inmates, even when limited to a consideration of defense mechanisms, was probably incomplete. Finally, the manner in which the death row environment shaped adjustment efforts, however adjustment was assessed, remained unknown. Thus, although it is apparent that many men were unable to cope effectively with death row confinement, their problems and crises of adjustment had not yet been explored.

We now know—from the original research reported in this book and from subsequent research by myself and others—that there are junctures in which individuals confined to death row feel immobilized, stymied, overwhelmed, or suffocated by pressure. The ingredients of these reactions offer insight into the human environment of death row. Coping failures illustrate transactions between the individual and the environment, highlighting occasions of stress that cannot be assimilated, managed, or endured. An analysis of problem and crisis sequences suggests stress management strategies that might be implemented on death row. Such an analysis also provides essential information on the totality or gestalt of the death row experience—information relevant to assessing the human costs of death row confinement and the death penalty.

Research Method

This book is based in large measure on in-depth, tape-recorded interviews conducted during September 1978 with 35 of the 37 men then confined on Alabama's death row.[41] The aim of the interviews reported in this book was to secure the prisoners' unexpurgated perceptions and thus obtain insight into the human experience of death row confinement. The interviews were thus open-ended and explored the dominant problems and pressures of confinement as perceived by the prisoners themselves. Subsequent research interviews conducted on contemporary death rows—by myself and others, on Alabama's death row and other death rows—are brought to bear as appropriate to update and amend the portrait of life on death row conveyed in the first edition of this book.[42]

The original study was part of a class-action suit on conditions of confinement on Alabama's death row. My job was to interview death row prisoners and capture and convey the experience of life under sentence of death as they experienced it. Over a two-week period, I conducted 35 interviews, each lasting between two and three hours. My interview room, with a picture window opening up onto the execution chamber, was the viewing room used for witnesses to executions. There was me, the prisoner, and, within direct sight, the electric chair. I have come to appreciate that the immediacy of the electric chair, and the tactless way prisoners were callously and gratuitously exposed to this formidable machine of death, added urgency and authenticity to the interviews.

The interview schedule used with the Alabama death row prisoners was modeled on procedures employed in prior research on acts of violence[43] and suicidal crises[44] among prisoners. Each prisoner was allowed to state, in his own words and in chosen sequence, his reaction to critical incidents or experiences during his confinement on death row. When needed, neutral probes ("Can you tell me any more about that?") were used to get the men to share as many details of their experiences as they could remember. The resulting material was then reviewed with the prisoners, this time through step-by-step, sequential ordering.

The interviews were focused, but without predefined sets of questions.[45] The aim was to elicit and examine critical junctures in each man's experience in which coping efforts were strained, impaired, or otherwise insufficient, as understood from each prisoner's point of view. The procedure remained constant, though adjustments of the interview format were required to accommodate differences among prisoners. Some men, for example, gave sparse or confused accounts of adjustment difficulties. More direct questioning was required in such instances in order to obtain a coherent description of the person's adjustment problems.

The interviews began with exploratory, open-ended probes designed to identify coping problems or crises. Opening questions were variations of the following: "Maybe you can start off by telling me what has been the most difficult problem you've had to face during your confinement here on death row?" or "Maybe you can give me some idea of what has been the toughest part of your confinement here on death row?" Such questions typically elicited a laundry list of grievances. In fact, complaints about routine features of death row confinement tumbled forth at the start of most interviews. The following reply to the opening query is typical:

> Every day it's something. Take food. Okay, like yesterday we got, I don't know what the stuff was—it looked like salmon patties. And the guard that brought the tray smoked cigarettes. He had dropped some ashes on the bread; he went ahead and brought me back another tray but that tray was probably the same tray. All he did was blow the cigarette ashes off. Mail situation. I got, well I ain't got it now, a little ole necklace, a religious necklace, that symbols the Pentecostal faith and the guard kept it for three or four days. And after he gave it to me he told me to let him see it. He kept it about 15 days and stuff like that. Packages. They bring packages back there and they claim that the post office people fuss with them. Like there'll be powder in 'em and powder smeared all over the floor. Just every little thing. Thing about the ink-pen situation. Due to filing writs, they take our ink pens back on surprise. They tell us that somebody was making knives out of batteries and they gonna take the radios from us.

Such preoccupations reveal the salience of mundane details to men confined in closed environments. Tainted food tastes even worse, many men reported, when it represents a major break in a routine of confinement. Obsession with the circumstances of prison existence may also have reflected the prisoners' knowledge of the interviewer's role in pending litigation (as noted in the consent form each signed). As good clients, they may have congenially keyed their early remarks to such issues, thinking perhaps that these were the only relevant interview topics. My interest lay elsewhere, however—not with the public abuses of power but with the private traumas of life on death row, an isolated milieu operating in service of the death penalty.

Follow-up questions, then, acknowledged complaints about prison conditions but were geared to encourage more introspective descriptions of stress and suffering. The prisoners were asked to reconstruct their thoughts and feelings in relation to their various grievances, and to examine in detail the personal consequences of these and other adjustment pressures that had emerged during their confinement. The interviews were not conducted to determine the actual quality of food or medical care, or to investigate harassment or abuse by guards, or to ascertain the length of time allowed for recreation. Instead, the condemned prisoners' subjective perceptions of these and other conditions were sought. The unanimity of perceptions in all respondents concerned with a particular issue and the personal consequences of shared perceptions were deemed especially significant. The interviews were thus designed to produce in-depth accounts of coping problems and crises experienced by the prisoners on death row, and to provide insight into the prisoners' world.

The interview procedure assumes that the personal significance of an experience can be ascertained by asking persons to reconstruct their frame of mind at the time of the experience, even though in their current perception that view may seem odd or obscure. Their premises at the time of the experience must be accepted, however unusual or artificial they may appear. Later, these premises can be explored in depth. In effect, each interviewee is enlisted as an expert researcher of his own experience; this empowering role provides added motivation for introspection.[46] Enlisting interviewees as experts on their feelings and experiences can be especially effective with incarcerated men because penal institutions discourage open consideration of personal problems or susceptibilities and discount or ignore the views of prisoners.[47] Factors that inhibit the development of trust, openness, and sharing among prisoners are pronounced on death row. Engaging death row prisoners as experts may be particularly appealing to death row prisoners and may account for the willingness of the prisoners in this study to explore their problems in the supportive context afforded by the interview. Simple loneliness and the desire for human contact and sympathy may also have encouraged men to participate openly and willingly in the interview. Said one prisoner, speaking both for himself and, he felt, for his peers:

> We're so happy just to get out of the cell to see anybody we can talk to from outside. It comes a time for all of us where we be needing someone like you to hold a conversation with about these conditions, and for you to be concerned about our conditions.

For these reasons, many condemned prisoners seized the opportunity for self-study and engagement presented by the interview, and a few inmates described the experience as personally rewarding and even therapeutic.

Information gathered under conditions of high participation, relevance, and involvement is likely to be relatively honest and complete.[48] Requests for step-by-step reconstruction of problems and crises as they unfold may also help respondents remember detailed sequences of stress. The open-ended interview sells itself, especially among persons not usually taken seriously or cared for by others. Respondents discover that there is no need to exaggerate or to otherwise regale the interviewer with sad tales and lamentations, that the facts speak for themselves because it is their world as they experience it that is at issue. Eventually they trust the interviewer, and they work hard to tell the "inside story" as they had known and lived it. Many of the interviews, in a sense, conducted themselves. When the interviewer got in the way or failed to understand a point, respondents did not hesitate to interrupt and correct, or to reiterate observations that might have been distorted or overlooked. Each respondent wanted to ensure that his thoughts were understood. As a result, the interviews better resembled intimate conversations than formal research procedures. They were more often painstaking explorations of significant human concerns rather than exercises in counting surface preferences or aversions. The prisoners were eager to talk informally—to be the experts, to set the tone of discussion, to speak their own minds. Their job was to talk openly and honestly. My job was to listen with care, probe gently when necessary, and, ultimately, to analyze their concerns in a manner that retained the cutting edge of authenticity conveyed in our discussions.

Analysis

The prisoners' perceptions were organized according to concerns that they identified as salient. These included concerns stated forcefully or given clear-cut priority by the interviewee. Matters given high priority were often indicated by statements such as, "This is important to me," "What I'm telling you is this," or "Listen, this is for real." As perceived by the inmates, these matters included the following: arbitrary rules, conditions of deprivation, and an assortment of daily frustrations: brutal or indifferent guards, some of whom seemed to take pleasure in teasing, threatening, and sometimes harming prisoners; alienated, apathetic families; and a general feeling of isolation and emptiness.

Concerns elaborated upon by respondents, as well as those spontaneously repeated during the interview, were considered salient and worthy of tabulation. Documentation of these observations was usually signaled by such statements as, "Here's an example of what I'm talking about," or "Let me show you how this works." Reiteration was often identified by such prefatory comments as, "Let me get back to this one thing," or "As I said before." Occurrences so documented or repeated included the following: attempts at change that were repeatedly ignored, or thwarted, or otherwise unsuccessful; memories of threats and abusive actions attributed to guards, or of incidents from which the guards' indifferences to inmates was inferred; and preoccupation with the details of painful visits, deteriorating family ties, and envisioned executions.

Salient concerns were also revealed in less direct ways. Inmates often provided information that contained a transparent dominant theme. This information was seen as indicative of an important concern. For example, one inmate recounted numerous specific examples of his death row experience in which the basic theme was oppression by the prison authorities. Other inmates provided either summary statements or metaphors that highlighted key dimensions of their death row experiences. These indirect references often underscored concerns that had been expressed in more direct ways. From their recounted experiences, I identified themes that occurred throughout the interviews.

Individual concerns were identified separately for each prisoner and then grouped across prisoners, with logically related or equivalent concerns clustered together. This grouping process permitted the identification of general psychological dimensions that capture significant interactions of man and environment on death row. The psychological dimensions were developed with an eye toward their plausibility. Validity was sought by comparing trends in the interviews with findings of prior research on the adjustment of condemned prisoners. Research on related subjects was also consulted to assess plausibility, especially studies on the varieties of personal adjustment to prison and to terminal illness. Psychological dimensions also had to be relatable to certain obvious objective features of the death row environment, particularly its isolation, its security, and its purpose of housing men sentenced to death. Above all, the dimensions had to remain faithful to the world of the prisoners, conveying the flavor and substance of the concerns expressed in the interviews.

Each interview, of course, was unique, not only in the way in which it proceeded, but also with regard to the nuances of each prisoner's concerns. Still, an outline of broadly shared features of the death row experience emerged from these discussions with disturbing clarity. This outline is shaped around three existential themes drawn from the interview protocols: powerlessness, fear, and extreme loneliness giving rise to feelings of emotional emptiness or death. These dimensions are defined as follows:

Powerlessness is felt in response to a controlling environment marked by seemingly omnipresent rules, regulations, and staff. The person feeling powerless believes he is unable to influence significant aspects of the living environment or to fight back and gain autonomy. A sense of helplessness and defeat is experienced as a continuing or dominant feature of adjustment to life on death row.

Fear is felt in response to a closed, high-pressure environment organized and run to facilitate the execution of its inhabitants. The person experiencing fear believes he is unable to defend himself against danger, or to ignore perceived threats or occasions of danger. Danger is often seen as widespread and diffuse, beyond the ability of any person to constructively cope or respond. A sense of vulnerability is experienced as a continuing or dominant feature of adjustment.

Emotional emptiness or *emotional death* is felt when one believes he is beyond the reach and support of significant others and has been abandoned or forgotten by them and the free community in general; it is a reaction to confinement in a setting in which human needs are discounted. The person feeling emotionally empty experiences loneliness, a deadening of feelings for self and others, and a decline in mental and physical acuity. A sense of apathy, passivity, and decay is experienced as a continuing or dominant feature of adjustment.

The image of confinement on death row as a *living death* was used by many inmates to capture the essential or cumulative experience of the condemned prisoner. Living death is here intended to convey the zombie-like, mechanical existence of an isolated physical organism—a fragile twilight creature that emerges when men are systematically denied their humanity, shorn of autonomy, security, and connection to others. The image, spontaneously and forcefully rendered by the prisoners themselves, serves as a dramatic summary statement of the death row experience, encompassing its central psychological features of powerlessness, fear, and emotional emptiness.

The psychological dimensions and corollary sources of environmental pressure on death row are indicated in Table 1.1. The following chapters examine the painful and sometimes heartrending experience of condemned prisoners as they struggle to cope. The goal is to track the prisoners' concerns in their own words, to provide the reader with an introduction to their world as they experience it. First, there is a brief consideration of the personal backgrounds of death row prisoners (Chapter 2). Analysis of the

TABLE 1.1 Classifications of Personal Reactions to Death Row Confinement and Cumulative Experience

Psychological Dimensions	Environmental Pressures	Gestalt
Powerlessness	Custodial regime (immobility and isolation)	Living death
Fear	Death work (chasm separating living from to-be-dead)	
Emotional emptiness	Human environment (interpersonal vacuum)	

impact of death row confinement begins with a depiction of the physical setting and custodial regime of death row (Chapter 3). The social world (Chapter 4) and mission (Chapter 5) of death row are next considered. A description of the cumulative human experience in this environment concludes the study (Chapter 6). The implications of the research, both for correctional reform and for the larger legal and moral issues posed by capital punishment, are summarized in a closing statement on the human costs of death row confinement and the death penalty (Chapter 7).

Death row emerges in this book as an environment in which prisoners feel impotent, afraid, and alone—defenseless against their keepers and unable to alter their fate. A few prisoners deteriorate dramatically; all experience, in varying degrees, a living death. This image of death row as a living death symbolizes the human environment of death row and the human consequences of confinement in this oppressive penal milieu.

Notes

1 See Johnson and Davies (2014: 669). Missouri is the exception to this rule. Missouri is a high-execution state that mainstreams condemned prisoners in the general population of a maximum-security prison; Missouri will be discussed in the concluding chapter.
2 Johnson and Davies (2014: 669).
3 Aldape, Cooper, Haas, Hu, Hunter, and Shimizu (2016).
4 Hinton (2018: 153).
5 For example, an unnamed death row inmate in Oregon described how he had hoped the death penalty would be repealed, but then with the recent presidential election, he now lives in fear (Death two inmate, 2016).
6 Of the 31 states that have the death penalty today, 20 of them permit prisoners less than four hours per day outside of their cells. Prisoners on death row, including Alabama's death row, regularly receive fewer hours out of their cells than indicated in official policies as a result of staffing constraints and the time-consuming logistics of prisoner movement in high-security settings. See Toch, Acker, and Bonventre (2018).
7 Hinton (2018: 139).
8 For a comprehensive review of the latest research on death row conditions, see Toch et al. (2018).
9 Even condemned prisoners mainstreamed into the general prison population in Missouri are not offered any meaningful preparation for the executions that await them, a point I will develop in the final chapter of this book.
10 For statistics on death row and executions, see the Death Penalty Information Center (2018). For a review of conditions of confinement on death rows, see Johnson and Davies (2014). See generally Toch et al. (2018).
11 Johnson (2014).
12 Remarkably, more than 200 condemned prisoners have been held on death row for more than 30 years (Toch et al., 2018: 4).
13 Snell (2014).
14 Some 55 percent of Americans in 2017 were in favor of the death penalty (Jones and Saad, 2017).
15 Toch et al. (2018: 3).
16 Eshelman (1962); Gallemore and Panton (1972).
17 Eshelman (1962); Gallemore and Panton (1972: 167).
18 Serge (1970).

19 Dostoyevsky (1892/1959).
20 Toth (2006).
21 Solzhenitsyn (1974).
22 Wolf and Ripley (1947: 180).
23 Des Pres (1977).
24 Hinton (2018: 241).
25 Levine (1972). For an account of other prisoners for whom death row yields growth through adversity, see Magee (1980); Kohn (2009), (2012); O'Donnell (2014); Jarvis (2015).
26 For discussions of deterioration, see Bluestone and McGahee (1962: 393); West (1975). It has been recorded that death row prisoners become increasingly apathetic and "progressively less suitable for reentry into a general prison population or the general public" (Gallemore and Panton, 1972: 171). Westervelt and Cook (2018) report continuing trauma in the aftermath of exoneration among death row prisoners.
27 Bluestone and McGahee (1962).
28 Gallemore and Panton (1972).
29 Aldape et al. (2016: 9–11).
30 Lewis (1979: 200).
31 Jackson and Christian (1980).
32 The significance of the views expressed by the condemned prisoners in Jackson and Christian's (1980) *Death Row* is hard to assess. The prisoners' observations are presented in the form of lengthy, essentially unexpurgated and unanalyzed verbatim interview excerpts. The reader is given little guidance in interpreting the interview excerpts. Nor is the reader informed about the interviewee selection process, the representativeness of the interviewees, or the nature of the interviews. A total of 26 condemned men were interviewed. No information is provided, however, on how these men were selected from among the 105 condemned men available for interview. Were there any refusals? What were the interviewees told about the research? What assurances were they given? What questions were they asked? These critical questions remain unanswered, detracting from the scientific value of this study.
33 Bluestone and McGahee (1962).
34 Gallemore and Panton (1972: 167).
35 Bluestone and McGahee (1962: 395).
36 Frankl (1977).
37 Kubler-Ross (1969).
38 Kubler-Ross (1969: 112).
39 Mausch (1975: 7).
40 Leigey (2015).
41 Access to Alabama's condemned prisoners was obtained through the author's association (as a consultant) with the Southern Poverty Law Center, a private legal organization located in Montgomery, Alabama. The author's obligation to the Center and the inmates of death row was to provide expert testimony in a class action suit contesting the conditions of confinement on death row in Alabama. The case, *Jacobs v. Bennett* (1978), however, was settled before trial.

One inmate refused to participate in this research. The other inmate was temporarily housed elsewhere in the Alabama penal system, participating in an appeal of his sentence. At the time of this study, only male capital offenders were held on death row. Consequently, only male inmates were involved in this study.

The following consent form was used:

On _____ I talked with Dr. Robert Johnson of The American University concerning my experience on death row. Our conversation was tape recorded. I hereby give my consent for Dr. Johnson to use my verbatim comments in published works. I understand that if my comments are included in published works, I will be given complete anonymity.

42 For further discussion, see Johnson and Whitbread (2018); Johnson and Lantsman (2017).
43 Toch (1969).
44 Toch (1975); Johnson (1976).

45 Merton and Kendall (1955: 476).
46 Bennis, Benne, and Chin (1969); Johnson (1976).
47 Sykes (1966); Toch (1992); Haney (2006); Johnson, Rocheleau, and Martin (2017).
48 Bennis et al. (1969).

References

Aldape, C., Cooper, R., Haas, K., Hu, A., Hunter, J., & Shimizu, S. (2016). *Rethinking "death row": Variations in the housing of individuals sentenced to death.* New Haven, CT: The Arthur Liman Public Interest Program: Yale Law School. Retrieved from https://law.yale.edu/system/files/documents/pdf/Liman/deathrow_reportfinal.pdf.

Bennis, W., Benne, K., & Chin, R. (1969). *The planning of change.* New York: Holt, Rinehart & Winston.

Bluestone, H., & McGahee, C. (1962). Reactions to extreme stress: Impending death by execution. *American Journal of Psychiatry, 119*(5), 393–396.

Death Penalty Information Center. (2018). *Facts about the death penalty.* Washington, DC. Retrieved from https://deathpenaltyinfo.org/documents/FactSheet.pdf.

Des Pres, R. (1977). *The survivor: An anatomy of life in the death camps.* New York: Oxford University Press.

Dostoyevsky, F. (1892/1959). *The house of the dead.* New York: Dell.

Eshelman, B. (1962). *Death row chaplain.* New York: Signet Books.

Frankl, V. (1977). *Man's search for meaning.* New York: Pocket Book.

Gallemore, J., & Panton, J. (1972). Inmate responses to lengthy death row confinement. *American Journal of Psychiatry, 129*(2), 167–172.

Haney, C. (2006). *Reforming punishment: Psychological limits to the pains of imprisonment.* Washington, DC: American Psychological Association.

Hinton, A. R. (with Hardin, L. L.) (2018). *The sun does shine: How I found life and freedom on death row.* New York: St. Martin's Press.

Jackson, B., & Christian, D. (1980). *Death row.* Boston, MA: Beacon Press.

Jacobs v. Bennett, Civ. No. 78-309-H (S.D. Ala., transferred May 25, 1978, settlement approved Feb. 22, 1980) (originally filed M.D. Ala., Civ No. 78-70-N).

Jarvis, J. J. (2015). *Finding freedom: Writings from death row.* Junction City, CA: Padma Publications.

Johnson, R. (1976). *Culture and crisis in confinement.* Lanham, MD: Lexington Books.

Johnson, R. (2014). Reflections on the death penalty: Human rights, human dignity, and dehumanization in the death house. *Seattle Journal of Social Justice, 13*(2), 582–598.

Johnson, R., & Davies, H. (2014). Life under sentence of death: Historical and contemporary perspectives. In J. R. Acker, R. M. Bohm, & C. S. Lanier (Eds.), *America's experiment with capital punishment: Reflections on the past, present, and future of the ultimate penal sanction* (3rd ed., pp. 661–685). Durham, NC: Carolina Academic Press.

Johnson, R., & Lantsman, J. (2017, November 16). Death row narrative study. Poster presented at the annual American Society of Criminology Conference, Philadelphia, PA.

Johnson, R., & Whitbread, G. (2018). Lessons in living and dying in the shadow of the death house: A review of ethnographic research on death row confinement. In H. Toch, J. R. Acker, & V. Bonventre (Eds.), *Living on death row* (pp. 71–89). Washington, DC: American Psychological Association Books.

Johnson, R., Rocheleau, A. M., & Martin, A. B. (2017). *Hard time: A fresh look at understanding and reforming the prison.* New York: Wiley.

Jones, J., & Saad, L. (2017, October). Gallup poll series: Crime. *Gallup News Service.* Retrieved from https://deathpenaltyinfo.org/files/pdf/GallupDeathPenaltyTopline171026.pdf.

Kohn, T. (2009). Waiting on death row. In G. Hage (Ed.), *Waiting* (pp. 218–227). Melbourne, Australia: University of Melbourne Press.

Kohn, T. (2012). Crafting selves on death row. In D. Davies & C. Park (Eds.), *Emotion, identity, and death: Mortality across disciplines* (pp. 71–83). London: Ashgate.

Kubler-Ross, E. (1969). *On death and dying*. New York: Macmillan.

Leigey, M. (2015). *The forgotten men: Serving a life without parole sentence*. New Brunswick, NJ: Rutgers University Press.

Levine, S. (Ed.). (1972). *Death row: An affirmation of life*. New York: Ballantine Books.

Lewis, P. (1979). Killing the killers: A post-Furman profile of Florida's condemned. *Crime and Delinquency, 25*(2), 200–211.

Magee, D. (1980). *Slow coming dark*. New York: Pilgrim Press.

Mausch, O. (1975). The organizational context of dying. In E. Kubler-Ross (Ed.), *Death: The final stage of growth* (pp. 7–24). Englewood Cliffs, NJ: Prentice Hall.

Merton, R., & Kendall, P. (1955). The focused interview. In P. Lazarsfeld & M. Rosenberg (Eds.), *The language of social research* (pp. 476–489). New York: Free Press.

O'Donnell, I. (2014). *Prisoners, solitude, and time*. Oxford: Oxford University Press.

Oregon Death Row Inmate. (2016, December 21). Death two inmate: Life on death row often means living in fear. *The Hill*. Retrieved from http://thehill.com/blogs/pundits-blog/civil-rights/311425-death-two-inmate-life-on-death-row-often-means-living-in-fear.

Serge, V. (1970). *Men in prison*. London: Gollancz.

Snell, T. L. (2014). Capital punishment, 2013. *U.S. Department of Justice Office of Justice Programs Bureau of Justice Statistics Bulletin*. NCJ 248448. Retrieved from www.bjs.gov/content/pub/pdf/cp13st.pdf.

Solzhenitsyn, A. (1974). *The gulag archipelago* (Vols. 1–3). New York: Harper & Row.

Sykes, G. (1966). *The society of captives*. New York: Atheneum.

Toch, H. (1969). *Violent men: An inquiry into the social psychology of violence*. Chicago: Aldine.

Toch, H. (1975). *Men in crisis: Human breakdowns in prison*. Chicago, IL: Aldine.

Toch, H. (1992). *Mosaic of despair: Human breakdowns in prison* (Rev. ed.). Washington, DC: American Psychological Association.

Toch, H., Acker, J. R., & Bonventre, V. M. (2018). *Living on death row: The psychology of waiting to die*. Washington, DC: American Psychological Association.

Toth, S. (2006). *Beyond Papillon: The French overseas penal colonies, 1854–1952*. Lincoln, NE: University of Nebraska Press.

West, L. J. (1975). Psychiatric reflections on the death penalty. *American Journal of Orthopsychiatry, 45*(4), 689–700.

Westervelt, S. D., & Cook, K. J. (2018). Continuing trauma and aftermath for exonerated death row survivors. In Toch, H., Acker, J. R., & Bonventre, V. M. (Eds.), *Living on death row: The psychology of waiting to die* (pp. 301–329). Washington, DC: American Psychological Association.

Wolf, S., & Ripley, H. (1947). Reactions among allied prisoners of war subjected to three years of imprisonment. *American Journal of Psychiatry, 103*(4), 180–193.

2

PATHWAYS TO DEATH ROW

Who are the condemned and how do they reach death row? The personal lives of capital offenders suggest that there are many individual pathways to death row, but virtually all of them were created by society long before the individual offenders embarked on their personal journeys to this bleak and forsaken setting at the deep end of our justice system. Each route is paved with failure, inadequacy, blocked opportunities, forlorn hopes, and broken dreams.

A fair summary of the research in this area would be as follows: Almost without exception, men on death row share a history of deprivation, neglect, and abuse rooted in dysfunctional families and often augmented by harsh punishments meted out in juvenile and adult confinement settings. Severe deficits in socialization and development, often including neurological impairment, are common expressions of the traumas that mark and mar their lives.[1] It appears that the greater the deprivation in terms of abuse and neglect, which in turn is associated with greater neurological impairment, the more heinous the capital crime.[2]

The men on death row also share infamy as a part of their grim biographies, at least for a short time. It is tragic that condemned prisoners draw public attention only at the time of their crimes, their trials, and as their execution dates draw near. As abused children, they are invisible; as poor citizens, they are neglected, even shunned. As death row prisoners, they are anonymous. Yet as murderers, they are public news, at least for a time. And the more gruesome the murder, the more newsworthy the criminal.

Deadly Stereotypes

Serious crime, of course, is a serious matter, deserving serious attention and analysis. The popular media, however, typically transforms complex human tragedies into simple morality plays. On the one hand, there is the detached inquiry that reports the bare facts surrounding capital crimes. None of the actors seem real or human. Disembodied figures populate a landscape riven by senseless violence. Capital punishment is seen as a calculated response to serious crime, a bureaucratic tactic deployed in an impersonal war on crime and criminals. We are led to believe that executions are undertaken only because nothing else works. On the other hand, there is sensational reporting of capital crimes and criminals, which may be more apt to capture the public mind than superficial factual accounts. Capital offenders are portrayed as deranged animals and psychopathic maniacs preying on unsuspecting and upright citizens. Execution, the reader learns, is too good for the monsters who rend the body social and send shock waves of fear through reputable communities like our own. Media coverage thus stifles or enflames feelings, further clouding the difficult problem of how to deal rationally with persons who kill.

Caryl Chessman, a long-term death row prisoner put to death by the state of California, studied the media distortion of capital offenders, particularly of the type likely to enrage decent citizens. Branded the "Red Light Bandit" during his lengthy tenure on San Quentin's death row, he summarized the public image of the condemned fostered by sensationalist journalism in the following terms:

> On the Row at the present time we have, according to no less an authority than the newspapers:
>
> 1.   Two "fiends" and three "monsters."
> 2.   One "moon-mad killer."
> 3.   One "cold-eyed, cold-blooded" leader of a "Mountain Murder Mob"; his alleged trigger-man, "The Weasel."
> 4.   One "sex-crazed psychopathic beast."
> 5.   Me.
> 6.   An assortment of "vicious," "sneering," "leering," "brutal," and "kill-crazy" murderers, plus a former private eye turned "diabolical" kidnapper.
>
> As the papers and "true" detective magazines tell it, we're creatures on the lam from Hell. Satan, in one of his most satanic moments, blew life into the figures on display in some sinister waxworks of horrors and presto! There we were.
>
> Here we are, an inhuman assemblage. Or so you are led to believe.[3]

Stereotypes of the capital-offender-as-a-monster are the product of what Chessman termed the media's "big buildup." This "big buildup" culminates in support for capital punishment as the necessary extermination of the monsters housed on death row. In Chessman's words:

> The big buildup usually begins with the commission of the crime and continues through the trial. If there's an acquittal, the promising candidate is dropped like a hot potato. If conviction carries with it a term of imprisonment, rather than the death penalty, he fizzles out as a monster after a few days or weeks. The elements of life, death, and violence are essential. The weirdest factor of all is this: if chance, fate, or circumstance had acquitted or imprisoned the "monsters" presently held on the Row, and had doomed those acquitted or imprisoned, the Row still would hold the same number of monsters. The headlines would remain as big and black; the editorials denouncing them would be as muscular; the demands for their necks would be as hysterical. Only the names would be changed.
>
> The legal niceties established, the monster is fair game. It's always open season on him. His crime or crimes are chillingly reconstructed, his imagined inhumanity is stressed. He's given a tag (red-light bandit, green-glove rapist, Manhattan maniac). Constitutionally and psychologically,

he's a sinister, mysterious and alien being. He's often under the sway of lunar influences. The forces that motivate him are brutally simple: he's "kill crazy," he's "sex maddened."

Enough bad things can never be said about him. The words used to describe him must always be scare words; they must always bristle with indignation. "Psychopath"—an epithet, not a diagnosis—is one of the best of these words; it's always proper to apply it to him and add the word "beast." It's fashionable to write to the editor of a newspaper who specializes in exposing and denouncing the monster and say, "It would be a pleasure to help exterminate [him]." It's an outrage to accord the monster due process of law.[4]

Capital offenders today may draw less sensationalistic media fanfare than in the 1940s and 1950s, the heyday of "detective" and "true adventure" magazines and the period about which Chessman wrote. The jaundiced character of many current depictions of the capital offender, however, is often essentially the same. As ever, there are those who "would have us believe that we are not discussing human beings at all, but rather "'beasts,' 'monsters,' 'mad dogs,' 'vermin,' or 'mutations.' . . . 'Do creatures like this deserve to live?'"[5] Editorials in some newspapers perpetuate the tradition of yellow journalism concerning capital punishment. Gary Gilmore was touted in one such editorial as a "psychopathic, self-destructive personality" whose "sordid drunken spree" effectively rendered him unfit for habitation in a prison.[6] "Hand-wringing sociologists" were admonished in another editorial to "lament all they like" over capital punishment. Execution, it continued, was "an act approaching judicial euthanasia"— a merciful gesture in which brutish criminals were presumably put out of their misery.[7] Remarkably, Hugh Nichols, then Chief Justice of the Georgia Supreme Court, characterized capital offenders in a newspaper in the following manner:

> You know, you don't put up a mad dog and feed him and take him home—you get rid of him. What good are they to society? They are incorrigible. Scientists prove now beyond any question that they are just born that way. You can't correct them. It's genetic. They're animals. There's no way you can do anything about them.[8]

In more sophisticated news reporting these days, murderers are not so crudely reviled as savages (though evocative terms like "fiend" can be found even today in descriptions of notorious murderers in major newspapers).[9]

Television and cinema, which have supplanted newspaper reading for many if not most Americans, offer a rich mix of popular shows and movies that serve to dehumanize and demonize offenders as "nonpeople . . . represented by the dastardly deeds they were shown committing."[10] A person who murders is thus a murderer and nothing more. "The American public," Haney notes, "has learned many of its 'deepest' lessons about crime and criminality through watching mythically frightening cinematic figures such as Hannibal Lecter—'Hannibal the Cannibal,' the sadistically mad killer, played with Oscar-winning skill by Anthony Hopkins in *The Silence of the Lambs*."[11] The implicit lesson is that

> murders are committed by persons who truly relish their deadly work; plot brilliantly, diabolically, and joyfully to perform it; and would just as easily polish off a meal of their victim's liver with a little Chianti as give you the time of day.[12]

To make matters worse, criminals and prisoners are increasingly being presented to the viewing public "as having 'animalistic and senseless' characteristics that stemmed from their 'warped personalities.'"[13]

The larger message conveyed in media of various types, as well as in some scholarly works, is that evil and failure are personal concerns, to be borne in isolation from one's fellow man; society takes credit for its heroes but attempts to stand blameless in the matter of its criminals. Legal scholar Walter Berns, for example, mocks Supreme Court Justice Brennan for contending that "even the vilest criminal remains a human being possessed of human dignity."[14] Berns asks, incredulously: "What sort of humanism is it that respects equally the [right to] life of Thomas Jefferson and Charles Manson, Abraham Lincoln and Adolph Eichmann, Martin Luther King and James Earl Ray?"[15] Taking this line of reasoning one step further, Blecker urges us to see capital offenders as moral monsters who command our righteous hatred: "Intuitively and emotionally," states Blecker, "we feel certain we have the right, if not the responsibility, to painfully punish monsters such as Morales [a condemned prisoner], because they deserve it. We rightly hate, yes hate, Morales and others like him."[16]

It may be satisfying to hate the authors of hateful deeds, but identifying the causes of capital murder as solely a matter of the personal responsibility of the offender is not only bad social science but dangerous social science. This wrong-headed view makes it easier to kill criminals because we can readily "distance ourselves from any sense of responsibility for the roots of the problem itself."[17] Developing this key point, Haney observes:

> If violent crime is the product of monstrous offenders, then our only responsibility is to find and eliminate them. On the other hand, genuine explanations for crime that include its psychological, social, and economic causes—because they sometimes connect individual violent behavior to the broader and more subtle forms of violence that inhere in society itself—implicate us all in the crime problem.[18]

Haney's view is convincingly seconded by Hinton, a now-exonerated Alabama death row prisoner. Drawing on his 30 years of firsthand observation of fellow condemned prisoners, Hinton sees dangerously flawed men made brutal by brutal lives:

> The outside world called them monsters. They called all of us monsters. But I didn't know any monsters on the row. I knew guys named Larry and Henry and Victor and Jesse. I knew Vernon and Willie and Jimmy. Not monsters. Guys with names who didn't have mothers who loved them or anyone who had ever shown them a kindness that was even close to love. Guys who were born broken or had been broken by life. Guys who had been abused as children and had their minds and their hearts warped by cruelty and violence and isolation long before they ever stood in front of a judge and a jury.[19]

Curiously, scholars like Berns and Blecker do allow capital offenders a measure of humanity. Berns, for example, supports capital punishment as a means to treat the condemned as "responsible moral beings" on whom society's righteous anger should be vented.[20] Capital punishment thus becomes a perverse way of demonstrating that society considers the downtrodden seriously. In light of what we know of crime causation and human behavior in general, this is a Hallmark Card morality, laced with black comedy: "Capital punishment, to show we care" for the dehumanized creatures among us.

The urge to deny the humanity of men who murder—and to seal this verdict with perpetual confinement or execution—may run deep in the human psyche (and is readily fed by media stereotypes).[21] Even sensitive clinicians dedicated to examining the origin and meaning of serious violence occasionally find themselves clinging to the hope that their troubling subjects are not human at all, but monsters who should be summarily dispatched from civil society. This self-deception, however, can be recognized and put to rest. Howard Wishnie's clinical observations are instructive in this regard:

> [W]hen sitting with some brutal and intelligent murderers, I have wished that they were locked up in stone-walled dungeons or executed. Then, I would be safe from them. At other times, I have found myself briefly charmed by their intelligence or conversation. In that fantasy, I become a special friend or ally. After all, he wouldn't hurt a friend? Nonsense! Such fleeting fantasies and physical sensations of tightness and coldness in the abdomen signal to me that I am deeply frightened. Here sitting with me is someone whom I would wish to appear as a monster. Then the difference between him and me would become all the more apparent. There should be something startling and different to set him apart from me! He has really done the things that I can only barely perceive in fantasy. All of my training and upbringing has led me to abhor real violence and murder. Angry feelings, rage-filled fantasies, yes, but assault and murder, NO! And yet he sits there talking calmly, comfortably. He has murdered and I am uncomfortable, not he! Having explored more deeply at other times what this confrontation touches within me (my own fears of rage and destruction) and having clarified my own responses, I usually proceed to explore the destructive events in the patient's life without the burden of my unreasonable fears.
>
> Once I have accepted into my consciousness that these events have occurred, that this man's frame of reference is different from mine with regard to these acts, we can begin together to understand their origin.[22]

Paradoxically, to deny the humanity of violent men is to deny a part of ourselves and our society. For violence, after all, is an all too common failing of individuals and societies.[23] Not until the basic humanity of the murderer is felt and understood can the work of explaining and ameliorating his violence begin. At this point one discovers that violence is not some specter or disease that afflicts some of us without rhyme or reason, but rather that it is an adaptation to bleak and often brutal lives. Violent offenders conform to the observation rendered by Vaillant that "the sons-of-bitches in this world are neither born nor self-willed. Sons-of-bitches evolve by their . . . efforts to adapt to what for them has proven an unreasonable world."[24]

Environments that spawn men who murder are indeed unreasonable—and unloving, unstable, unreliable, and replete with occasions of verbal and physical violence.[25] Some people get along reasonably well in these arid human milieus. Nurturing families, more often than not, afford them a safe harbor against a stormy and tempestuous world. Somehow they find shelter, the human love and concern that "facilitates our perception and toleration of painful reality and enriches our lives."[26] Others are less fortunate. For them, harsh lives fracture self-esteem, leaving a sense of self-doubt that undermines personal adaptation. Belittled by others, they feel both angry and insignificant. Rewarding relationships, which might make possible the rebuilding of self, prove difficult to achieve because they are not able to take others seriously—other human beings simply mirror the emptiness of their lives. Moreover, low self-esteem and mistrust of others make manipulation and deception the primary ingredients of interpersonal life.[27]

Violence constitutes tangible evidence that one is really somebody, a person of consequence who can make things happen, a man substantial enough to inspire awe and fear in others. Such evidence may be sought repeatedly to assuage doubts and fears, and to reaffirm a strained image of competence. For this reason, Wishnie observed,

> any minor slight, intentional or accidental, becomes cause for serious confrontation. Their fragile sense of self-esteem is always hanging in the balance. Behind it is the question, "Am I really a valuable person?" Because of this nagging self-doubt, there are constant efforts to substantiate the external image without resolving the internal doubts. Thus, an individual will risk physical danger or imprisonment at the slightest provocation, in order to maintain his self-esteem.[28]

The following incident is provided by Wishnie to make his point:

> Bill, a short man, was leaning against a ping-pong table. He was asked to move by Wendell, an extremely tall, muscular individual. Bill, sensitive about his size, thought he detected an insult in Wendell's voice. While Bill knew he was in the way, he refused to move and challenged Wendell to move him. The two were stopped just short of a fight. At a minimum, both risked leaving the hospital and returning to prison; at a maximum, death, for each acknowledged that he had been prepared to kill the other. Bill later explained in group, "I'm nothing, but it would kill me to let those suckers know it. I've gotta show them all the time. It would just kill me if they knew. Then I'd really be nothing."[29]

The violence of violent men is not promiscuous or blind. They may habitually resort to violence, but they are not consumed by hate or racked by uncontrollable destructive urges. With few exceptions, violent men are purposive in their violence. They strike out in self-defense, to shield themselves from real or imagined insults and injuries encountered regularly in their dealings with others. They strike out also to avoid confronting their personal inadequacies and facing directly the hopelessness and helplessness that permeates their lives.[30] Their violence is adaptive, however tragic its origins and consequences.

Although murder sometimes results, it is not the objective of this violence. Most violent men do not kill; most men who kill do not receive capital sentences—and those who both kill and receive death sentences are not necessarily the most violent of the violence prone. Indeed, the real lives of condemned men are considerably different from their counterparts in the popular press or in the works of social scientists who impugn their humanity. Gettinger's sensitive study of eight condemned prisoners showed them to be fully human.[31] Each sought relationships, status, and support. None was devoid of human feelings or human foibles. Each failed and turned, regrettably, to violence. Gettinger intentionally skewed his sample to include as wide a range of offenders as possible; yet virtually all of the men he studied were products of poverty, family instability, foster homes, and prisons. Condemned prisoners tend to be garden variety, run-of-the-mill felons. If anything, their criminal backgrounds are less pronounced than those of most felons. For "despite the popular image of the murderer as a drooling beast (or automaton) . . . murder is a once-in-a-lifetime crime," often committed by persons new to serious crime and highly unlikely to continue in serious crime after release from prison.[32] Several studies confirm and extend these generalizations.[33]

Like those men studied by Gettinger and others, Alabama's condemned are less notorious and alien upon examination of their personal backgrounds. Their statistical profile reveals the capital offender to be 29 years of age, Southern born and bred, and educated through grammar school. More often than not he is black (59 percent black vs 41 percent white) and a Baptist with professed evangelical leanings. He hails from a dysfunctional family replete with neglect and abuse. He was married or involved in a common law relationship at the time of his arrest, but formally separated or divorced after a few years on death row. His work history, comprised of brief stints at unskilled laboring jobs, was occasionally punctuated by bouts with the law. His criminal career was relatively short, though it included both juvenile and adult crime, including assaults. He stands condemned for murder but has not killed before. In a state without capital punishment, he might have faced a sentence as short as 10 to 20 years. Parole would likely have been available at some point. Even in Alabama, a notably punitive state, there was a good chance that he would have received a prison term rather than a date with the electric chair.

Some capital offenders, of course, have more damaging records than the statistical average. A few have killed before. They have long criminal and prison records; their credentials as dangerous men are in order. Others have histories of major and minor crimes short of homicide. Yet some have much less troublesome pasts than the typical capital offender: 1 in 5 has no prior felony convictions, a few are first offenders, 1 in 3 had never seen the inside of a prison before confinement to death row. There was even a teenage first offender among Alabama's capital offenders. It cannot be denied that the condemned have many faces, not all of them persistently menacing or malevolent, however difficult and even disabling their experiences during their formative years.[34]

Background statistics paint a more neutral picture of the capital offender than that purveyed in lurid journalistic accounts, but behind these statistics reside human beings who somehow turned explosively violent. Each killed other men, and a few killed women and children. Some may have murdered cold-bloodedly, cruelly, without mercy. A psychotic haze may have blurred the sense and sensibilities of others. Most seem to have acted in rage or panic. Yet they all killed, and they all face execution. How did they come to this violence and counter-violence?

This subject was occasionally broached in the interviews with Alabama's condemned prisoners. Though the focus of inquiry was on death row confinement, some prisoners felt they could not explain fully the meaning of their death row experience without relating it to their prior lives. Personal flaws, nagging doubts and inadequacies, a recurring sense of injustice, consuming passion—all were mentioned to explain, in part, how one could become a prisoner on death row. The crimes themselves, though, were rarely discussed. All prisoners had their cases on appeal, and many were reluctant to explore this dimension of their lives. A fair number of men, however, were voluble in describing their passage from free citizen to condemned prisoner. The lives thus partially revealed hint broadly at the indifference and brutality that may have shaped the prisoners' violence. A few of these accounts elaborate on concerns raised in muted or passing fashion by other prisoners. They are offered here, tentatively, as pathways to the death-in-life that is death row.

Violence and Maturity

Some condemned prisoners grew to adulthood with few restrictions and little guidance. Afforded the premature autonomy frequently conferred on children of the very poor,[35] they enjoyed the freedom of an adult without being equipped to handle adult responsibilities. They remained children in adult bodies. Eventually, the impulsiveness of the child, coupled with the power of the adult, proved lethal to others and destructive to themselves.

Their lives had all the ingredients of an adolescent's extended party. Apartments, girls, alcohol, and drugs were available early. School and work seemed inordinately dull in comparison with the life of the streets. Crime was easy and fun, drugs were a kick, everything was cool, until one day the games took an unscheduled turn and ended, abruptly. Along with their victims died this adolescent abandon. Now suddenly grown up, they hope for reprieve and for the chance to forge, for themselves and their loved ones, the constructive lives they might have had.

> I think if I had just stopped when I was young, maybe I would have been somethin'. I don't know. Why did I grow up like this? Was I supposed to grow up like this, you know? Was it meant for me? I'll be askin' myself, "Was it meant for me or did I just come into it." People said I was a devil. Was there a devil in me? See, I was caught up in you know, like in two worlds when I was out there. I knew my potentials and I knew my levels. I knew I had great ability, but at the same time, I couldn't pull myself together. I used drugs for about eight years, you see. I started out very young, when I was 15, 16 years old. That's the only thing that really bugs me. Why I couldn't cope with that problem? I understood this what was holding me back, but I couldn't lick it. And I see now where it got me . . . But then everything was a good time, man. I felt like "Hey, I'm a man now, 13 years old, a man." By the time I was 14 I was able to get my own apartment. I went out and got my own apartment at 14 years old. I did crime to pay the rent and get drugs. It was easy, man. The ease of doin' it, that was it. Everybody say, "Robbery, that's something hard to do." But I break in. It's the simplest thing in the world to do. Just don't be thinkin' about bein' caught, you know . . .
>
> It was just me. I didn't think about it at the time, I didn't want to, to be different I, I loved the way it was. Now it's somewhere where you can think about it and you got time to think, think what you could have done. And it's somethin' like people already have told me. They told me, "you could have been a mechanic" ('cause I like working on cars) and I would say, "Hey, that's a dirty job, though." I guess I don't know. I get upset about somethin' like this, 'cause I knew I could have done it . . . Oh, I think about my past; I think about my future. I think about a little of everything. I get a lot upset because I know things could have been different. I know I could have been like all my sisters and brothers. I think everyday. Every time when I'm not talkin' about it, I'm thinkin' about it, thinkin' about maybe if I get out of here, I'll go back. Since my mother has died, you know, I thought I'd go back and take my little brother and sister up, you know, and raise them, since I've been through somethin' like this, and keep them from becomin' somebody like me. I want to prevent them from this. 'Cause I call 'em and write them, I try to tell them this is no place to be. All they can think of is, you know, they think I'm the greatest. I'm not lettin' 'em. I'm here and it's not nothin' to be cool about, nothin'. I don't want 'em to come here. 'Cause if you come here, something can happen to people—always cut up or beat up or somethin'. I don't want nothin' like that for them.

Other men recall a more serious, feverish search for excitement. Each day was a constant pursuit of the psychological high that satisfied, reminding them that they were still alive and still their own man.

Crime provided the best high. In crime there was danger, risk, big stakes and big rewards. But crime also provided admission to prison—a setting more boring, eventless, restricting, and irritating than anything in the free world.

Prison weakened further any interest in living within the law. More crime meant more prison, and prison meant again being boxed in, suppressed, bursting with unharnessed energy. Then, a final explosion occurred. Like Wild West cowboys, these hope-to-die kids aimed to ride out in a blaze of glory. Failing that, their death wish is granted in the form of a death sentence.

PRISONER: I was 26 up there when I was doin' time. I would have been 26 years old. This was my second time in prison, ya know? My situation had reached a point where, where I can't make it inside. It's like being a trained animal. Go to bed when someone tells ya you can go to bed. Eat when they tells ya you can eat. Watch television when they say ya can. Just all of that. That's being caged like an animal. This animal don't cage good at all . . .

I've never done anything constructive, ya know? I don't really want to do anything constructive. I don't care. I'd reached a point in my life where I didn't care about anything, anybody, including myself. Ya know? And I think when you've reached that point, ya know, I think there's nothin' left in life, really. Fuck the restrictions, ya know, put on you by a job, family, government, laws. I'm just gonna go out there and I'm gonna live like the hell I want to live, for as long as I can get away with it. Ya know? And, ya know, when it's over, it's over. Ya know? But I don't want to have to be around to face the consequences.

It just seemed like every time I would turn around there was, there was responsibility there and I had never been geared up to responsibility. With accepting it, or to handlin' it, really. So, ya know, you all the time run, ya know. I can't handle that, ya know. That's too tough for me, ya know. And most guys will sit there, and I did for a while, and try to laugh at the chumps that live the straight life, 9 to 5, with all the bills, the responsibility. Ya know? "That's not for me." You laugh at them. Ya know? What's to laugh at? You're the chump. You can't handle it; they can handle it. Well, so I learned to accept that in myself and once I really got down to the nitty gritty I thought well, if you can't accept responsibility, and if you don't really want anything out of life, ya know, then there's nothin' here for you . . .

I was robbin' savings and loans, ya know, good money! Livin' the good life, ya know, and all that. That gets boring. Man, it gets boring. And you think about that ya know, and so like this last trip out we went through 25,000 dollars in two and a half months. Well, it wasn't the money to me, ya know. It was the kicks. It was the fun. The excitement you got. That's all that was left for me. The money wasn't anything.

It got so that everything in life bored me silly. I looked around, some friends of mine, they're married. The guys, they're happy. They're really happy and it blows my mind. It blew my mind because I thought, "I can't never have it." That type of happiness that they seem to have, and uh, I guess I've never been a happy person in my life. Ya know? Not really. So like I say, you sit there and ya think, ya know. There's, there's nothin'. Ya know? So when I got in prison this last time, like I say, ya know, me and my partner, we rapped it over and, well, felt pretty well the same type thing. There's nothin' out there for us. So let's just go til it's over. And, then when they get us, then I thought, ah ha, ya know, well, these suckers sit there, they think that I'm gonna spend all these years in prison, they're crazy! I would rather die than stay locked up here.

INTERVIEWER: Yeah. So you made this decision then to go on a hold-up spree.
PRISONER: Risking death.
INTERVIEWER: And it ended up with a capital sentence.
PRISONER: Yeah.

Some capital offenders were born to poverty, spent their childhoods in orphanages and foster homes, passed their teens in the reformatory, and entered adulthood in prison. Their lives were circumscribed by impersonal institutions, and it is almost as if their development was arrested at the stage of impulsive, aggressive adolescence that is a common feature of adjustment in these environments.[36]

These men typically suffered abandonment by family and state. Children of prison, the free world was novel and threatening while prison was familiar and threatening. Survival was a struggle featuring violence and crime. Violence ensured reputation and safety; crime meant food and shelter, and a sense of self-respect. Serious violent crime grew almost imperceptibly from the ethic of force that shaped their lives in reformatories and prisons.[37]

These men originate in poverty and ignorance and have been sharply excluded from the larger society that hides them in urban ghettos, rural hamlets, and penal institutions. They speak the language of slum streets, backwoods bars, county lockups, and state prisons, and inherit the despair wrought in these settings. An element of self-pity, too, sometimes emerges, an unappealing trait that is nevertheless understandable when life for them has been unending trouble. Death row, in any case, is simply a variation on an enduring existential preoccupation with survival in a dangerous and unstable world.

> There are, I believe, nine people in my family. My mother and father are dead. Now, our family grew up in orphanage homes because our father died when we were mostly all kids and our mother, she had to give us up because she couldn't support the nine of us being a house maid at the time—making $7.00 a day. So we were all scattered over the state of Mississippi in orphanage homes. And we were abused by orphanage parents, being beaten and made to pick cotton and all of this stuff and we were shut off from associating with other people of society because we were orphaned as children. So we were kept under discipline since the time we were children. And I've never really had two whole years—I would say three whole years—of freedom, since we were put in orphanage homes, and I was 6 years old then and I'm 28 years old now. I was 6 years old when I was put in foster homes and I'm 28 years old now and I have not had straight, three years of freedom.
>
> I was in foster homes from the time I was 6 until I was 13. When I turned 13 years old, they transferred me from a foster home to reformatory school and I was in reformatory school from the time I was 13 until the time I was 17. When I was 17, I ran away. They caught me the same night and two weeks later they transferred me to a more severe institution—a penal farm. And I was there until I was 18 years old. So, I've really had no freedom—from the time that I was 13 until I was 18 I was confined in reformatory schools and penal farms. From 13 to 18. When I turned 18 I enrolled into the Job Corps. My mother had passed away, you know, all my brothers and sisters I didn't know where they were because we were scattered when we were all kids, so I was actually in a world all by myself. I didn't have nobody to help me and so forth. So all I knew then for survival is trouble, you see; like burglaries, trying to steal some food, trying to

steal some clothes, because I hadn't really had the opportunity of getting an education, going to school and having the things that most kids have today. So in Job Corps, when I left Job Corps I came back and got one of these here jobs and they actually was paying me $38.00 for a whole week's work and the work was tough. But $38.00 a week wasn't holding me up too good and I committed a couple of burglaries to sort of even things up and that's when I got my first sentence to prison when I was 18. I got a three-year sentence. And instead of making parole, they let me stay the whole three-year sentence without getting a parole. So, I was 21 years old when I was paroled and I stayed in Job Corps for two months. So, that was two months' time that I had been free since I come up to the County Farm, actually two months since I was 13 years old. And I was 21 years old at the time. I hadn't had but two months' freedom since the time I was 13 until the time I was 21. And then I went and got this here crime and find myself on death row.

In this prisoner's reasonable assessment, "I've never really never had a straight shot at life, and now here I wind up with a death sentence."

Violence and Sanity

Gazing on a doomed soul on route to the gallows, John Bradford is said to have uttered the now-famous phrase, "There but for the grace of God go I." Bradford lived at a time when capital punishment was a popular disposition for offenses considered trivial by today's standards. Other citizens, perhaps, could readily put themselves in the condemned person's shoes. Who would not steal a loaf of bread to feed his family? Who might not default on a loan? Everyman, surely, was envisioned in many men condemned to death for minor crimes. Small human fallings from grace punished in so harsh and final a manner must have been a chilling spectacle of great personal import.

Yet Bradford's truth is a deeper truth than mere empathy for those whose social situation approximates our own. At bottom is the recognition that chance and circumstance dictate much of one's life; that any one of us could have been dealt a life that ended in the ignominy of a death sentence. Nowhere is this more apparent than in the case of seriously mentally disturbed persons—persons whose actions seem beyond their own comprehension or control, seemingly dictated by urges that impel bizarre and sometimes violent conduct. Who can be held responsible for these acts? Who is immune from the pressures and constraints of mental illness? Who takes comfort in the execution of such persons?

Only a handful of prisoners among Alabama's condemned may have been actively psychotic at the time of their crimes.[38] The man chosen to represent this group descended from the security of the middle class to the forgotten world of the condemned prisoner. His blurred memory, searching confusion, and palpable despair convey the struggle of men who must reconstruct and make real their involvement in crimes of raw and occasionally gruesome violence. The private failings and doubts that moved this man, though, may be familiar to many of us. We have seen the guilt that plagued him in others, perhaps in ourselves. The shock and revulsion he felt at his crime would surely ring true for us, too. His frailty, however, marks him as different and susceptible. By his own account, life problems were felt as crises and crises had the impact of disasters. A broken marriage thus sparked vengeful destruction of those who, sensing his limits and mindful of his needs, nevertheless abandoned him to the world, naked and defenseless.

The crimes of psychotics often display purpose that relates to deep-seated and volatile needs. These crimes are felt to be senseless because making sense of them is too difficult or painful. Characteristically, this man speaks of his inability to comprehend his crime. Yet he is obsessed with remorse. Suicide, an escape from the crime and from himself, is a constant preoccupation. His crime and remorse bespeak a man past the edge of sanity. The crime is monstrous, but its author is better described as confused, inadequate, and mentally ill. Society, however, has not bothered to seriously pose the question of why this man killed. Instead, his life is demanded in payment for his crime—collected, preferably, on the day of execution, or squandered over years of imprisonment.

I think about killing myself every day. For one thing, see, I didn't, I didn't even know I killed my wife or nothing like that, you know. I didn't even know. It was just a senseless crime, it's just senseless. And that eats on my, that's why when something like that happens, "Why is the world like it is?" She just got her a new old automobile, and I was real happy for her. She, she went through high school, but nothing, never did get in the lunch line, you know, always the freebie line and all that kind of stuff. That embarrassed her, you know. I didn't have nothing but sympathy, love for my wife, and a lot of opinions for my mother-in-law. She had had a hard time raising the three girls, and she had just come into some money that was going to make her life easier too, for the rest of her years. She inherited some land from her daddy and sold it. And there's no reason, no way in the world I'd have took those peoples' lives. If I'd had to, if I'd known, or had any inkling or any idea that I was going to do something like that, I'd have killed myself before I ever allowed myself to (kill them) . . .

I think of suicide all the time. It's hard to live every day knowing that I had a good life up until—I had everything that most people didn't have, you know, all through my life. I was an only child, and I guess I was what you called spoiled rotten and all this kind of stuff. I was given everything I wanted: cars, motorcycles, whatever. All the money I wanted to spend. And I never did, you know, get involved with stealing or anything.

I had an accident when I was young, and it kind of, it's been eating me up all my life. I had a baseball practice with a young boy, when I was about 15 or 16 years old and he was, I don't know, 9 or 10, whatever. He was pitching and I hit the ball with the bat and hit him in the head. And that's had me, kept me from really enjoying things I was given all these years. I, I, I felt guilty about everything I've ever had. All my life every day I've prayed for God, if he could to take me instead of somebody else, another child that might be dying with leukemia or whatever. And of course that never does happen.

Like I said, I felt guilty all my life and really haven't been able to enjoy life as most people should have that's had all the benefits I've had. I had the ability to play professional baseball. The coach and a lot of people told me, and I signed a contract but just couldn't ever play. I just had what you'd call a bad head. Couldn't ever get straightened out, got to drinking and staying out and not practicing like I should, and I didn't make it. Everything that come up in life like that, I'd put out a lot at first, you know. Going to college I made As and Bs my first year. Then just something happened to me. I don't know if I just felt like I wasn't worthy or whatever. I don't know what it would be really. But many times I look back on my life and that's what I come up with. Just get to feeling guilty and then flunking out or whatever, you know . . .

I've had what you'd call a couple of nervous relapses or breakdowns or whatever you want to call them. You're nervous, you feel like you're in an ant bed, and my mouth closed up like a little hole—I couldn't open my mouth. Once was when my little girl fell out of a trailer and we thought she'd broke her back. Another time was hunting with my daddy. My daddy's a big hunter, and my granddaddy's a big fisherman. In fact, my daddy, he's such a big hunter, he leases a lake every year with several guys where he works for dove hunting and all. He's in a hunt club and all that stuff. He's real involved in it. But several times I've been; I guess I've been deer hunting probably four times in my life. I went to sleep all four times. One time a deer come within spitting distance almost, you know. I couldn't, couldn't bring myself to shoot the deer. And I've had dogs, you know, run out in front of the car and run over them. I've even had birds. I've had tears running down my eyes when a bird ran into the car. And yet I killed three people. I, you talk about something, I don't know if you've ever, how, what the situation with you is, but I just can't understand that. Why? Why? It don't make sense.

Pathways to death row involve familiar scenarios of human defeat, often compellingly articulated in the literature on capital mitigation over the last few decades: lives that begin too soon, forcing children into alien adult roles; lives that never materialize, spawning self-destructive rage; lives that turn sour, leaving trails of shock and regret.[39] There are no monsters or mutants, no creatures beyond human comprehension, as the media would have it. There are, instead, human violence and human indifference—both on the part of the offenders and the society. Capital offenders, to be sure, are not passive victims of circumstance; they are implicated in their fates. But society, too, is at fault, for it confronts these men with challenges for which they are not equipped to cope competently, humanly, even sanely. Born and reared in environments rife with violence and trauma, many of these men exploited violence-promotive norms because few other means of ego support or status were open to them.[40] As individual men of violence, they may indeed have played hideously caricatured roles, but the stage and script of each violent encounter were of society's making.

It is a continuing source of sadness that each man's journey to death row takes him over terrain comprising human failures that recur regularly, and with disastrous results. But nothing is done until it is too late and tragic fates have once again been sealed. When tragedy takes the form of murder, there is a predictable outcry of anguish and indignation. Blame is allocated, vengeance is sought, men are condemned to die. In the interim, condemned prisoners spend long and empty years awaiting execution on death row under conditions that often mirror their traumatic, tortured pasts.[41] Haunted by lives steeped in despair, awash in loss and grief and even madness, Hinton reports that condemned prisoners learn firsthand a harsh truth: "Hell was real, and it had an address and a name. Death Row, Holman Prison. Where love and hope went to die."[42]

Notes

1   Lewis (1979); Debro, Roebuck, Murty, and McCann (1987); Light and Donovan (1997); Lisak and Beszterczey (2007). The latest research on what has been termed "the cycle of violence" (Widom, 1989) linking abusive treatment in childhood to adult violence, broadly applicable to condemned prisoners, has concluded that neglect in the home, even more than violence, "emerged as the most robust predictor of adult violence" (Myers, Lloyd, Turanovic, and Pratt, 2018: 266).

2 Van Soest, Park, Johnson, and McPhail (2003). The authors compare the life histories of 37 men executed in Texas in 1997. Childhood neglect and violence are ubiquitous in this sample, as prior research would suggest. The worst crimes were committed by those men who suffered from neurological deficiency and severe child abuse. For other studies exploring pathways to death row paved by deprivation and abuse, see Jones, Savel, and Radelet (1996); Lezin (1999); Cunningham and Vigen (2002); Schroeder, Guin, Chaisson, and Houchins (2004). Note that the effects of childhood trauma are cumulative and become progressively more severe if untreated (Anda et. al., 2005; Shonkoff and Garner, 2012). None of the prisoners I interviewed reported any helpful interventions in their childhoods.

3 Chessman (1972: 4).

4 Chessman (1972: 11–12).

5 Gettinger (1979: XXI).

6 "Editorials" (1977).

7 *The Montgomery Advertiser* (1975).

8 Quoted in Gettinger (1979: 265).

9 As recently as March 30, 2018, A *New York Post* headline, in full caps, announced with outrage that "The fiend behind one of the most infamous shootings in city history—the 'Palm Sunday Massacre' that left eight children and two young moms dead in Brooklyn in 1984—has been quietly released from an upstate prison" (Cohen, Feis, and Celona, 2018).

10 Haney (2005: 84).

11 Haney (2005: 92).

12 Haney (2005: 92).

13 Haney (2005: 90).

14 Berns (1979: 163).

15 Berns (1979: 163).

16 Blecker (2008: 995).

17 Haney (2005: 99–100).

18 Haney (2005: 99–100).

19 Hinton (2018: 133).

20 Haney (2005: 162). For a more recent interpretation of arguments on the notion that capital punishment as practiced today in an error-prone and often brutal justice system nevertheless respects rather than violates personhood, see Blecker (2008) and Blecker (2013).

21 Haney (2014).

22 Wishnie (1977: 145). The violence dynamics explored by Wishnie can be found among prisoners, especially hard-core prisoners who see themselves as convicts committed to violence as a way of life. Their world "is populated by men who doubt their worth as human beings and who feel they must constantly find occasions to prove themselves by dominating others"; indeed, many convicts see violence as "their *only* means of becoming men of consequence who are taken seriously." See Johnson, Rocheleau, and Martin (2016: 148–149).

23 Sadly, the adage "violence begets violence" may apply equally to individuals and societies. See Archer and Gartner (1978: 219).

24 Vaillant (1977: 371).

25 Wishnie (1977: 37).

26 Vaillant (1977: 28).

27 Wishnie (1977: 44, 54).

28 Wishni (1977: 41).

29 Wishnie (1977: 41).

30 Wishnie (1977: 40). See generally Johnson et al. (2016); Toch (2017).

31 Gettinger (1979).

32 Gettinger (1979: 116).

33 For pertinent literature reviews, see generally Haney (2005); Bohm (2015).

34 Comparable profiles are available elsewhere. For Florida's condemned, for example, see Lewis (1979: 200). See also Debro et al. (1987); Light and Donovan (1997); Johnson (1998); Toch, Acker, and Bonventre (2018).

35 The subcultural values and concerns underlying premature autonomy among the very poor are discussed in Miller (1958: 5). The ego adaptations typical under these conditions are indicated in Toch (1971: 386).

36 Some of the attributes of this group are discussed in Irwin (1970), under the heading of "state-raised youths."

37 Jones et al. (1996: XIV): "We know something about what causes people to become murderers. Many are victims of physical, sexual, or emotional abuse, of a lack of resources or responsible role models. Instead of talking about the justice of the death penalty, perhaps we ought to talk about the thousands of children who never get much of a chance in life. In this sense we all bear some responsibility for the high rates of violence that plague our society today." See also Lisak and Beszterczey (2007: 118): "A majority of these families had multigenerational histories of either physical abuse or sexual abuse. Almost every family had a history of mental illness and substance abuse, and many were characterized by long-term instability and histories of criminal behavior ... Nearly half of the sample suffered some form of neurological impairment; nearly all manifested psychiatric symptoms of some kind (other than substance abuse), and nearly half were suicidal. Almost all of the men had serious problems in school, and strong minorities manifested the typical signs of severely troubled adolescence: delinquency, running away, and homelessness." Further, Smith (2005: 369) states that: "It is the rare serious perpetrator who was not also a victim ... It is the rare death row inmate whose life does not read like a case study of extreme deprivation and abuse. It is the rare juvenile incarcerated in an adult prison for rape or murder who has had anything other than the cruelest of childhoods."

38 There undoubtedly are other psychotics housed on death rows in other states. See Miller and Radelet (1993). The following excerpt from a letter published in an informal newsletter by the Illinois Coalition Against the Death Penalty is a case in point. It is important to note that this letter was not published to impugn the mental health of its author, but simply *as one of a series of communications from death row prisoners to coalition members. This unfortunate prisoner's pleas, despite their mental health overtones, are quite moving.*

    "THE GOOD ... IS LOVE, TRUTH, PEACE, FREEDOM, & JUSTICE." THE TRUE REFLECTION OF JESUS; FOR "JESUS!! MEAN JUSTICE," AS HIS SPIRIT WAS FREE, HIS SOUL—AT PROFOUND PEACE, & ... HE ONLY SPOKE THE "SOOTHING TRUTH"; SAYING ... HE LOVE ALL LIVING CREATURES OF THIS WORLD.

    "THE BAD ... IS—MURDERING, THIEVE"

    "THE BAD ... IS—MURDERING, THIEVERY, ROBBERY, RAPE, LIEs & DECEPTION. ETCETERA ETCETERA, ETCETERA. (LUCIFERS) ROLES IN LIFE.

    &!

    "THE UGLY" ... IS THE INJUSTICE THAT'S POURED UPON THE INNOCENT AND RIGHT. YES—the ill acts of man towards man for POLITICAL FAVORS & POWER.

    "THE GOOD ... THE BAD ... AND ... THE UGLY."

    Greetings ... my natural brothers and sisters. This day I'm speaking to you of THE GOOD, THE BAD, & THE UGLY; while standing between questions and answers. KNOWING & KNOWING NOT WHY such ugliness are now living within our so-called JUSTICE SYSTEM? And know not why—the BAD has changed places with the GOOD? Of the three (3) I prefer the GOOD as all of my life in retrospect up to this day—10/25/80 ... I can yet view myself caressing DEEP WANTS, UNEXPLAINABLE NEEDS to hear and share truth while—LOVING IN PEACE. I've always possessed a special tenderness for the aged and infant; and I've always cared about animals but now I'm made to suffer from their absences period, and the possibility of never again ENJOYING the BEAUTIFUL SCENERY of a BABY'S SMILE, A CHILDS laughter, and the wisdom of the aged.

39 Haney (2008). I have testified as a mitigation expert in a fair number of capital cases and have seen these dynamics at play firsthand.

40 Wolfgang and Ferracuti (1967); Toch (2017).

41 The notion that death rows likely mirror the traumatic pasts of condemned prisoners is an insight drawn from the work of Kupers (2018: 61): "Because prisoners on death row, on average, have experienced more traumas in their lives than almost any other subject of citizens, we should make every effort to make certain that their experiences in prison do not mirror their traumatic past." With time on their hands and little help with the scars of their childhoods, it is little wonder that that death row can be described, in the words of a death row prisoner in North Carolina, as "an endless sorrow and hurt that's refused to heal," leaving him feeling "like a dog about to be euthanized." Significantly, this man resides in a congregate solitary confinement death row in the nation.

42 Hinton (2018: 95).

References

Archer, D., & Gartner, R. (1978). Legal homicide and its consequences. In L. Kutash & S. B. Kutash (Eds.), *Violence* (pp. 118–149). San Francisco, CA: Jossey-Bass.

Anda, R. F., Felitti, V. J., Bremner, J. D., Walker, J. D., Whitfield, C., Perry, B. D., Dube, S. R., & Giles, W. H. (2005). The enduring effects of abuse and related adverse experiences in childhood: A convergence of evidence from neurobiology and epidemiology. *Pediatrics*, *129*(1), 174–186.

Berns, W. (1979). *For capital punishment*. New York: Basic Books.

Blecker, R. (2008). Killing them softly: Mediations on a painful punishment of death. *Fordham University Law Journal*, *35*, 969–998.

Blecker, R. (2013). *The death of punishment: Searching for justice among the worst of the worst*. New York: St. Martin's Press.

Bohm, R. (2015). *DeathQuest: An introduction to the theory and practice of capital punishment in the United States* (4th ed.). New York: Routledge.

Chessman, C. (1972). Trial by ordeal. In S. Levine (Ed.), *Death row: An affirmation of life* (pp. 5–26). San Francisco, CA: Glide Publications.

Cohen, S., Feis, A., & Celona, L. (2018, March 30). "Palm Sunday Massacre" killer quietly freed from prison. *New York Post*. Retrieved from https://nypost.com/2018/03/30/1984-palm-sunday-massacre-killer-quietly-freed-from-prison.

Cunningham, M. D., & Vigen, M. P. (2002). Death row inmate characteristics, adjustment, and confinement: A critical review of the literature. *Behavioral Sciences & The Law*, *20*(1), 191–210.

Debro, J., Roebuck, J., Murty, K., & McCann, C. (1987). Death row inmates: A comparison of Georgia and Florida profiles. *Criminal Justice Review*, *12*(1), 41–46.

Editorials and comments. (1977, January 18). *Tuscaloosa News*.

Gettinger, S. H. (1979). *Sentenced to die*. New York: Macmillan.

Haney, C. (2005). *Death by design* (Kindle ed.). Oxford: Oxford University Press.

Haney, C. (2008). Evolving standards of decency: Advancing the nature and logic of capital mitigation. *Hofstra Law Review*, *36*, 835–882.

Haney, C. (2014). Media criminology and the death penalty. *DePaul Law Review*, *58*, 689–740.

Hinton, A. R. (with Hardin, L. L.) (2018). *The sun does shine: How I found life and freedom on death row*. New York: St. Martin's Press.

Irwin, J. (1970). *The felon*. Englewood Cliffs, NJ: Prentice-Hall.

Johnson, R. (1998). *Death work: A study of the modern execution process* (2nd ed.). Belmont, CA: Wadsworth.

Johnson, R., Rocheleau, A. M., & Martin, A. B. (2016). *Hard time: A fresh look at understanding and reforming the prison*. Hoboken, NJ: Wiley-Blackwell.

Jones, L., Savel, L., & Radelet, M. L. (1996). *Final exposure: Portraits from death row*. Boston, MA: Northeastern University Press.

Kupers, T. A. (2018). Waiting alone to die. In H. Toch, J. R. Acker, & V. M. Bonventure (Eds.), *Living on death row: The psychology of waiting to die* (pp. 47–69). Washington, DC: American Press Association.

Lewis, P. W. (1979). Killing the killers: A post-Furman profile of Florida's condemned: A personal account. *NPPA Journal*, *25*(2), 200–211.

Lezin, K. (1999). *Finding life on death row: Profiles of six death row inmates*. Boston, MA: Northeastern University Press.

Light, K., & Donovan, S. (1997). *Texas death row*. Jackson, MS: University Press of Mississippi.

Lisak, D., & Beszterczey, S. (2007). The cycle of violence: The life histories of 43 death row inmates. *Psychology of Men & Masculinity*, *8*(2), 118–128.

Miller, K. L., & Radelet, M. L. (1993). *Executing the mentally ill: The criminal justice system and the case of Alvin Ford*. Newbury Park, CA: Sage.

Miller, W. (1958). Lower-class culture as a generating milieu of gang delinquency. *Journal of Social Issues*, *14*(3), 4–19.

The Montgomery Advertiser. (1975, March 28). Page 4.

Myers, W., Lloyd, K., Turanovic, J. J., & Pratt, T. C. (2018). Revisiting a criminological classic: The cycle of violence. *Journal of Contemporary Criminal Justice, 34*(3), 266–286.

Schroeder, J., Guin, C. C., Chaisson, R., & Houchins, D. (2004). Pathways to death row for America's disabled youth: Three case studies driving reform. *Journal of Youth Studies, 7*(4), 451–472.

Shonkoff, J. P., & Garner, A. S. (2012). Lifelong effects of early childhood adversity and toxic stress. *Pediatrics, 129*(1), 232–246.

Smith, A. (2005). The monster in all of us: When victims become perpetrators. *Suffolk University Law Review, 38,* 367–394.

Toch, H. (1971). The delinquent as poor loser. *Seminars in Psychiatry, 3*(3), 386–399.

Toch, H. (2017). *Violent men: An inquiry into the psychology of violence* (25th anniversary ed.). Washington, DC: American Psychological Association.

Toch, H., Acker, J. R., & Bonventre, V. (Eds.) (2018). *Living on death row.* Washington, DC: American Psychological Association Books.

Vaillant, G. (1977). *Adaptation to life.* Boston, MA: Little, Brown.

Van Soest, D., Park, H. S., Johnson, T. K., & McPhail, B. (2003). Different paths to death row: A comparison of men who committed heinous and less heinous crimes. *Violence and Victims, 18*(1), 15–33.

Widom, C. S. (1989). The cycle of violence. *Science, 244,* 160–166.

Wishnie, H. (1977). *The impulsive personality.* New York: Plenum.

Wolfgang, M., & Ferracuti, F. (1967). *The subculture of violence.* London: Tavistock.

PART II

The Experience of Death Row Confinement

Life on the Row is a blending of the real and the unreal; it's a clash of internal and external tension, the tension of everyday living magnified a hundred times. You're a prisoner in a strange land. You are and you aren't a part of the larger whole around you. You form friendships and your friends die. You dream and your dreams die.

(Caryl Chessman, former death row prisoner, San Quentin Prison, executed May 2, 1960)

I've spent over 5,000 days on death row. Not a single waking hour of any of those days has gone by without me thinking about my date with the executioner . . . All that thinking about it is like a little dying, even if you're on the best death row on earth.

(Willie Turner, former death row prisoner, Virginia State Penitentiary, executed May 23, 1995)

I was headed to Holman Prison. The House of Pain. Dead Man Land. The Slaughter Pen of the South. It had a lot of names. I was terrified.

(Anthony Hinton, former death row prisoner, Holman Prison, Alabama, exonerated April 3, 2015)

3

ROOTS OF POWERLESSNESS

The Physical Setting

Death row is meant to be imposing, stark, and austere. Alabama's death row, the setting of this inquiry, is no exception.[1] Perhaps the best description of the setting was given by one of the death row prisoners I interviewed, a self-styled prison "connoisseur" who has done time in various prisons across the nation:

> Now I been around and I never seen a prison in my life or heard of one as nitshit and rule-crazy as this motherfucker here . . . I'll take this penitentiary right now and put it back, say, in the early 1950s, back when it was sure enough rough, sure enough a chain-ganging way of life. That's where it should be at, instead of the late 1970s along with your other prisons and things. It's still in the 1950s where they're kicking ass, feeding slop, and harassing you any way they possibly can.

The physical setting of death row in Alabama is intimidating. To get there, at the time of this study, one had to pass through five locked gates: The first marked the entrance to the Holman Prison compound; the second protected the prison proper; the third separated the outsider from the living, working, and feeding areas of the general prison; the fourth gate separated the special housing unit devoted to isolating prisoners from the rest of the prison; and the fifth set off death row within the isolation unit, making condemned prisoners pariahs within even the constricted world of the solitary confinement housing area. Alabama's death row has grown over the years, consuming more tiers, but the general feeling of isolation—of being buried alive—remains the same. "You got to go some to get in here," remarked one inmate, referring to the arsenal of security that confined him and his peers on death row.

The fact that one has to "go some" to get out of death row may be more to the point. On death row, one feels deeply embedded in the prison—lodged, figuratively, in its bowels, and shut off from light and liberty. The setting is like a tomb, which parallels the psychological experience of death row confinement. The description offered by Bryan Stevenson captures the isolated and isolating quality of Alabama's death row today:

Condemned prisoners on Alabama's death row unit are housed in windowless concrete buildings that are notoriously hot and uncomfortable. Each death row inmate was placed in a five-by-eight-foot cell with a metal door, a commode, and a steel bunk. The temperatures in August consistently reached over 100 degrees for days and sometimes weeks at a time. Incarcerated men would trap rats, poisonous spiders, and snakes they found inside the prison to pass the time and to keep safe. Isolated and remote, most prisoners got few visits and even fewer privileges.[2]

These harsh conditions regularly give rise to a lived experience marked by daily and nightly horrors, which are vividly captured by Hinton, a now-exonerated veteran of Alabama's death row:

Every night, I could hear the rats scratching and scurrying across the floors. I imagined the roaches swarming the walls at night and hiding back in the vent during the day to watch me. I was the trapped insect. Those roaches had more freedom than I did. The sounds at night were like being in the middle of a horror movie—creatures crawling around, men moaning or screaming or crying. Everyone cried at night. One person would stop and another would start. It was the only time you could cry anonymously. I blocked out the sound. I didn't care about anyone's tears or their screams. Sometimes there was laughter—maniacal laughter—and that was the most frightening. There was no real laughter on death row.[3]

The living area of death row is divided into tiers of cells arranged in cell blocks. Each cell block holds two tiers of cells. The cell blocks are arranged diagonally and are close together. Even so, with the density of steel and concrete, communication between cell blocks is almost impossible. Communication between tiers in the same cell block is difficult. The prisoners are only vaguely aware of events that occur in areas of death row other than their own tier. In a sense, each tier is a miniature death row, with its own prisoner population, social climate, cultural history, and character.[4]

Death row has a number of unpleasant physical features. The cells are narrow, dark, and close, and without amenities. The toilets are small and cramped, little more than metal pipes wedged in each cell floor. The aesthetics of this arrangement leave much to be desired, since these crude toilet surrogates flush poorly and resist cleaning. "My cell always smells like shit," complained one man. This sentiment is seconded by his fellow prisoners.

The smells of death row are not offset by the aroma of prison food or by other qualities of the prison diet, though sometimes the scent of the food is said to mask the odor of feces, urine, and sweat. Death row inmates eat what other prisoners eat, but they contend that because they are located far from the kitchen, the food they receive is invariably cold, stale-smelling, and tasteless. The food portions seem quite modest for grown men, and many inmates complain of hunger as a novel and difficult aspect of their confinement. The inmates also maintain that their sparse food allotments are adulterated by staff, who allegedly add dirt and other contaminants to the standard prison fare to express their contempt for the offenders who populate death row.

The death chamber, the death witness chamber, and the silent cell (for men whose executions are imminent) are located in a ground-level tier that supports one of the cell blocks comprising death row. (At the time of the original study reported in this book, all prisoners were executed by electrocution.)[5] This tier is not part of the living area of death row. It is, however, both a hub of social activity for staff and a tangible reminder to the prisoners of the purpose of death row confinement.

When I conducted the interviews in the death witness chamber, each inmate would arrive at the chamber door with his hands cuffed behind his back, and with two or even three officers in tow. At my request, the inmate's hands would be cuffed in front to allow for a more comfortable interview session. Introductions would be exchanged between myself and the prisoner, and the officers would be thanked for delivering the prisoner to my care. No officers were present or even in the vicinity of the chamber during the interviews.

The death witness chamber is a small concrete room, painted an institutional gray. Often, the overflow of water from an adjacent toilet drained into the room. Although the floor was cleaned and mopped daily, it remained damp and musty. With the added smell of dead cigarette butts, of which dozens accumulated each day, the odor of the room grew foul. The inmates and I smoked almost continuously during our conversations, partly to reduce tension and partly to share a common ritual. Cigarettes became a modest gift of thanks to prisoners who shared so much of their lives with me in the brief span of one or two hours, in a closed room where temperatures routinely registered over 95 degrees, and not infrequently passed the 100-degree mark. The prisoners, at least, were dressed appropriately for the occasion—some shirtless, others barefoot, all clad in hand-me-down prison clothing, often tattered, well ventilated for life in such close quarters.

The obvious discomforts and our shared reactions to them, such as smoking constantly and sweating profusely, may have helped establish a bond between myself and the prisoners. Of greater import, however, was the presence of the electric chair—"Old Sparky"—just one room away from us, visible through picture windows enabling official guests of the state of Alabama to witness without obstruction the executions being carried out. The chair was an awesome sight—a giant yellow structure embraced by thick black leather straps, connected by tubes of encased wire to an unseen generator, and crowned with a prominent circular sign, on which was inscribed in bold red letters the simple command: READY. The stark presence of the chair reinforced the gravity of the situation, added to the interviews a tone of high seriousness, and provided a catalyst for discussions of life in an environment that draws its meaning and purpose from such an instrument of death. We had here, then, not the pristine sterility of the laboratory, but a complex and ugly real-life situation, with human beings and their human problems demanding attention and concern.

Many of my impressions of the physical setting of death row are the product of a tour taken before I conducted the interviews. It is always a troubling experience to venture through prison tiers inspecting the cells and their occupants; many visitors, I was told, turn their gaze from the prisoners they are purportedly there to view. The prisoners, for their part, play the expected roles with élan, often providing gratuitous shows of hostility or abusiveness for their uninvited guests. In a sense, the impotent inmates get their say for a while, on their own stage. A tour of the cells on death row, however, is much worse than that of a regular prison compound. Men who shall become research subjects, colleagues of a sort, correspondents, even friends, look somehow bloated in puny cells, pressed in by living continuously in spaces not much more substantial or inviting than attic closets. The effect is of a staged presentation of a new and dangerous species, held secure for clinical scrutiny. My job, I knew, was to explore life in what was later described for me as a "mausoleum for the living." Notwithstanding the macabre connotations of the assignment, the death row prisoners were expansive and eager to use me as an audience for their private rage and despair; analysis of the impact of death row confinement is, essentially, little more than a translation of the accounts given by these men.

The Custodial Regime

Death row is a prison within a prison, physically and socially isolated from the prison community and the outside world. Condemned prisoners in Alabama at the time of this study lived 23½ hours alone in their cells, punctuated by 30 minutes devoted to private exercise in a closely guarded outdoor cage designated for high-security risk inmates. The regime today offers prisoners an hour a day out of the cell, which includes small-group recreation when staffing permits. However, chronic understaffing results in a daily regime much like the one I studied in 1979, and essentially the same as the regime offered to Texas death row prisoners today.[6]

On Alabama's death row, and on solitary confinement death rows in general, inmates try to fill empty time with exercise, reading, reverie, radio, television (if available),[7] or conversation with their neighbors. Strategies vary. For some men, a tightly patterned sequence of private activities and accomplishments is required to reduce anxiety and maintain self-control. For example:

> I'm trying to compile a crossword puzzle dictionary to try to get published. And I'm working on writing a cowboy western. I think anybody can write one of those. Just have to pick up a few words, you know, cowboy type words. I think anybody can write a cowboy plot. And I'm also working on a history novel. And I do a lot of reading, and I stick my head in the law books every day. I try to, you know. And I try to read a chapter or two out of the Bible every day. Try to write a letter every day. I've got an exercise list up on the wall, I try to do those. And I've also got a list of things in personal hygiene stuff I need to take care of every day. If I don't have that list to check off, I forget to do it. Now I try to have enough up there to do to keep busy, to keep my mind occupied while I'm awake. In a situation like this, I think it makes you regress back to your childhood, and you do little childish type things. But I've been able to stop myself from doing it. I think if I didn't have such a list up there that I could look at sometime during the day, whenever I would have done some things like that, I probably would have gotten out of control.

Others find a measure of relief in loose configurations of activities, the object of which is simply to occupy otherwise irksome time.

> Sometimes I turn to reading the scriptures, you know, and reading other religious literature, which I find very beneficial . . . I've been into it for quite some time, you know, and I love the scriptures, really. So, I either turn to talk to a friend or reading the holy scriptures, you know. Or if the television is playing I try and watch some program on TV and try to gain some benefit out of it, rather than just keep on pacing and being irritated with the thought of this cruel sentence.

But the war against boredom, the death row prisoners' intimate companion, typically ends in defeat. Few men can bind themselves to artificial programs of work or study that must extend over years of life on death row. Were television regularly available, many prisoners would no doubt retreat into the fantasy life of soap operas, a monotonous but addictive routine. For Alabama's condemned, however, books and radios are the principal stuff of recreation. Moreover, since most condemned prisoners prefer action over contemplation, a regimen of musty library books and country music leaves them feeling they have literally nothing to do with their time. Somehow, they make do with the help of insects and other creatures who share their cells, or with unlikely (and unrewarding) reading selections, such as Webster's dictionary, which reveal the poverty of their formal educations. The quality of their prison lives is demonstrated, in part, in the insipid diversions they employ to pass time.

PRISONER: I have got so bored at times, I used to hook cockroaches together, sort of like they was a team of mules, to drag a matchbox around on the floor to pass time. I mean that may sound weird to you or somebody else, and it might be. Matter fact I just flushed a little frog down the shit jack the other day that I had back there. It came up through the shit jack. I kept him back there a couple of weeks and I kicked roaches and things to feed him. Just any little old thing.

INTERVIEWER: Just to keep you busy.

PRISONER: To more or less keep your mind off the damned chair and the things that you're seeing around you. Anything to occupy your mind.

■ ■ ■

I got a big dictionary. I look in there and I read—just look at words, I can't even pronounce the words I be looking at, you know, but I read the meaning to them. I like doing stuff like that. It's hard to stay at that thing, you get sleepy—without moving—you can't stay up but an hour at a time, you have to lay back down. I can't seem to settle down in my cell. Like, I spend 23½ hours in there and I can't ever come to peace with myself. It irritates me all the time.

The prisoners are effectively isolated from one another. "I talk to a guy next door," said one prisoner, "but if I didn't get out and see him as I pass his cell when I shower, I wouldn't even know what the guy looks like. I hardly know what he looks like now." Men locked in adjacent cells are barely able to make physical contact. "You can pass objects to each other and you can virtually touch hands then if you wanted to," stated one man, "but that's as close as we come to each other. At any time—24 hours a day, 365 days a year—that's the situation. You can't even play cards with a guy, like to kill time."

The routine of the death row prisoner is a grinding, dull, and redundant existence, a life of solitude and pressure. The experience of one of the more vulnerable inmates is particularly painful, and highlights the lower-order stresses experienced by other inmates:

PRISONER: I sit in that cell, you know, and it seems like I'm just ready to scream or go crazy or something. And you know, the pressure, it builds up, and it feels like everything is—you're sitting there and things start, you know, not hearing things, things start to coming in your mind. You start to remember certain events that happened, bad things. It just gets to a person. It's a strain on a person. I sit up at night, you know. You just sit there, and it seems like you're going to go crazy. You've got three walls around you and bars in front of you, and you start looking around, you know, and it seems like things are closing in on you. Like last night, when I sit in there and everything's real quiet, things, just a buzzing noise gets to going in my ears. And I sit there, and I consciously think, "Am I going to go crazy?" And the buzzing gets louder; and you sit there and you want to scream and tell somebody to stop it. And most of the time you get up—if I start making some noise in my cell, it will slack off. And it sounds stupid, I know, but it happens.

INTERVIEWER: It's almost like you've got to break this cycle somehow?

PRISONER: Yeah, stop it. Get something else started. Get your mind off it, because it's real quiet, and it's pretty hard to break the cycle. You know, you're sitting there, and I don't know, I reckon it's, if you don't, sometimes I wonder if I don't get it stopped, I'm going crazy or something.

INTERVIEWER: That must be a pretty frightening thought.

PRISONER: It is. Like if you're in something you can't get out, and you're sitting there and you're trying your best to break the barrier, and it just won't break. And you know, maybe tonight when I lay down it's not going to break when I get up and try to make some noise.

The theme of custody permeates and circumscribes death row and the setting is run with disciplinary precision. The men are considered dangerous, both to themselves and others, and are automatically classified as "escape risks." Watched closely and frisked often, death row prisoners have their hands cuffed behind their backs and are heavily guarded during the rare excursions from their cells. Typically, only one prisoner is moved at any particular time. Death row inmates exercised alone at the time of this study. They were afforded free run of the modest outdoor recreation cage, in which they could pace and engage in calisthenics. These experiences often proved unrewarding, however, because they were so obviously an extension of the close confinement in which the prisoners live. In the words of the prisoners,

> We get 30 minutes a day to go outside. But that's in isolation, too. You walk around. You got a little place they set aside for us, but it's a cage. And you walk around like an animal does. And you know you're no different. You just go out there in another cage and you walk around.

■ ■ ■

> Even when you leave your cell to go to the exercise yard to try to get your mind off things, you really don't 'cause you're just in another confined place and you don't really have room to walk around. And the way, you're carried out there and brought back—two guards, you handcuffed behind your back. Fuck it.

Reforms put in place since the original study allow some prisoners to exercise in small groups, when staffing permits. As it happens, understaffing at Holman makes recreation less readily available in practice than on paper; some prisoners, I learned from interviews at Holman conducted in the summer of 2017, are too anxious about their safety to join in small-group exercise, preferring to stay in their cells or recreate alone.

It is important to note that custodial measures on death row are not experienced by inmates as neutral facts of life on death row or as necessary responses of the prison administration to the task of holding condemned and arguably dangerous men. Instead, inmates experience the environment as a series of assaults. The physical setting is seen as punitively spare; surveillance and security are viewed as ways to inflict pain. The quality of life on death row, according to the inmates, is intentionally substandard.

Filth, inedible food ("food I wouldn't feed my dog"), and worn out clothing are cited as planned features of the death row regime.

> It's unsanitary. They come down there with our [food] trays, and they're coming down with cigarettes in their mouths, ashes dropping down in our trays. I've had hair in my tray. They're talking about us being trash, and they're being unsanitary toward us.

■ ■ ■

> They bring around those trays and the tray is filthy. And you know they can get clean because they got scratch marks all in the dirt there. You know that a wet rag or whatever can get it out. In fact I've asked several of the guards to, just to give me something to do, something physical to do. I'm a machinist and I've always liked doing stuff with my hands, working with wood or whatever. And I told them to bring the trays up there to me and I'd go and scrub them off. But they'd rather bring them up dirty.

■ ■ ■

> Since coming here, I have not been furnished a change of clothes. The only thing in the line of clothes since I've been here is the pants that I have on now and this shirt that I have on now. If you will notice, this shirt has only one button on it. And it's really an old shirt and it's been worn by probably 25 or 30 different people. And the pair of pants that I got is busted in the seat right here and it's the only pair of pants that I have been issued and I have been here 90 days now.

Custodial procedures also include restrictions on mail, visits, and other contacts with the outside world. Packages, whether mailed to the prisoner or delivered by visitors, are limited in weight and number and are carefully searched for contraband, which can be anything from too many items of clothing or books to drugs, alcohol, or weapons. Purchases from the prison "store" are similarly limited and carefully monitored by staff. The isolation of the prisoners, and the resulting emotional and material deprivation, alert men to the joys of conversation and consumption. A chance to place an order at the prison store becomes a major event: a day of liberation from various forms of hunger, but also a symbolic affirmation of the constraint that envelopes the prisoners, terminating their autonomy as adults and undermining their resistance to the prison.

> They have one day that is a store day. The one day actually is to these people on death row like Christmas and all they actually get is cigarettes and candy or cookies, and that's actually become to be a thing like Christmas. I've surveyed it from watching the guys and everybody gets excited and they are actually more happy on Tuesday when they get that little store package. But, you see this is actually what we have been reduced to as far as being men, trying to be a man, finally enjoying a little thing like a cookie. To me it's actually absurd, this actually affects me to that point and there is no way out of it, there is no way to rebel against it.

Some custodial procedures affect the prisoners' relationships with their families and friends. A package "returned to sender" for technical violations of abstruse prison regulations may be seen by the prisoner as an attempt to disrupt the vital flow of support from loved ones. The inmate thus deprived may react with bitterness and hatred.

> OK, my family is not rich. Now, my wife bought felt-tip pens for me to use here. I used to draw her flowers and put them on letters and envelopes and send them to her. This was our way of communicating between my family. I used to draw those pictures of flowers and they were pretty good and they commented on it, the whole family all of a sudden wanted some of these drawings that I was making. But, what happened, what I'm trying to say is that after she bought the pens and she sent them to me, she spent her money to send them to me and they sent them back. I'm saying to myself, "My family is actually wasting their time trying to show me that they care and these people are actually preventing them from even showing me a little affection in the sense that they care." That's enough to hate them. I mean really hate them.

Restrictions on visiting are frequently cited by inmates as disrupting their relations with loved ones. The men are limited to one hour per month of "contact visitation." During contact visits the handcuffed inmate can sit in a guarded room with his visitors. Prisoners are also allowed noncontact visits in which the inmate, sitting in an enclosed oval-shaped structure, is physically separated from his visitors by a metal grid. Noncontact visits are more liberally available because they are easier to monitor and pose fewer security risks than contact visits. These visits, however, often leave the prisoner emotionally drained and bitter at having expended energy and hope in fruitless attempts to sustain ties to loved ones, who may be equally upset about the quality of these visits. Prisoners describe noncontact visits in the following terms:

> My wife, she comes and you have got to sit on that hard stool and holler at the top of your voice so that she can hear you because the little holes, they are clogged up with paint and you can't hear and your voice echoes in the room—you can't even hear yourself. It would be something different if you could talk without screaming at the top of your voice, you know, and then they only allow you to stay there an hour, too. So it's the same thing all over again. You didn't accomplish nothing.

■ ■ ■

PRISONER: You have to talk through little pencil holes in the glass. There's no closeness, ya know? It's not like touching. You can't reach out and touch somebody or hold their hand or anything like that.

INTERVIEWER: Does that discourage your family from coming?

PRISONER: I think it does a lot. I think, I think it puts them in a hopeless situation. They sit there and feel like they're isolated, ya know? They think they're taking it out on us but it's affecting our family. It hurts a lot especially where family goes. Now if your family was allowed to come see you like they do in the penitentiary on Saturday and Sunday and spend all day with you, it would maintain some family ties. Help strengthen them instead of weakening them.

Most inmates feel an enhanced need for human contact and support to help them through their ordeal, and restrictions on visits interfere with their strong desire for outside supports. Loved ones are also affected. Seemingly arbitrary restrictions on the length or intimacy of visits prove painful for both the prisoners and their visitors.

> They say, "A lot of people are here and we've got to take you back so he can come in" . . . To me this is ridiculous, because my wife has to drive a hundred and some miles to come down here and she has two kids to support and she is only making $90 some dollars a week or $80 or whatever, and she can't afford to keep coming out here and be turned away after a 30-minute visit. I hate what they are doing to my family.

■ ■ ■

PRISONER: You know how people give, bring food and everything like that when people die and stuff like that. My mother does all the time. Anybody gets sick or something like that, she always carries a bunch of food over there to feed all the visiting people and all that kind of stuff. Well, it tears her up that she can't bring food down here. I mean that, that, to me, she gets more upset about that than me being down here. (*Laughs*)
INTERVIEWER: Because she can't be hospitable, in other words.
PRISONER: Well, she thinks when somebody's sick or whatever or shut-in or something like that, she's supposed to bring food to them. That's just the way her mother taught her to do, I guess. My grandmother, you know, they're country people there, you know. She brought a ham sandwich down here one time. And they wouldn't even let her bring that in. Ain't no sense.

One prisoner described his visits as his emotional lifeline. Because visits were interrupted or strained, he suffered; should they be terminated, he would be unable to go on. In his words:

> I get a lot of encouragement from my wife. This is why I basically need to be near her or talk to her more often, because she gives me strength to hold on to this thing. She tells me that she's not going to give up and she believes God can make miracles. This kind of stuff helps me, man. And believe it or not, from talking to her—if I could talk to her once a week, I could get through years of this. But if I am cut off from her . . . Even my mother, if I am cut off from these people, you know, it's going to be my downfall because I, in a sense, depend on them for strength to hold on. And when these people [prison staff] mess with that, you know, when they tell me I can't see this person or I've got to talk to them through a metal partition, it's just ridiculous. I can't accept that. I want to be close to them. I want to know that, hey, these people are concerned about me . . . This is all that I have and if they are going to take all of this away from me, I'm dead anyway.

Emotional lifelines are exceedingly fragile and are subject to much stress in the arid milieu of death row. Men find, for example, that otherwise rewarding visits can be ruined by the staff's security procedures. If visits temporarily free the prisoner from his confinement, the accentuated reentry into the world of close custody can be psychologically devastating. For some prisoners, reentry security arrangements translate into costs that outweigh the acknowledged substantial benefits of visits.

> Your people come to this place. You go down and you sit down for an hour or whatever you stayed and you get your mind away from this place. And just as soon as you come in after having enjoyed yourself for a little bit, just as soon as you get up from out there and walk in here, they strip you, look up your asshole and in your mouth and strip search you and handcuff you behind your back and drag you back up that hall. Well, you see, they just broke your whole fucking visit. You would have been better off, in a way, if you'd just stayed in your cell and if you could have slept through that hour . . . I mean that's the kind of attitude that leaves you with after they fuck with you. Knowing your people drove and went through all this trouble to come see you, to give you an hour or something. Then they have taken the fucking time to figure out a way to fuck it up for you.

Most prisoners are nevertheless eager for human contact and willingly comply with prison rules to secure visits. They are troubled, however, when visiting restrictions infringe on their families, who may desperately need supportive contact with their condemned husbands, fathers, brothers, or sons. The pains of confinement on death row can be felt by the prisoner's entire family. "We've all got to face it," said one prisoner, "it's not only me facing the death sentence, it's my whole family." Consequently, the inmates suspect that the officials' motives involve keeping prisoners and their families apart. In the words of one inmate:

> There is no call for this separation between people. You are inside of this institution with all kinds of metal and guards; they are not worried about you escaping, and then if you've got something, I mean, they have you covered 100 percent, to a point where you couldn't escape or hurt somebody. And then, why are you going to hurt your family, anyway?

The custodial regime appears to have taken its toll on family relationships. Ties to the outside world become tenuous for many prisoners, fostering doubts about the integrity of staff (who allegedly interrupt visits, withhold phone calls, and tamper with mail) and the fidelity of family (who may visit or write too little or not at all). Some prisoners, caught between an uncaring staff and a wayward family, despair of achieving support from loved ones. They question whether they can endure the lonely confinement that stretches out before them. One such prisoner observed:

> They won't let you make a phone call. They mess with your mail. They won't let you have your mail, and then you look at yourself . . . Well, my brothers and sisters, they haven't written me and my wife hadn't written me, and I didn't know what was happenin' and maybe she's given up on me and she's done got tired of waitin' and maybe they got tired of comin'. It looked like everything had turned against me, you know? I couldn't get a letter, and I couldn't get a letter out to nobody, and I sit in here. I said, "What are you layin' here for? You ain't got nothin' to look forward to." And so why don't I just get it all over with, you know? Just put it to an end, and then it won't bother me or nothin'.

To make sense of the environment, such as it may be, is to make endurance easier. From the vantage point of the inmates, custodial measures can only be understood as reflecting a policy of routine harassment. The following observations concerning mail, visits, food, showers, and physical abuse are representative of the prisoners' complaints concerning their treatment.

Every day is harassment. Problems with the mail, visiting, food. Since I've been here, roughly a year, they may have four or five visiting lists. They tell you who you can bring and who you can't. They've got a list now where you can only have a partial family visit. In other words, so many people, I think it's eight, that you can do. But some of these guys have like 15 or 20 family members that, that they can't see. Or they can't receive money orders. Nobody that's not on your approved correspondence list is allowed to send you money orders. Money orders have been sent back. And they stop our packages from home containing not necessarily like food, but coffee, cookies, and stuff like this. Well, they stopped feeding us this stuff (from packages) because the guards didn't want to pass them out.

■ ■ ■

The way they do their thing, you know, little old mediocre thing, they may pick at you, do little things that get you. Like when they bring your food, waste all over the tray. Come shower time, time when you take your shower, they give you maybe four minutes, five minutes, four minutes and a half in the shower to shower. You got to wash you head, then take your soap and shave. Then another thing, going to the yard. They come and get you and yell at you, "walk time." First thing in the morning, as soon as the daylight break, "walk time." OK, you got out of bed, it's still dark on the outside.

■ ■ ■

We're treated just like animals put in a cage. You know, like sometimes they come by with their sticks and they poke at you like you're an animal or something. That's the way they feel around here. And once you pick at an animal long enough, he starts fighting back. And we're not in a good place to fight back, and we can't fight back through anybody else.

The prisoners feel doubly aggrieved because they are abused, in their view, as a result of their status as capital offenders. Their behavior in prison has little bearing on their treatment. "We're up here because of our sins," observed one man. "We're not here in the institution being locked up and harassed because of something we've done in the institution." The men portray themselves, not without irony, as well-behaved prisoners. There is merit to this claim, though their obedience to the guards may reflect the high level of fear on death row, a concern that will be examined in detail in Chapter 4. Nevertheless, the fact remains that many condemned prisoners readily comply with the wishes of the staff. Oppressive custodial procedures, as they see it, discriminate against them and impugn their character as inmates. "It's just the idea of being treated so differently," stated one man, "like you're less than the other prisoners. That's enough to just drive you up the wall. You feel so fucking helpless. I've come to the point a lot of times that I want to cry about it. I do, occasionally."

In the main, the prisoners feel powerless to stem the abuses they depict as regular features of their existence. They point to a history of failed reform stratagems, including a hunger strike and various legal campaigns. These actions seem more often to have produced added harassment rather than relief. The men have become cynical. Their experience has taught them that helplessness is a dominant feature of their prison lives—that their thoughts and concerns are of no consequence to prison officials or the general public.

> We had a hunger strike back in February. We had 21 men up there at the time. Fourteen of them started it, and they dropped out a few at a time. After ten days we had about ten people left. Nine or ten. And we decided, the hell with it. You know, just cut it off now because the Board of Corrections wasn't coming off nothing. We'd already had a couple guys pass out from not eating, and people were getting sick, and they weren't paying any attention. They were running all this stuff in the paper: "It's a big joke, they've got food saved up that they're eating," you know. Nobody hears our side of it, it's really depressing.

■ ■ ■

> I can sit here and talk about harassment all day but there's nothing going to be done about it. The guards, they know they got us beat. Because we're criminals. We could go down there to the courthouse and tell everybody all day long, you know, all 37 of us. We could say we're being harassed. One guard could get up there and say, "All those guys—they're criminals. They're going on griping about something. Don't pay no mind."

Few prisoners, however, feel totally devoid of coping options. Some try to frustrate the staff as a kind of quid pro quo for the abuse they suffer. The persistent writ-writer or jailhouse lawyer sometimes adopts this stance. One such inmate said: "Even if I don't get a damned thing done, I've caused them some trouble. They've been causing me so damn much trouble; at least this is a little revenge." Other men openly challenge the guards, on the premise that fire must be met with fire, at least occasionally. Some refuse to play at all, neither harassing nor responding overtly to harassment. More commonly, however, prisoners express their resentment in passive-aggressive efforts at counter harassment. Two typical ploys are recorded below:

> OK, when they bring the food at the bottom, I pretend to read the Bible. It don't take you no more than 10 or 15 minutes for me to read. And durin' that period of time, they go around and take up the trays. OK, so they can't give us any more time? "Why you always last to be finished with your tray?" I said, "Well, number one, because I read the Bible every morning. Number two, I'm gonna read the Bible before I eat and I don't want you to disrupt me from readin' the Bible. And when I finish eatin', I'll send the tray back to the bottom."

■ ■ ■

> Well I'm sitting there the other day at night writing a fucking letter. The old fucking guard come along and says, "I want that pen." I just broke the son of a bitch in half and laid it up there on the door. Told him I'm through with it. Now, it's childish to break a pen just for the hell of it. It's childish for a grown fucking man to walk up and see another grown person sitting there writing a letter and say, "I want that pen." Knowing it's the only fucking one that's in there. And I'm writing

somebody out there on the streets that might do something for me—knowing this stinking son of a bitch ain't gonna do nothing for me. So I figure, why the fuck should I give it to him in writing order. If you give it to him, give it to him where it won't do no fucking good.

Perceptions of harassment, whatever reaction they evoke, make for a volatile social environment. Resentments fester and threaten to erupt. The potential for violence is obvious—so obvious, in fact, that most inmates see this as another part of staff design. A sampling of their views is reflected in the following interview excerpts:

> We're afraid that a situation is gonna be brought about where the guards are gonna set somebody up. When I say set somebody up, they're gonna try to push him to the point of no return, you know? And we've talked about that quite a bit here lately. Guys can see it. They see it happening. And it breeds an atmosphere of fear. Because, am I gonna be the one, you know, that they're gonna single out? If so, how am I gonna handle it?

■ ■ ■

> A man condemned to die, but a person's still pushing him straight on, a man who never did nothing to him . . . They try to get everyone in death row to explode, you know.

■ ■ ■

> The state of Alabama's done spoken for our ass, you know. And so there's not a whole lot left for us. We're caged up like an animal 23½ hours a day, we caught all kinds of flack, you know, from the guards themselves, we caught it from the prison administration by messin' with our privileges and our visits . . . It seems almost like they're trying to drive somebody into pulling something. They're really messin' up. And we sit there and everybody sticks together, trying to keep everybody cool. And it's not easy back there living under that type of strain.

The prisoners may work together to control explosiveness, but as one inmate asserted, "Everybody has a point he can be pushed to and that's it."

Most death row prisoners are not as tough or promiscuously violent as one would suppose and could be managed under conditions less reminiscent of a battle garrison. Despite the pervasive custodial measures, the guards know this. They appeared to be confident of my safety on the occasions they abandoned the tier on which I conducted the interviews; each time I had to hunt them down to return a (presumably dangerous) prisoner to their care. Even were they not assured of my safety, I was. The prisoners' reactions are largely reasonable, even tame. I have noted that some are first offenders or have very brief criminal records. These men appear in shock, searching for ways to comprehend their situation. As newcomers to prison, they are naive and frightened, seeking a magic formula to secure "easy time" and avoid harm. The tougher offenders calmly watch and wait. Seasoned veterans of the courts and prisons, they bide their time, hoping for a loophole in the law, a reprieve, or a miracle.

Of course, it would be a mistake to assume that prisoners on death row do not require close supervision. All have killed at least once, and a few claim the ability, if not the disposition, to kill again.

Hard lives produce hard men, and most of these men have lived close to the bone. As seen in Chapter 2, virtually all are poor, most are illiterate, and many are from ethnic and racial minorities. Virtually all of them have been maimed by lifetimes of neglect. The putative legality of their sentences neither soothes the sting of injustice the men feel nor quells their anger. When provoked, these inmates can pose a substantial risk—and some of them are not all that hard to provoke, if one believes their accounts. Thus, in a sense, custody provides reassurance. But tight, oppressive security may ultimately defeat its own purpose, spawning prisoners made meaner and more vindictive by arbitrary and impersonal treatment. One prisoner maintained, "If I wasn't dangerous before I came here, I'm dangerous now because I've developed these hatreds." Another claimed, "You grow to hate any man in a uniform or any man you see toting those sticks." "They fuck with me," stated one prisoner with obscene bluntness, "and I'll fuck with them. It's just that simple." This man then elaborated the simple yet potentially lethal code of violence that locks him and his keepers in silent combat:

> I look at myself like this: I leave them the fuck alone and I'm going to make them let me alone. I'm going to demand them to never put their fucking hands on me. Now as long as I is inside that cell and going on—damn what they say and do out there. But if they ever spray me in the face with that mace or [a guard] puts his hands on me—if he ever comes back through there, I'm killing that motherfucker. And I don't care if it's him, the warden, or who it is . . . Now they haven't put their hands on me since I been here like I said. But they ain't gonna handcuff my hands behind my back and bring me around and slap the shit out of me and carry me back, because I'm gonna take him off. See, because sooner or later he will forget about it and he'll walk back in front of that door. When he do, I'll pluck that son of a bitch. And if I can't pluck him I'll pluck his fucking brother because I look at that out there as a family, 'cause that's exactly the way they look at it. Because if they got to come and get me to drag me out there and put me in that fucking chair, everyone of them, everyone that's necessary for them to take, they'll come.

Officials of the Holman Prison contend that the constraints of the physical plant and the prison staff have combined to make the death row regime a reasonably safe way to confine condemned prisoners. The prisoners see the matter differently. From their standpoint, fear motivates the guards, feeding an ethic of custody and preventing the development of any genuine communication with the prisoners or authentic concern for their needs.

PRISONER: There seems to be too much security. There seems to be an abnormal amount of fear in the guards simply because we have a death sentence and that makes it hard for us to have the same courtesies that we should—that other inmates have. For example, the guards are so afraid of us where they won't get close to us or they won't come up and talk to us when we need something done seriously. It could be a medical problem or something. And because of this fear in the guards, we don't get the assistance we need like other inmates do.
INTERVIEWER: I see, and you think the main reason for that is fear?
PRISONER: Right. You can easily tell it's fear in the officers and other employees in the institution. Just because we have this death sentence, people are so afraid of us that they don't want to get close to

us and because of this very thing we just don't get what I would say the compassion that we need or the assistance that we need. Sometimes it's hard to find the right word, but I know that it is something that we don't get that every man, regardless of his condition, should have.

Regardless of the forces sustaining the custodial regime of death row, rigid and impersonal procedures separate inmates and guards, contributing to an environment marked by indifference and neglect. Widespread feelings of abandonment result. These feelings hurt different prisoners to varying degrees and in different ways. For some, the abandonment they suffer on death row leads to a conscious abandonment of society, to a decision to become the alienated, antisocial, and dangerous persons they are expected to be.

> When I look at the attitude of the guards toward us death row inmates, I feel it is society's attitude also. Now, I know that there are some in society who do care and who feel that we are people just like them, but when I look at the guards' attitude toward us, that gives me the impression that the majority of society doesn't even care for us and that would treat us the same way in that respect. . . When such peoples like this surrounds me day in and day out—hey, that works on me and other inmates on death row. It changes us, really from normal people into people who are no good and not fit for society.

For others, abandonment leads to efforts at self-insulation and self-protection—the angry, impotent "lone wolf" stance against a world of predators.

> The people here make you feel isolated from the world. After a time, you don't want to trust nobody for nothing. Now you know that if a man gets to feeling like that, he just going to back off into a corner and he is going to protect that corner. He ain't going to let nobody enter that corner. That's the way I feel. Since I've been on death row, I feel like I have to protect myself because ain't nobody else going to help me . . . I feel like I have lost faith in everybody.

Many condemned prisoners lead palpably empty lives. They feel isolated and lonely. Visits are scarce or nonexistent. Exercise provides little relief, and may become, instead, a burdensome departure from inactivity. Alone and uncared for, some condemned prisoners are consumed by apathy, emerging as stuporous, inert figures who do little more than survive each day. The following interview sequence conveys the tone and substance of such a life and reveals the pathos of men who meet death row on its own terms—with resignation and defeat.

PRISONER: My sister, she came once . . . My momma she got, let me see, she got eight or nine children and really, ya know, she just ain't able, ya know.
INTERVIEWER: That sounds kind of lonely, not being able to have visits.
PRISONER: Right, 'cause I always be up there locked up and stuff.
INTERVIEWER: Do you go out for exercise during the day?
PRISONER: Most of the time I just feel so bad that I just don't do it.

INTERVIEWER: Do you talk to anybody up there? Like other guys up there, other inmates.

PRISONER: Every now and then. Sometimes they just think something's wrong with me, 'cause, ya know, I just be sittin' back quiet.

INTERVIEWER: So you spend most of your time just sitting there.

PRISONER: Right.

INTERVIEWER: Would you like to talk more to inmates? Maybe get some advice from them? Or do you feel they can't help you?

PRISONER: No, sometimes I just don't feel like talking.

INTERVIEWER: I see. How about the guards? Can you talk to the guards at all?

PRISONER: I rarely do say something to them. The guards play too much. Every time ya do something, they're playing. That's why I just stay back and just cover up and, ya know, just turn to the wall when I hear them coming.

INTERVIEWER: So up there, there's not much help for you then.

PRISONER: Right.

INTERVIEWER: So you're always like locked up by yourself, and that's about all there is for you here?

PRISONER: Right.

INTERVIEWER: I see. How does it feel being locked up here every day?

PRISONER: Really bad.

INTERVIEWER: Can you give me a little more detail about how you feel bad? I mean, do you feel tense, depressed, or angry, or all those things?

PRISONER: Yeah, I do feel it all. Right. 'Cause I'm real sick and stuff. You know, I've got bad nerves.

INTERVIEWER: I see. So in other words you sit up there and you're tense all the time. Is that it?

PRISONER: Right. Ya know, it's like feeling just really sick.

INTERVIEWER: Okay, why do you think you're shaking? What do you think it is that makes you shake?

PRISONER: It's my nerves.

INTERVIEWER: What is it that gets your nerves going up there on death row?

PRISONER: Oh, I've always had bad nerves. You know, I was getting something for it outside. It's that up there, ya know, they just don't give me nothing for it.

INTERVIEWER: So you used to get medication for your nerves but now you don't.

PRISONER: Ya know, I told the doctor to give me something. Really, he gave me aspirin, that's about it.

INTERVIEWER: Okay, now why do you think that they're not giving you medication that's strong enough to help you?

PRISONER: Really, I don't know. Sometimes, ya know, they act like they just don't have time and stuff, just don't care . . . Ya know, when I was in the jail, I just felt better about things, 'cause being around people, you know, walking around people and stuff.

INTERVIEWER: So you were more social back in jail?

PRISONER: Right, ya know, most everybody knowed ya and I knowed them and stuff. We knowed each other.

INTERVIEWER: Besides feeling lonely here and not having friends here and not getting enough medication, have you noticed any changes in yourself since you've come to death row?

PRISONER: Really I got tired and real lazy, ya know, since I've been here. I feel sleepy, don't want to do nothin'.

The condemned prisoners' experience of isolation—of being cut off, abandoned, forgotten, even dead—is a central feature of their existence on death row. The palpable sense of injustice seen in the condemned prisoners quoted in this chapter reflects, in part, the stark fact that "there is nothing they can do to improve their situation"; this objective helplessness, in turn, makes condemned prisoners "exquisitely vulnerable to the harm of the solitary confinement,"[8] as we shall see throughout this book.

The findings reported in this chapter have been vividly reaffirmed in research on contemporary death rows, my own research and that of others. Feelings of isolation and abandonment, against which one is powerless, emerge in the published writings of condemned prisoners, in blogs maintained on behalf of condemned prisoners, in the correspondence of death row prisoners, and in interviews with condemned prisoners conducted by researchers and journalists.[9] The consensus view, then, is that death row is a barren human environment—a grave for the living.[10] To live in that grave, reports Hinton, is to live with "death and ghosts everywhere," to inhabit a surreal world that was "haunted by the men who died in the electric chair" and by those who "chose to kill themselves rather than be killed." Blood, real and imagined, Hinton continues, "flowed in the cement cracks of the floors like a slow river, until it dried and then split apart under the weight of the creatures that crept over it in the night." In this world, against the backdrop of filth and grime and "men moaning or screaming or crying" at all hours of the day or night, condemned prisoners must struggle to retain their dignity and integrity in a world in which they are treated as more dead than alive.[11]

Notes

1 Johnson and Davies (2014).
2 Stevenson (2014: 53).
3 Hinton (2018: 94).
4 See generally Hinton (2018).
5 The current method of execution in Alabama, as in most states today, is lethal injection. Alabama prisoners convicted before 2002 can choose electrocution as their method of execution, though none have done so to date.
6 Johnson and Davies (2014: 669). See also Mann (2010) for a discussion on the negative effects of prolonged isolation on death row inmates; and the Human Rights Clinic (2017).
7 Obsession with television, and to a lesser degree, radio, have been noted as a common adaptation among death row prisoners and prisoners generally (Levine, 1972; Jackson and Christian, 1980). For a discussion about television as a means of coping with the extreme social isolation of contemporary prisons, cut off as they are from the technological interconnectedness of modern life, see Johnson (2005).
8 Kupers (2018: 60). Those harms stem, in part, from the fact that prisoners in isolation cannot regularly "check their ruminations and beliefs . . . in conversations with others" in the environment (Kupers 2018: 53). Without such reality checks, extreme perceptions and behaviors are likely to flourish, including irrational thoughts and behaviors, to the detriment of the mental health and general well-being of the prisoners.
9 For a comprehensive review of the ethnographic literature on death row, see Johnson and Whitbread (2018). For an examination of death row blogs and a poster describing preliminary findings, see Johnson and Lantsman (2017).
10 As O'Donnell (2018: 193) reminds us, Arthur Koestler, writing on his experiences as a condemned prisoner in Spain in the 1930s, "drew on the image of the grave to describe how it felt awaiting execution in solitary confinement." His solitary cell, Koestler writes, "was like a vault enclosed in three-fold armor-plating: the threefold wall of silence, loneliness and fear." The notion that one is buried alive on death row, a grave for the living, is seen in the many references to prisoners condemned to death row as having a living death. See generally O'Donnell (2014).
11 Hinton (2018: 94).

References

Hinton, A. R. (with Hardin, L. L.). (2018). *The sun does shine: How I found life and freedom on death row*. New York: St. Martin's Press.

Human Rights Clinic at the University of Texas School of Law. (2017). *Designed to break you: Human rights violations on Texas' death row*. Austin, TX. Retrieved from https://law.utexas.edu/wp-content/uploads/sites/11/2017/04/2017-HRC-DesignedToBreakYou-Report.pdf.

Jackson, B., & Christian, D. (1980). *Death row*. Boston, MA: Beacon Press.

Johnson, R. (2005). Brave new prisons: The growing social isolation of modern penal institutions. In A. Liebling & S. Maruna (Eds.), *The effects of imprisonment* (pp. 255–284). Devon, UK: Willan.

Johnson, R., & Davies, H. (2014). Life under sentence of death: Historical and contemporary perspectives. In J. R. Acker, R. M. Bohm, & C. S. Lanier (Eds.), *America's experiment with capital punishment: Reflections on the past, present, and future of the ultimate penal sanction* (3rd ed., pp. 661–685). Durham, NC: Carolina Academic Press.

Johnson, R., & Lantsman, J. (2017, November 16). Death row narrative study. Poster presented at the annual American Society of Criminology Conference, Philadelphia, PA.

Johnson, R., & Whitbread, G. (2018). Lessons in living and dying in the shadow of the death house: A review of ethnographic research on death row confinement. In H. Toch, J. R. Acker, & V. Bonventre (Eds.), *Living on death row* (pp. 71–89). Washington, DC: American Psychological Association Books.

Kupers, T. A. (2018). Waiting alone to die. In H. Toch, J. R. Acker, & V. M. Bonventure (Eds.), *Living on death row: The psychology of waiting to die* (pp. 47–69). Washington, DC: American Press Association.

Levine, S. (Ed.). (1972). *Death row: An affirmation of life*. New York: Ballantine Books.

Mann, D. (2010, November 10). Solitary men. *Texas Observer*. Retrieved from www.texasobserver.org/solitary-men.

O'Donnell, I. (2014). *Prisoners, solitude, and time*. Oxford: Oxford University Press.

O'Donnell, I. (2018). Psychological survival in isolation: Tussling with time on death row. In H. Tock, J. R. Acker, & V. M. Bonventre (Eds.), *Living on death row: The psychology of waiting to die* (pp. 193–211). Washington, DC: American Psychological Association.

Stevenson, B. (2014). *Just mercy: A story of justice and redemption*. New York: Spiegel & Grau.

4

DEATH WORK AND THE CRUCIBLE OF FEAR

Death row prisoners know well that they are impotent before the power of the guards and feel tightly held in the grip of the custodians' regime. These perceptions are especially salient among condemned prisoners held in solitary confinement death rows in states like Alabama and Texas, among others, in which executions are carried out with regularity.[1] Condemned prisoners see guards as both agents of custody, who seek to maintain life, and agents of execution, who oversee and inflict death. Inmates are very sensitive to this duality and equally sensitive to the fact that their keepers are part of a regime organized to take their lives. A deep and perhaps unbridgeable chasm separates condemned prisoners from staff.

Inmates know that the guards who watch them daily are part of the execution process, broadly defined. Officers who work on death row may not serve on execution teams in some states; indeed, death row guards are typically excluded from execution teams.[2] However, for many prisoners, the line that separates death row officers from execution team officers is a thin one, maybe even an illusory one. On Alabama's death row, unlike in some other states, executions are held in the death row cell block and death row officers do sometimes serve on the execution team. This means that execution team officers, some of whom are regular death row officers, rehearse on death row, sometimes marching in front of the cell of a prisoner slated to die. The effect on one Alabama prisoner, reports Hinton, was stark and simply heartbreaking:

> He cried as the Death Squad practiced marching in front of his cell, and he cried as they went into the death chamber and turned the generator on to test Yellow Mama [the electric chair]. He cried as the lights flickered, and he cried at night when the lights went out.[3]

The man was put to death soon thereafter.

Whether the "death squad," as the inmates call the execution team in Alabama, includes death row officers is academic to condemned prisoners. On Alabama's death row, at least, many prisoners have come to believe that officers who work on death row, let alone in the death house as members of the execution team, are "mental" types, eager to use coercion to control prospective victims. Some take a more extreme view. The image of guards conveyed by these inmates is one of persons not only anxious to see prisoners executed, let alone to participate in those executions, but also in search of interim outlets for violence (both psychological and physical) well before the prisoners' legal deaths are sanctioned and carried out.

> We know within ourselves that no matter how courteous a guard tries to be to us, we know what he will do in the end. And so that right there makes us guard against them. This is their domain, where they can come and have some say so, they can tell other people what to do and force people to do what they want. I feel that's why they are here. They just have that ability; they want to kill. They want to see people go through hardships. That's why I say they are mental.

■ ■ ■

> It's a job to them. Right, okay. But when it comes to taking a human's life, that they should, you know, for them to accept this, to me, is a deficiency on their part. That they themselves have been brainwashed to the point that they can't see what is actually happening. You know, what the system is actually doing and by them having a desire to participate, I look at them like they are crazy. You know, because they seem to be doing it for the pure pleasure of it. It's not only fear that they would indeed struggle or help in bringing you and strapping you in this chair anytime the word came down, but they would also—given any kind of slight cause—break your head open with those sticks. So, a lot of them more or less look for an opportunity to use those things. When you go into the shower, the guy actually has the thing drawed back. Sometimes you feel like if you even look back he'll clobber you. And it will be his word against yours that you moved or made a menacing move toward him.

Some prisoners suggest that the hostility of the guards stems not from individual defects of character, but from intensive on-the-job training provided by those in command of death row.

> They got us one sorry motherfucker right here and that's the only ways I know how to put it. One of the most sorriest motherfuckers right here that could be working in a penitentiary. Now he comes to work and sits his ass down right up there, and sits there and tries to figure out a way to fuck somebody back there on death row. And he's the one that shows the others how to do us . . . It's just like father teach son—that's their routine. When a guard comes here, instead of giving him [formal] training and everything and teach him how he should cope with these things in prison and stuff, they bring him right up here, put him under one of the worst sons-of-bitches there is here. Then father teach son. Then it's just a very short period of time until they have built up this attitude and they look at you the same way he does . . . Now I been in down here since way back. So a whole lot about the outside, I don't know nothing about it. But about these son-of-bitches, I do. And that's why I say, when a guy come into here and he say, "Well, there goes a good guard." Shit. It won't be three days before he's just as sorry as the next motherfucker.

Few inmates, however, issue blanket indictments against staff. Most prisoners admit that good guards exist, although they feel the odds are against them. As the prisoners see it, decent guards (not unlike the officers in the Stanford Prison experiment) must fight an uphill battle to retain their humanity on death row. A good guard must contend with abuse from his peers and rejection by some inmates. "You have some officers around that would really like to help you," stated one prisoner, "but the rest of them be reprimanding him and all this until he gonna come around to their way of thinking." The maverick guard is seen as vulnerable to dismissal. "The good officers are the little officers. If they help us too much, they gonna lose their jobs." The "good officer" may also be vulnerable to abuse by the prisoners, who may confuse concern with weakness and proceed to con or intimidate him.

> All right now, most people on death row, instead of respecting him or being kind, they take advantage of him. That happens. It can make the best officer just about the worst. I expect a year, maybe two years at the most, somebody's going to take advantage of this officer. If they do, then it's going to turn him against everybody else.

■ ■ ■

> It takes a certain kind of person to deal with people such as death row inmates. You have some, not all, death row inmates that think they're God. You have some, though, that because they've got the devil in 'em, ya know, now that classifies them as being No. 1, Top Cat. And some of them try to project that image, as a real tough guy, you know? And see the tough guy, he might make it hard on the fellow (guard) that's tryin' to help the men.

Even if he surmounts these hurdles, the good guard may be reassigned to another section of the prison. "The ones that try to be different and treat us as humanly as possible," observed one prisoner, "they get them out of here as fast as they can. They don't let them stay here." At any rate, the potential benefit to inmates of a humane guard is largely lost because of the magnitude of the negative attitudes and actions of his more typical peers. These guards, in the words of one inmate, "take it upon themselves to be your judge and your jury and your executioner. This is their pleasure."

Paradoxically, death row is a lawless world, or, perhaps more properly, it is a law unto itself.[4] In Alabama, rules and regulations cover every contingency, but inmates contend that, as a matter of practice, there were no formal written rules or regulations specifically governing death row. Instead, in the view of the prisoners, the regular prison rules and regulations were used as a general starting point—custom, convenience, or simple arbitrariness subsequently guided the development of operating policy concerning the care and handling of condemned prisoners. Tremendous discretion was therefore given to the death row commander (the "sorry motherfucker" referred to above) and his guards. Authority was, then, essentially a personal matter. As the inmates saw it, guards were free to implement what amounted to a totalitarian regime. Their word was law, and their law, by inmate accounts, was a crude rendition of "might makes right."

> He got the winning hand and you got the loser. And from their point of view, you're wrong—right or wrong. That leaves you in a hell of a situation to start with. Say if he hit you or something, and he was wrong. He would never apologize to you. Because he wouldn't want, he wouldn't no way want another guard or another convict to hear him apologize to you, see. It just don't happen that a guard will apologize to a convict and say he was wrong, see. Because they can't be wrong.

■ ■ ■

> They're tryin' to carry things back into what the prison was in the 1950s and 1940s, and things like that. They tryin' to go back to the inmate ain't got no rights. He had no privileges. He had nothin'. He had a cell, and he said, "Yes sir, boss," "no sir, boss," "yes sir, captain," and all this. He done whatever ya said, whatever the officer said was right, and whatever he told ya to do, ya did. If he told ya to jump, ya jumped and on the way up ya asked him "how high." If they come to you, they look at you and say, "I don't like the way you look." And you say, "Boss, I'd change it if I could." That's the way they wanta get it back to bein'.

Total authority may intimidate but it does not necessarily confer an image of competence. The death row prisoners may fear their keepers, but they do not respect them. Indeed, guards are portrayed as rubes, dupes, or mindless machines of punishment. The following scenario captures the scorn many condemned prisoners feel for the guards, and provides a glimpse of the humor that may help the prisoners come to terms with their own impotence.

> We got a cell downstairs—a cell upstairs. All right, if the man upstairs tunnels a hole in his floor—where's he going except fall down into the next floor, into the cell that's underneath him? All right, they come in to shake you down. He goes and gets him a hammer and goes up in the next tier on the second floor and starts banging on that floor just there looking for a tunnel on the second floor. It never did dawn on him, he never did realize that, well, fuck it, if they tunnel out of here, they ain't going nowhere but downstairs. They don't never tunnel out of the second floor. Hell, they tunnel out as low as they can get to the ground. So that's the kind of people you got to deal with. They're so fucking dumb they got to be told when to breathe and who to breathe with. And whatever they're told to do, well they just go right on and do it.[5]

Though it may be gratifying to attack the character and intelligence of the guards, the prisoners never forget that the death row regime is grounded in the custodians' superior force.

The inmates' perceptions suggest an aura of violence that surrounds death row, contaminating routine encounters and setting the stage for campaigns of intimidation. "They're going to pick at you no matter how quiet you are, how obedient you are to the rules, and how well you try to behave," observed one prisoner; others complained of the guards' basic disrespect for the inmate as a person.

> When you are in prison, everybody wants to be treated like a man. A real man; a macho man. And officers want to treat you like you are a boy . . . They want you to look up to them and say, "Yes sir," and "No sir." But they want to call you, "Hey, boy."

■ ■ ■

> They're saying "I've got you, you know, and I'm going to get my respect. And if I don't, I'll just write you up for insubordination or beat your ass, and anything I say is going to go." So your morale is just shot, because you know that they've got you and there's not a whole lot you can do about it.

Some inmates maintain that the prison staff especially abuse those who are obviously unable to cope with stress. For example, one man described the abuse of a neighboring inmate as follows:

I ain't no doctor or nothing, but something is wrong with him. Something is wrong with him. He sleeps next to me and he just talks. He just talks, and the way he be talking he be answering himself and it be like five or six people in the room, but it ain't nobody in there but him. One day he ripped the sink off the wall, throwed it at them. He been throwing his trays lately. He won't eat. So they [staff] say something to him like, "Hey I went for a walk today and the Room told me to tell you 'hello!'" The guard knows this is going to set him right back off and he is going to do something. And they do this instead of trying to help him ... Something is wrong with him and instead of them trying to help him or encourage him or something, say tell the psychiatrist when he comes around to speak to him especially because he got a problem—instead of doing that they comes around there and say, "Well, Moon is going to take you out." Just little funny remarks and they know that will set him right back off. Like late at night at the two o'clock count, they come up to the bars and he is asleep, they come up to the bars and take the bat and just—boom, boom, boom—and just hit the bars and they wake him up out of his sleep. And he is already sick anyhow, you know?

Another prisoner described his own experience at the hands of staff:

PRISONER: They ask me, "Am I ready?"
INTERVIEWER: What? They ask you, "Are you ready?"
PRISONER: Yes, for the chair.
INTERVIEWER: So, they come up to your cell and they say, "Are you ready to go?" and that kind of thing. And then what do you say?
PRISONER: I stay back in the corner and say, "No."
INTERVIEWER: You say, "No." And . . .
PRISONER: And I start crying and get nervous.
INTERVIEWER: Well, I don't blame you. What do they do next?
PRISONER: Hit the lock and walk on. They laugh about it.
INTERVIEWER: So, in other words, the guards are just sort of having fun, kind of—come down the cell, give you a hard time, and then move on?
PRISONER: Yes.
INTERVIEWER: Is this most of the guards, or just some of them, or just one guy, or what?
PRISONER: It's most of them.
INTERVIEWER: This happens a lot, does it?
PRISONER: Yes.

Interviews suggest that bids for respect may not buy immunity from alleged staff abuse. Actions that reflect autonomy, or that can be construed as manifestations of adult independence, may be viewed by staff as acts of disobedience and may increase the risks inmates face in encounters with staff. Inmate accounts suggest that the guards may fear and hate the prisoners as much as the prisoners fear and hate them. Guards appear to flex their muscles for reassurance—to steady taut nerves and to allay anxiety. They may flex them often, and on exceedingly flimsy pretexts. According to one prisoner, "The guards say, 'Well, you was outside and you did this and you did that, but I'm running this motherfucker down here now. When I say crawl, you best crawl.'" An authority that stands or falls on minor acts of disobedience is a brittle authority, its agents prone to overreactions and abuses.

> I sometimes wonder why a person do us like that, you know. You locked up, you know, you can't defend yourself. Like I got maced, you know? The dude squirted a whole can of mace on me 'cause I asked the dude for some matches. Asked one of the guards for some matches and he told me he wasn't a flunky for the state. And we exchanged words. He told me he wasn't gonna let me get out of hand like—he named somebody else on death row—that he wasn't gonna let me get out of hand. So he squirted a whole can of mace. At one time, all of it.

From the viewpoint of the inmates, this type of conduct appears senseless. Another prisoner provides an example in which a verbally aggressive inmate was allegedly mobbed by a group of guards. Although violence was apparently averted, the account underscores the vulnerability felt by condemned prisoners.

PRISONER: Well, I'd gotten into an argument the day before with one of the guards. And I cussed him out. I figured that was the end of it. And the next day we had a shakedown. Normal procedure is, you come out of your cell and they get your hands cuffed behind you. Now they finished searching my cell and then [he] and five others told me I was going to come out here and get a haircut and all that. And I knew right away that a haircut wasn't the reason they were bringing me out here. So they did cut all my hair off, then lined me up against the wall and started pounding on my chest and slapping me around. The whole thing was with the idea that I was supposed to try and fight back, because the first time you try to defend yourself—like they're standing in a semicircle around you with pick handles and baseball bats and all kind of stuff—and the first move I would've made, I would've been killed right there, you know, or beat senseless, one or the other. So I, I just stood there and took the whole thing.

INTERVIEWER: I see. How long did it go on for?

PRISONER: Um, about five or ten minutes. Can't be sure.

INTERVIEWER: Did it ever get very serious?

PRISONER: No it never, you know, I wasn't hurt bad, but I was scared. Damned scared.

INTERVIEWER: Sounds extremely intimidating.

PRISONER: It was one point that was really bad. The one that was doing all this, his name was _____ and that's the one I had gotten in the argument with before, he was handling the whole thing. At one point [he] kicked me on the shin, which is the signal for "Let's kill him," you know. I thought, "Here it goes," you know, "I've had it now." But I don't know why, but they all held off.

INTERVIEWER: I see. You think if you had struck back . . ..

PRISONER: If I would've made any move towards any of them, they would've wiped me out.

Many prisoners express fears of guard violence. "They can do anything they want to you," said one man. "Who's going to stop them?" Elaborating on this widely shared belief, another inmate described the dangers associated with death row confinement and the potential for irreparable harm these dangers are thought to entail.

You have to more or less watch what you say to these guys because if they want to get you back, they could easily do that. You're on your way out to the yard, the guy could say as soon as you get out of the center—around that little bend—where the rest of the guys couldn't see you, they could easily claim "well, he turned around and hit me," "he turned around and I thought he was attacking me," or "he pushed me." And one whack with one of those axe handles up against your head, if you're not going to be dead, you're going to be insane for the rest of your life. And then you're not going to be able to help no one. That's what happened to one of the fellows over there. I understand he got beat in the head so much, he doesn't even know which way is up now.

These perceptions give rise to the continuing dread that the same fate might easily find him.

I am really afraid of that. I'm trying to hold on to my own common sense, you know, because I feel that is one of the main factors that I do have that is still mine. My knowledge that I can think and my ability to learn and do my own research on my own case. I feel that if I got hit with one of those sticks, I wouldn't have that much sense. So, I live in constant fear of that actually all the time.

Terror does not discriminate. "Everybody's the same," stated one prisoner.

You would think, well, that a black guard would be better than a white guard. But, hey, the black guard is badder than the white guard. Officer Jones [pseudonym], I don't know what he is. He seem like he's here to kill somebody or something. He don't care nothing about nobody.

Attitudes are polarized on death row, pitting one group against the other. The guards are armed with heavy wooden batons[6] that inspire fear in lone, handcuffed prisoners. The custodians also control the prison's justice system; they are seen as dispensing punishments at will. Catch-22 situations are said to be routine. The harassed prisoner who reacts with angry words may be punished for insubordination. More ominously, the beaten prisoner who defends himself may be punished for assault.

If anything goes wrong, they's ten officers jumpin' around the cell with sticks and all those type of things. That prove to me, I feel in my opinion, that they messed up men. Number one, they want to jump on a man and beat on a man when he handcuffed. Secondly, they are gettin' attention. And that's the only reason why they get attention—because they got us in lock-up, in handcuffs, and there isn't but so much we can do to defend ourselves. Now I'm on 60-day restriction. I was beaten by eight guards and I was written up for an assault on the officers. It didn't, it didn't state what officers was assaulted. It didn't state no procedures or no content of the results of the assault I supposedly committed. I mean now I'm aware of the fact that I'm [allowed] due process of the law, you know, proper hearin' and proper procedures. I didn't receive nothin' but a statement from the warden sayin' that I'm on 60-day restriction.

Prisoners contend that custodians of death row are unwilling to tolerate any act that might be interpreted as disobedient or challenging to their authority. Inmates support this contention by arguing that even expressions of opinion contrary to those of staff have produced beatings. "These people are something else," stated one prisoner, "it's just whatever you get, you just be satisfied with that, because if you voice your opinion about it, you're going to get a whipping." Inmates see themselves as helpless victims of tyrannical control. "If you retaliate," observed one man, "you know you're going to die."

Psychological survival on death row can be compared with walking a long tightrope, where even slight deviations from expected behavior can produce disaster. Safety derives from inaction; action becomes a matter of risk. A person feels safest in his cell. Outside the cell he is handcuffed and vulnerable; guards can force him to private areas of the prison and subject him to beatings. Nonessential excursions are therefore to be avoided and essential excursions are undertaken with apprehension.

> They come around and they say, "Come on, let's go such and such place," you know. And you get kind of paranoid, 'cause you don't know whether to go or whether to just say, "Well, whoever it is, just tell 'em to go ahead on, I don't want to see nobody," you know? . . . They handcuff [your hands] behind your back. You're rendered in a helpless position when you got your hands behind your back. It kind of throws you off balance, so you can't do nothin' else but be open to whatever kind of attack they want to make on you.

An invitation to venture from the cell to respond to requests for interviews, as in this research, may elicit a battery of questions designed to assure the inmate of his safety.

PRISONER: Not ten minutes ago they came up there and they said, "Come on, we're taking you downstairs." I said, "What for? To see who? You know, unless I know where I'm going, I'm not leaving this cell, not with you." You know, I got to know somethin'.
INTERVIEWER: So, in other words, in the back of your mind there's the possibility of abuse?
PRISONER: Yeah, yeah. Well, like I say, if they get you out there, you know, and well, your hands are handcuffed behind your back, the guard is going to give a push, and back down the stairs you go. But you tripped and fell, you know, no witnesses, no nothin', you know. And you know the situation.

Fear accompanied many of the prisoners into the interview room. Of course, the death witness chamber—my interview room—was not a reassuring setting. For some prisoners, however, a more immediate concern was reprisals for participating in the research. "If they heard what I was saying," said one prisoner, "I'd probably be next on their list." A number of prisoners spoke in low and muted voices to avoid being overheard, even though the door to the chamber was closed and the guards were stationed well out of earshot. One man would only whisper his responses to my queries. The following illustrates the prisoners' fears.

INTERVIEWER: You mentioned before that you almost have to be afraid all the time in this kind of place. Are you pretty afraid right now?
PRISONER: Right now, yeah. That's why I talk so low because they are going to be—like last time another man came in here and the next two days after I went on the walk—I can't remember the

name of the officer that asked me, but he said, "Have a cigarette." So, I took the cigarette. He said, "What did they talk to you about up there?" So, I just played dummy on him and I said, "Oh, it ain't nothing. Some old man talking about they are going to do something. They ain't going to do nothing; they are full of shit." So, I walked on the walk. So by telling him like that, he didn't even question me no more. He just took it for granted. He say, "Well, it ain't nobody." But they always looking for a threat.

Nevertheless, even fearful prisoners spoke to me of their concerns. This implied a degree of perceived security; they felt safe enough to discuss sensitive subjects in the sheltered context of an interview. Few men can be assured of their safety on death row, however, and some become paralyzed by fear. Fearful inmates strive to maintain a low profile. Adaptation includes efforts to sleep away the day, which leaves the relative peace of the night for the person to savor, or to hide in the corner of one's cell, seeking sanctuary from the danger perceived beyond the cell door.

> I stay up all night a lot of the time. And I sit there and read at night because that's the onliest time that I really can, you know, feel at ease a little bit, two or three hours at night. In the daytime they're always coming by, looking in on you, saying stuff to you. At night, most of the time the guards at night, they stay out at the desk and they almost never come in, down the aisles of the tiers. And that's about the onliest time a person can really be able to rest his mind, to be at ease.

■ ■ ■

PRISONER: If I sit in my cell and one of them says something that I don't like, I'd rather sleep than get my brains beat out over nothin' . . . I want to live as long as I can. I mean, heck, if I can sleep, then I won't have to worry about getting my head beat in.
INTERVIEWER: So you'd rather sleep . . .
PRISONER: Yeah, and when I'm not sleeping, I always try to stay away from my door. I get, I get in the back of the cell and get on the bed and go to write. They're going to have to come through the door and come all the way back there to the bed . . . It scares you sometimes. It makes you worry; it makes you wonder what, what's going to happen and when it's going to happen. You never know.

A few men feel completely overpowered by the pressures of their environment. "You tryin' to be brave," stated one such prisoner, "but you don't know what they gonna do to you. There's nowhere to hide. Every day you gonna see them; you can't hide nowhere." More immediate fears merge into the ultimate fear of the execution of one's sentence.

> When you're on death row and you're laying down in your cell and you hear a door cracking you'll think of where it comes from. When you hear it crack. And when you hear the keys and everything, when something like this happens, the keys come through there: I'm up. I'm up, because you don't know when it's going to take place. The courts give you an execution date, that's true. But you don't know what's going to take place between then and when your

execution date arrives. You don't know when you're going to be moved around to the silent cell over here. That's right down the hall, what they call a waiting cell. Up there, you don't know when you're going to be moved down there. And this keeps you jumpy, and it keeps you nervous, and it keeps you scared.

Fear is not an accidental feature of the death row regime. It serves the interests of staff, for it is integral to maintaining order. Obedience, in fact, is the only coping strategy many prisoners see as viable. As one prisoner said: "I got to take whatever they dish out—be quiet and just take it all, and that's about the only choice I got." The formula is simple: obedience provides a sense of security. The motivation is even simpler: self-preservation.

I try to go along with everything the best I can and make the best out of everything I can. It's rough, it's hard, but still, the more you gripe and grumble and complain, the more trouble you cause, the worse they're going to make it on you, see. So, I go along with them, cooperate with them 100 percent. Because if you don't, you're going to get your tail beat. With sticks, pick handles, clubs, and everything else. I mean when you get beat, you're going to get beat, they're going to beat you.

■ ■ ■

A person has to, you know, kiss the guard's rear end. And that's something I don't want to do. But it's something I'll do to keep from getting beat up . . . Well, you know, they ride you bad. Which, I've got somewhat of a bad temper. It's been pretty hard for me to keep it down. And you sit there and grit your teeth. If you don't grit your teeth, you're going to lose them: Going to get beat up. It's just something that you know you'll have to do, because you know they'll get away with it.

Most prisoners describe their obedience as feigned deference to the power of the guards, as distinct from anything remotely resembling respect for their person or authority. A few of the black prisoners take this one step further and play a shuffling "Uncle Tom" to the guard's arrogant "Massah." The mechanics and impact of this deception were described by one prisoner:

It's real simple the way we do it. When you come down in front of his face, well, he don't know what you are thinking. A person can't tell what you are thinking. So, if you are giving him a smile, you know, whitey got that bat and stuff on his side and feel all that superiority in him, he feels so big, and if you smile at him, you know, with "yassah" and he wouldn't give himself a thought of, "Well, this man is thinking against me." He say, "I've got him where I want him, you know, and he will stay in line."

The ploy may work. But like all adaptations rooted in involuntary obedience, it exacts the psychological cost of shame and suppressed rage.

To be sure, some men demand and get respect from the guards. Projecting an image of themselves as men who must be reckoned with, they keep their distance from guards to minimize interaction and thereby reduce the likelihood of abrasive encounters. "I don't associate with the guards," stated one man. "I don't try to get on a first-name basis with 'em or nothin'." Observed another prisoner:

> I don't laugh with 'em, I don't play with 'em, and I don't give 'em no room to laugh and play with me. So they don't have any other reasons to come up to me other than to bring me my mail, carry me to the yard, or carry me to the shower.

Aloofness is meant to convey a message of calm and strength. According to one prisoner, a man who keeps his distance from staff broadcasts that "he ain't the type that you bother." The message may need to be reinforced occasionally, such as by carefully orchestrated confrontations that show guards that the prisoner is without fear.

PRISONER: When I first come here I had an attitude of respect. I respect whoever come, whoever gonna come up, and they respect me. Well, now this is the type image that I try to cast, ya know. Whoever confront me, I give 'em respect. I give the officers respect. I either call him officer or maybe sometime I might even call him Mister. But now when he speak back to me, I'm gonna look for him to call me by my name and not by some little ol' boy or, ya know, some other kind of terminology they use on other inmates. Ya know? Well, I look for them to respect me and I'm a demandin' man. The rest of 'em don't demand that but I demand that.

INTERVIEWER: Have you been successful in these demands?

PRISONER: Well, like one of the officers, one time he came here and he decided he'd call me Mickey, and that was not my name. And so I told him that I respect him as an officer and I called him by his name, and I expect him to call me by mine. Don't try to put more tags on me. Ya know? And he apologized and he said he wouldn't do it no more . . . See, when they takes ya out to the shower they put your handcuffs in front, and when they opened the door and I stepped out there, I stepped right close to 'em and I told him. And the distance I was from him didn't leave no room to do nothin' and so he got caught that one time and said, "I'm sorry and I won't do that no more."

It is essential that prisoners seeking the respect of staff maintain poise and self-control. Emotional outbursts must be avoided as they may "invite" a guard into an inmate's cell, justifying, in the perverse idiom of the prison, whatever violence may occur.

> I never put myself in the position to where I invited one of them in my cell. Well, if you invited the son of a bitch in and he kicked your ass, you deserve it. If a man ain't got no better sense than to stand there and cuss one of them and say, "Well, then, come in this fucking cell and kick my ass." Now, if he goes in there and kicks his ass, he deserves it, because he invited him into his house. Whatever that man does to him, he deserves it. So that's what I try to not do.

The role of the tough, fearless, and self-reliant convict is hard to play on death row. Feelings reveal themselves through carefully cultivated facades. Fear is particularly difficult to mask. According to one prisoner, "You can tell a person as if he glowed like a lantern; you can tell if he got any fear in him or not." Because everyone on death row lives in fear, the tough guy image is always an assumed role. The cool exterior uneasily masks emotional turmoil, and the effort exacts its price in discomfort and anxiety.

> Sometimes you get a little down and depressed and you [feel] kind of frustrated because you gotta, you feel like you have to keep on proving yourself to people. And sometimes it deals with your mind and it gets ya in a real confused state at times. And ya just don't know what to do or how to do it. I can't sometimes get relaxed. I can't write no letters or I can't read a book or I can't find nothin' that hold my interest or nothin'. It's just a nervous, jittery feelin'.

A few prisoners seek relief from the siege mentality of death row through their willingness to alter constructively the character of staff/inmate relations. Mutual respect among guards and inmates, according to some men, can provide a framework within which the tension and violence of death row might be eased. The inmates say they are willing to meet the staff halfway, and some have a history of reciprocity in their dealings with receptive members of the prison staff.

> It's a two-way street. Just like some of the officers coming up there treated the inmates halfway decent. Of course, they don't show no favoritism or anything; they don't do any favors. It's just their attitude, you know? And in return they get a lot better respect from the guys. It don't hurt for a guard to be halfway decent.

Others are more pessimistic about the prospects of planned change. They strive to accept death row for what it is, rather than attempt to change it. "You have to make compromises," observed one man, "because it's the only system we have. Some states are better; some states are worse. Alabama is the only one we have."

More abstract variations on this theme assume a neutral and indifferent universe in which death row is "just a different part of life." These views amount to pretexts for graceful defeat, invitations to accept impotence—to endure because endurance is what life allows. At best, the stoic may objectively analyze the world in which he lives. The difficulty is that in oppressive settings like death row, detached inquiry may fall short of yielding neat, rational, and digestible pictures of one's world.

> I try to switch over and look at it from the staff, from their side. It's really involved to think of it. I sit up here and find myself making a study of it sometimes—make little observations here and there, noting the responses and what stimulates a prisoner to say one thing, you know, interactions between the prisoners and guards. But some of these guards . . . I don't know. I just can't make sense out of them. What kind of people are they? What kind of place are they running?

Religion offers a mode of adjustment pursued by some prisoners that may supplement more worldly efforts at self-control. Belief in God fosters belief in a larger mission for one's life and one's suffering. A sense of peace, calm, and strength is one apparent result. "I look at myself as somewhat of a rock," stated one prisoner. "I feel like it's Him strengthenin' me that enables me to stand up under pressure." A few prisoners endorse simplistic religious beliefs. They claim that God will reimburse them in kind for their losses, that deprivation on death row will be recompensed by wealth after their reprieve. More modestly for example, one prisoner awaited a radio the Lord would proffer as a replacement for one stolen by another prisoner (a nonbeliever). Most prisoners concerned with religion, however, seem to be sophisticated consumers, at least from a psychological standpoint. They spoke of belief in God as affording a freedom no man can deny. They wish to take the Lord as their garment, to shield them from the excesses of an ugly and overwhelming world.[7]

> I found an escape route—that's what I will call it—the escape route is that when it gets to bothering me so bad, you know, I go to the Bible. Then you will think again, you know . . . And it will ease you down. You will find some good in it and you will find some bad in it, but it will ease the pressure. You ain't dealing with man no more. Man don't have a chain on this, he can't handcuff this here. I can leave when I want to and that's where I go.

■ ■ ■

> He tells ya that if they do bad to you, they've done bad to Him before they done it to you. If they punish you because of what you've done, well, then they punished Him before they punished you. And what ya try and do is you try to become more Him and less of you. And you see He's able to withstand any pressure that they put on Him. But it's when you're more Him, well, then there's less of you, so they're unable to work on you. You're safe, ya know, you're covered.

Adaptation in this unstable world is possible. Most prisoners, after all, survive their ordeal without breaking down or succumbing completely to the pressures of life on death row, though the experience may leave scars. In the final analysis, most prisoners exercise what may amount to a kind of existential detachment—transcending the material restrictions of the present and retaining a degree of personal choice. One prisoner put the matter in the following terms, speaking for himself and, in his view, for many of his fellow death row prisoners:

PRISONER: I wouldn't let their attitude, or what they possibly could do, or would do, stop me from doing *anything*. That's like if I was so scared I wouldn't come out to take a shower, you know? That's silly. I'm not going to do it. If they beat me every day, I'm still gonna come out.

INTERVIEWER: Why is that?

PRISONER: I don't ever want them to think they've got total control. I want the last word . . . See, that's the only freedom we got. I think it's the only thing that keeps us going. Just knowing that in the end, it's our choice and they can't do nothing about it.

Prisoners retain an element of choice in relation to how they perceive their keepers—"that's the only freedom we got," said one man—but that is a fragile freedom. It was my sense from the interviews that every prisoner fears that violence may ultimately consume him. The inmates know that there is nothing they can do to avoid it, to defend themselves, or to retaliate. In the words of one prisoner, "You get depressed. You get angry. You're feeling helplessness. You can't do nothing. You can't fight them. They can do what they want to. Anything." In this world, the logic of despair reigns supreme. The inmates feel trapped and helpless, "pinned to the wall," as one man stated, "waiting to be shot."

***

The crucible of fear examined in this chapter is a central finding of ethnographic research on death row conducted since the publication of the first edition of this book in 1981. Gabe Whitbread and I, reporting on a comprehensive review of ethnographic research on death row confinement as of 2018, reported the following:

> Prisoners on death row are in a constant, exhausting state of high alert that starts when they arrive in this threatening setting and continues on into their daily lives in the cell, where feelings of vulnerability can reach great heights.[8]

Fear on death row, we found, is pervasive and insidious:

> On death row, offenders fear for their sanity, safety, and everything in between. They feel that there are myriad ways that they can be harmed, and that they cannot turn anywhere for help or protection. They fear the staff, their fellow prisoners, and emotional turmoil building within themselves, threatening destructive or self-destructive violence.[9]

Fear is central to what is sometimes called "the death row phenomenon," which includes "living for years with the knowledge that one is going to be executed, living among prisoners who will likewise be executed, and watching one after another of one's neighbors on death row undergo execution."[10] Hinton, who established an unusual rapport with death row officers on Alabama's death row, observed: "I knew that the guards would kill me if I got an execution date. They knew it too. There was no way around it."[11] In this macabre world, shadowed by violence, officers and inmates alike "were all in this dark, dank, tiny corner of the world acting out some perverse play where we laughed together six days of the week, but on Thursdays, they killed us."[12] In the view of Lezin, who conducted in-depth case studies of six prisoners on different death rows, the death row environment is "surreal in its desolation," giving rise to "a living hell" in which, for most prisoners, "fear, fed by threat and uncertainly, bleeds into hate."[13]

Notes

1 Johnson and Davies (2014). For a vivid description of the salience of executions in the minds of condemned prisoners on death row in Texas, see Human Rights Clinic (2017).
2 Johnson (1998).
3 Hinton (2018: 100).
4 Isolated units in prison often work as though they are beyond the reach of the law and hence able to meet out harms with relative impunity. See Haney (2003).
5 Joseph K., a famous fictional character in Franz Kafka's (1956: 282–283) portrayal of totalitarian regimes, held his keepers in equally low esteem. Describing the guards at his execution, the main character, K, observed "I am grateful for the fact that these half–dumb, senseless creatures have been sent to accompany me on this journey, and that I have been left to say to myself all that is needed."
6 Prisoners see batons as the official weapons of the guards. The prisoners claim that the guards also routinely arm themselves with pickax handles, rubber hoses, and other unofficial weapons.
7 Recent evidence suggests that using religion as a coping mechanism likely grows over time on death row, and is among the most salient themes of last words (Smith, 2018).

8 Johnson and Whitbread (2018).
9 Johnson and Whitbread (2018).
10 Kupers (2018: 60).
11 Hinton (2018: 216)
12 Hinton (2018: 216)
13 Lezin (1999: 63); Rossi (2004).

References

Haney, C. (2003). Mental health issues in long-term solitary and "supermax" confinement. *Crime & Delinquency*, *49*(1), 124–156.

Hinton, A. R. (with Hardin, L. L.) (2018). *The sun does shine: How I found life and freedom on death row*. New York: St. Martin's Press.

Human Rights Clinic at the University of Texas School of Law. (2017). *Designed to break you: Human rights violations on Texas' death row*. Austin, TX. Retrieved from https://law.utexas.edu/wp-content/uploads/sites/11/2017/04/2017-HRC-DesignedToBreakYou-Report.pdf.

Johnson, R. (1998). *Death work: A study of the modern execution process* (2nd ed.). Belmont, CA: Wadsworth.

Johnson, R., & Davies, H. (2014). Life under sentence of death: Historical and contemporary perspectives. In J. R. Acker, R. M. Bohm, & C. S. Lanier (Eds.), *America's experiment with capital punishment: Reflections on the past, present, and future of the ultimate penal sanction* (3rd ed., pp. 661–685). Durham, NC: Carolina Academic Press.

Johnson, R., & Whitbread, G. (2018). Lessons in living and dying in the shadow of the death house: A review of ethnographic research on death row confinement. In H. Toch, J. R. Acker, & V. Bonventre (Eds.), *Living on death row* (pp. 71–89). Washington, DC: American Psychological Association Books.

Kafka, F. (1956). *The trial*. New York: Schocken.

Kupers, T. A. (2018). Waiting alone to die. In H. Toch, J. R. Acker, & V. M. Bonventure (Eds.), *Living on death row: The psychology of waiting to die* (pp. 47–69). Washington, DC: American Press Association.

Lezin, K. (1999). *Finding life on death row: Profiles of six death row inmates*. Boston, MA: Northeastern University Press.

Rossi, R. M. (2004). *Waiting to die: Life on death row*. Harrisonburg, VA: Vision Publishers.

Smith, R. A. (2018). The functional use of religion when faced with imminent death: An analysis of death row inmates' last statements. *Sociological Quarterly*, *59*(2), 279–300.

5
CONTEMPLATING EXECUTION

The grim prospect of death by execution dramatically affects the human environment of death row, sharply dividing guards, who work in service of the death penalty, and inmates, who hope desperately to live. This seemingly unbridgeable chasm breeds an atmosphere of mistrust and fear. The death sentence itself is also an independent source of stress and suffering for condemned prisoners, worrying them by day and haunting them by night.

The possibility of execution, for example, gives rise to intense preoccupation. "I spend a lot of times, you know, analyzing and fantasizing and visualizing my condition as a whole," stated one man. "My main worry is about being here and not knowing if I'm going to come out of it alive." The future is uncertain. For some prisoners, even thinking about the death sentence can aggravate fears and set in motion an obsessive reaction bordering on anxious panic.

> When that sentence comes across my mind, that brings quite a bit of fear. It brings quite a bit of fear and worry, you know. Upsetting of the conscience. Causes the person to pace back and forth, become nervous, you know. Can't sit down. It's hard for such [a] person to sleep. This happens to me at times, you know, when I think about, you know, the fact that my sentence might not be commuted or the death penalty might not be thrown out. This causes me to grow nervous. Can't sleep. You are full of anxiety and really it's insanity.

The prisoners' reflections on the death sentence often center on the uncertainty that characterizes their condition. Not uncommonly, there is a painful oscillation between hope and despair. According to one prisoner: "It's just like you are in the middle of a vise, and one part of the vise is pulling you this way and one of them is pulling you the other way. And the vise is sharp." With the parameters of one's existence cast in terms of uncertain hope and uncertain despair, arduous and recurring battles for peace of mind ensue.

> Well, like sometimes I look at it and say I got a pretty good chance of beatin' this thing, ya know. And times when I get confused and nervous, I look at it and say, "Well, man, they railroaded me

down here, ya know, and why should I look for the same people that railroaded me down here to give me any kind of break?" It's hard. You try to reason it out; you try to push one idea out. You might try to turn the radio on, or turn it up, or cut it to blast one of the two ideas out of your head. And then if that don't work out, well I just get down and I try to do a lot of exercise to get off some of the pressures that way . . . At times it helps relieve it. Ya know? But sometimes you gotta just stay down and stick with it and it'll blow on over sooner or later. And sometimes you might work it out. But a great number of the times, it just hangs on with ya until you can't do nothin' except fall out and sleep.

There is a "domino theory" of capital punishment espoused or endorsed by many inmates, where the execution of one person will lead to the executions of others. This theory is wrong; each capital case proceeds on its own independent schedule through the appellate courts. But from the vantage point of death row, and giving due consideration to political and other pressures that affect executions, executions can appear to be connected in some way. Common sense on death row seems to make this connection unassailable. The assumption held by condemned prisoners is that death rows in America are full to overflowing; all that is needed to empty them is for the pro-death penalty forces to regain momentum. A few executions, according to this theory, might be enough to precipitate a tidal wave of state-sanctioned killings. Summarizing these sentiments, one prisoner spelled out a somber scenario:

> If they go ahead and execute one, what's going to stop them from doing the whole thing? So, there's always a cause for fear. They could come and get me at any time. There's no future. You know, like hell, they could pass a law tomorrow and burn everybody, you know. They could come in and start electrocuting. Of course, it's unrealistic, but at the same time, it could be done.

Executions in other states feed the prisoners' fears. John Spenkelink's execution in Florida in 1979, during the period of the original research for this book, for example, both frightened and saddened the Alabama prisoners. (It also moved them to send flowers and a note of sympathy to Spenkelink's mother.) When John Evans, one of their fellow-condemned, actively sought his own execution, some of the men were fearful that they would be the next to go. For example,

PRISONER: See my case is riding right along with Johnny Evans's case—in the same court right behind Johnny Evans.
INTERVIEWER: Oh, and he wants to get executed.
PRISONER: He wants to go—okay. Now I don't.
INTERVIEWER: Right. I understand that.
PRISONER: But now my case is riding right behind his—okay. Now, there's a chance that if he goes, I go—you understand?
INTERVIEWER: I do.
PRISONER: All right. Now I've looked at the situation; I've talked it over with John Carroll. John said, "No, it ain't got nothing to do with your case." But it *does*. It's all up on the same law. And I'm not going to—like I told John, I said, "Man, come clean with me," because I wanted to *know*. All right, and the more that Evans talks over the TV and so forth that he wants to die—or radio or whatever

he's been talking on—OK, now this pushes this same law that John Carroll and the Southern Poverty Law Center has been trying to fight to get overturned. Okay. It's a whole bunch of them fighting against it, I understand. But you take one person on death row that wants to die, and that's gonna turn it. That gonna leave it just like it is. All right now, if he goes, I go. I got enough sense to realize it. And that does shake me up, it does keep me worried.

Some years later, Evans was executed. That execution was botched and brutal, replete with three separate administrations of electricity and the insidious smell of burnt flesh and clothing that accompanied failed attempts to kill him. These repugnant odors wafted up to the tiers holding the condemned prisoners.[1] This event, a tragedy for Evans and his fellow prisoners waiting to die, lasted a full 14 minutes. This tragedy, implying to the prisoners that the authorities would stop at nothing in their bid to conduct executions, also added to the sense that the execution of one prisoner might one day pave the way for the execution of others, that executions themselves might degenerate into acts of torture, and that condemned prisoners can do little more than sit and wait for their fate, on whatever arbitrary schedule that fates unfolds.[2]

Anxieties about execution are nourished by various experiences, some seemingly benign. Condemned prisoners discover reminders of their fate in likely and unlikely contexts. The rejecting guard, the loving family member one might never see again, the advocate of the death penalty, the recreation cage that affords a tantalizing taste of freedom—each one, in a different way, forces the prisoners to examine their predicament. In the words of the prisoners:

> When guards show so much neglect and cold attitudes towards me, that brings the sentence to my mind. When I look at the picture of a beautiful niece of mine that I have there on my table, that brings it on, knowing that I probably will be executed. You know, here it is, I have got beautiful relatives who love me and I love them and that brings it on, you know, me not being able to be with them anymore in life. And when I hear people, you know, over the news, talking about the death penalty like talking about criminals—mainly that they are unfit, that the doors ought to be shut and never opened again—that brings on worries about my sentence. Seems like I live with the death penalty every day.

■ ■ ■

PRISONER: The baddest part about it, I hate to get off into just thinking about it. Just really finding out where I'm at, 'cause sometimes I go out in the exercise yard and it dawn on me where I'm at. And this hurts real bad, you know. So I don't want to think about nothing like this.

INTERVIEWER: I see. Every once in a while it just hits you that you're in this situation?

PRISONER: Yeah. I mean it really hits me. You know like on television, you know, you see the people who is for the death penalty get up there and talk about how the death penalty deters crime and stuff like this. Way to capitalize on the prisons—what they gonna do. It hurts. Like I say, I don't try to escape reality now, but I just hate to think about it.

Unquestionably, the most potent and virulent sources of death anxiety are staff efforts to remind inmates of their impending executions. Upon admission to death row, prisoners are given tours of the death room during which they view the electric chair as though it were an exhibit in a museum. In uglier encounters, new prisoners may be graphically reminded of their date with the chair, and then summarily locked in their cells to consider their fate.

> I was down here in 20 minutes [after sentencing]. I was looking at that chair and they said, "Bring him on in here." They showed me the chair and they said, "Yeah, we are going to sit your ass in there." You know, they were calling me nigger and shit. They were asking me why I did what I done, and did I want to die . . . What they want to do, they want to scare you. It fucked me around. The chair, that's just like seeing a childhood ghost. That's what that is, a ghost. I went upstairs, you know, they put me in a room and I didn't say nothing to nobody for a whole day trying to get that, trying to get the chair off my mind. But I couldn't, you know. I was thinking too hard trying to get it off and I wouldn't say nothing to nobody. Didn't nobody ask me too much because I guess the same thing probably happened to them.

Routine admissions procedures may acquire ominous connotations. Prisoners are apprehensive when they first enter death row, a setting that has symbolic connotations that play on their fears. Death row is "the end of the line," "a box canyon," and "a tomb," to borrow some of the prisoners' metaphors. Many prisoners are confirmed in their fears from the outset. For one thing, upon admission they must pass the death room. With or without an official "tour," viewing the chair proves unsettling. Subsequent procedures as innocuous as fingerprinting can produce fear; the most mundane formality is likely to provide reminders of the prisoner's fate. With anxiety and imagination working in tandem, the incoming prisoner may imagine that he is being prepared for a proper execution.

> They brought me down here and they fingerprinted me. I filled out this slip and it said "Death by electrocution," you know. And they've got a thing that was tellin' you to determine how long you'd be shocked, short time or long time. It made me realize, you know, it was actually happenin'. They're getting ready for me. It just got me more depressed and afraid.

At the time of the original study examined in this book, the electric chair figured prominently in the experience of condemned prisoners, a fact some attribute to staff design. "It's strangely odd how a lot of times they bring you down here," stated one prisoner, "and there it is, plain as day. I would not be surprised if it's not the intent that they want you to see that chair—as a sort of suggestion."[3] The chair also figures prominently in some tours of the prison made available to outsiders. Some guards were showing the chair to a visiting law enforcement officer during one of the interviews. The death witness chamber allowed full view of the scene, where I was conducting an interview, though the words of the participants were inaudible. There was much nervous laughter among the officers, apparently elicited by antic rehearsals of what a real electrocution would do to the victim—the paroxysms of the would-be victim producing paroxysms of laughter. The reaction of the interviewee was moving. For him, this was one more example of his keepers' preoccupation with violence. The scene also brought home his inability to comprehend people who seek out death work as a career. At the conclusion of his account, he wept openly.

PRISONER: Isn't that weird how them people like to come see that? They got some kind of fixation that I can't understand that, that's something else. I just don't really want to live in a world where people are like that. I'd rather be dead and gone. That, that don't make no sense. Look at them (*laugh*). Looking at people like that, now I get tickled wondering what in the hell, why he, what he gets out of seeing that. I can't figure it out. I get tickled looking at them guards like that.

INTERVIEWER: Well tell me, when you laugh at that, what is it you're laughing at?

PRISONER: I've tried to figure it out. I think what it really comes down to is I have to put it in a comical vein to keep from getting that much more depressed. I don't think it's actually, I think it's something in my mind that puts it there to keep me from going over the deep side.

INTERVIEWER: I see. So you've got to detach yourself from it almost.

PRISONER: I think that's it exactly, if you want the truth. I think that's what it. I'm about to cry now that I think about it. What in hell do people want to live like that for?

Official tests of the electric chair are another source of death anxiety on death row. These trial tests, undertaken when an execution date draws near, create noise and vibrations that can be heard and felt by inmates in cells located above the death room. Some inmates believe that staff tests of machinery are attempts to "fire-up" the chair and scare them, especially those whose execution dates are imminent. These rehearsals severely upset the prisoners,[4] and this is intensified by the comments of some guards, such as, "That baby's working real good today," or, "That judge gonna fry you for them murders." Although, for the most part, staff do not act malevolently in these instances, affixing the precise source of culpability is of little more than academic concern to the inmates, who are made to feel the cruelty and inhumanity of an environment that deals in death.

Death work, from the viewpoint of the prisoners, is an unavoidably morbid business. The sentence of death by electrocution seems to them particularly demeaning. "This is the way you do a beast when you are killing him," stated one prisoner, "like a hog at slaughter." Inmates speculate about the mechanics of electrocution and its likely impact on the body, which they visualize in vivid detail. The specter of electrocution brings to mind the frying and melting of organs and the general disfigurement of the body. "It messes up the body terrible," concluded one prisoner. Others analyze the experience in more detail. As indicated in the following excerpts, individuals who face death by electrocution ponder the raw physical violence of the sentence and seek to fathom the personal meaning of the experience.

PRISONER: How am I going to approach and sit in that chair? How am I going to take it? What's it going to be like? How is it going to feel? I already have an understanding about electricity, you know; it's not hard for me to imagine what an experience it would be.

INTERVIEWER: I see. It's a very ugly sounding experience.

PRISONER: Definitely. Just think about the insides of your body, you know, how such organs could be burned, you know, thousands of high voltage. Think about the precious brain that is in your head, you know? Think about your eyes? What will become of them through such hundreds of volts being run through your body? It's just really unpredictable what all can happen through such an experience, and what it will be like to go through it, to die right there, strapped in the chair.

■ ■ ■

The body sears when the currents start going through the body; this makes a guy shiver to think of it. Does he feel it? What does he feel to start off with? When the current goes through, does he, is he unconscious right when it strikes him? Or what really happens? I'm pretty sure he's struck unconscious. But still it's just something. A person don't know what the soul feels or nothing else. But one of these days all of us might feel that. And we're there wondering about it. You know, I think about it quite a bit, and it goes through my mind. And I wonder what's really going to happen.

As it happens, the prisoners' fears are well founded.[5] Warden Lawes of Sing Sing Prison, New York, a frequent witness and host to executions during the 1920s, described the impact of electrocution in the following manner:

As the switch is thrown into its sockets there is a sputtering drone, and the body leaps as if to break the strong leather straps that hold it. Sometimes a thin gray wisp of smoke pushes itself out from under the helmet that holds the head electrode, followed by the faint odor of burning flesh. The hands turn red, then white, and the cords of the neck stand out like steel bands. After what seems an age, but is, in fact, only two minutes, during which time the initial voltage of 2,000 to 2,200 and amperage of 7 to 12 are lowered and reapplied at various intervals, the switch is pulled and the body sags and relaxes, somewhat as a very tired man would do.[6]

Electrocution has been described by one medical doctor as "a form of torture [that] rivals burning at the stake."[7] Electrocutions have been known to drag on interminably, literally cooking the prisoners. In one instance, a man's brain "was found to be 'baked hard,' the blood in his head had turned to charcoal, and his entire back was burned black."[8] One man somehow survived electrocution and was returned months later, with the approval of the Supreme Court, for a second (and unsuccessful) encounter with the chair.[9] John Spenkelink's electrocution, carried out during the period of this research study, lasted over six minutes and required three massive surges of electricity before he finally died. Although we have no accounts of the damage to Spenkelink's body caused by his execution, allegations that Florida prison officials stuffed his anus with cotton and taped his mouth shut suggest that they may have anticipated the forbidding spectacle typically provided by electrocution, and made every effort to make the sanction cosmetically acceptable.[10] As noted above, the execution of one of their own, John Evans, a few years after the study, lasted 14 minutes and required three administrations of electricity.

Beyond the expected physical indignities and pain, the death sentence calls for a trial by ordeal in which the inmate is expected to complete his last walk under his own power and face his sentence with some poise and composure. Most prisoners, in fact, walk to their executions with surprising calm. Some fall apart during their last walk, and must be dragged kicking and screaming to their deaths. But "the rule," as attested to by many observers, "is for the condemned to walk toward death passively, in a sort of dreary despondency," as though resigned to their fate.[11]

Prisoners facing the death sentence, however, have no advance assurance that their last walk will fit the general rule. Norms, patterns, and analyses of prevalent behavior all fail to capture the concerns of the individual men who must struggle to make sense of their private and unique predicament. "That time between when you leave your cell until you get to that chair," stated one prisoner, "that's all your hurt . . . that's the main thing." A number of concerns weigh on the minds of the prisoners when they envision walking to their executions. One is simply whether or not they can, in fact, maintain enough self-control to walk to their deaths. "I'm not saying I'll *walk* by myself," said one man, "but I'm going to try." Others fear they may become violent and then be hurt by the officers. "I'd rather go around here and set in that chair than grab one of those officers," stated one prisoner. "It ain't going to do me no good to get my brains beat out and maybe die there in the cell." Perhaps the most common fear is of breaking down during one's last walk and thereby leaving behind a reputation of weakness. For a few prisoners, this fear was reportedly greater than their fear of execution itself.

PRISONER: Don't nobody want to sit in that chair. They are saying the reason they don't want to sit in the chair is because it messes the body up terrible. I say that too, out loud. But deep down inside, the real reason is because I am afraid that I might break down before I get to the chair. You've got to walk to that chair.

INTERVIEWER: I understand. You mean you might panic?

PRISONER: Yeah, panic and show your feelings. I'm not a freak for publicity. Don't nobody want to go out and the word you left behind is that you broke down.

The ultimate issue raised by the last walk, however, is the painful and almost incomprehensible process of participating in one's own demise. This point was illustrated in the prisoners' ruminations on their executions. For example:

> I have thought about the walk from my cell to the electric chair that certain day. It's hard to rehearse it. And you wonder, how are you going to react? Are you going to go crazy on the way down there? A person's not going to be able to act calm, I don't believe. It would be pretty hard for me to do. I can't come down here smiling. That's just not natural for a person. I mean, if he does, he's got a pretty strong mind. But I think about that quite a bit, you know, the walk that I'd have to take from the cell to the electric chair. And I wonder what's going to be going through my mind, the whole time I'm coming down here. And once you get seated in that chair; you're sitting there, you know, and you're not saying nothing. The whole time you're sitting there you're getting prepared for your death. And lots of other guys said when I first come down here, they said, you get to sign your death warrant . . . That don't make you feel too good. You sit there and you wonder about it, you know. Just sitting there seeing yourself signing your own death warrant.

Dwelling on the details of the death sentence, and on its physical and emotional consequences, naturally creates tension, anxiety, and fear. One man, for example, is plagued by recurring nightmares in which the ritual of execution is played out to its lethal conclusion.

> I go to sleep and I dream of me sitting down in that chair. I mean it's such a fearful thought. Me walking down the tier, sitting down in it, them hooking it up and turning it on . . . 1 don't know. I can wake up, my heart's beating fast, I'm sweating like hell, just like I'd rinsed my head in water . . . I feel I'm gonna have a heart attack.

A few men become preoccupied with putting their affairs in order. "I thought a lot about saying who gets what," stated one prisoner. "I've even given thought about how to be buried." A kind of material and spiritual housecleaning is undertaken. The goal is closure—tying loose ends and perhaps giving coherence or purpose to an often otherwise aimless life. Distributing one's worldly possessions, however meager, can be both an act of charity and a way of repaying debts and obligations. The act of giving can secure, or be thought to secure, the forgiveness of persons one has hurt. Spiritual housecleaning, however, may be more difficult to accomplish and less certain in its rewards. Christians on death row may have problems squaring their conduct with the mandate to live a Christian life. Uncertainty about where one stands with the Lord can be a source of substantial stress for some condemned prisoners.

PRISONER: Well, you've always been taught to live right. I haven't been a Christian all my life. I have studied the Bible while I'm here. That's one thing I want to be able to do is be right with the Lord, whenever I do leave this world. Because I've read quite a bit of the Bible and understand a lot. But now as much as I wish I feel like you can be saved. I feel like I've sat down and prayed and communicated with the Lord that I believe that if I act like a Christian, I'll be able to spend eternity in heaven.

INTERVIEWER: Is that a comforting thought for you?

PRISONER: It's not a comforting thought, because you don't never know. I'm accused of killing somebody. That's a bad sin. It does say that the smallest sins—you know, they're all equal; the sins are equal. You know, you wonder about it. A person, you know, it's always on your mind, too, that you took another life. And you've got to give yours in return. And that's the way I think . . . I sometimes wonder whether I will go to heaven. It's not, like I said, a comforting thought. Because I'm not sure how I am with the Lord. Nobody's perfect, you know. Nobody knows the Lord too good.

Of even greater concern, however, may be the human legacy of execution. The image left behind for loved ones to contemplate and remember the prisoner by—the ugly memory of the seared and burned body mechanically processed by the state, and, if the prisoner breaks down, the humiliating testament of cowardice—may make suicide an attractive option. Suicide, after all, offers a means to die a more dignified death than does execution—at a time and in a manner of one's choosing. Just under half of the prisoners, in fact, entertain the possibility of suicide in lieu of execution. Some are unquestionably serious in their deliberations. The sentiments expressed in this interview excerpt embody their concerns:

> Well, in consideration of these people having planned to electrocute me, suicide has run across my mind, for this very reason: I would rather take my own life than have someone take my life by means of an electric chair or electrocution. I feel that it is [a] more decent and considerable way of dying; rather than having to go and sit in that chair . . . When a man is electrocuted, you see, there are memories left in other people's mind, who are still alive, of how this person was killed, you see. And me considering the fact that it is a lot of relatives of mine out there who are still alive and would have to think about the fact that I had to go down and sit in a old, cruel, and ugly electric chair and was killed, you know, by some authority. What if I go and break down? I wouldn't want

to let nobody get their pleasure seeing me break down. I wouldn't want my people thinking of me having died that particular way. I would rather have them thinking that I died by an overdose of pills, or by cutting my wrist or something of the sort, rather than to leave this world and leave them thinking that I was killed by being electrocuted . . . I wouldn't want to leave such an ugly memory on their conscience, to know that I was electrocuted.

To the condemned, their sentence is a major concern, a source of worry, anxiety, fear, and even dread. For some, this concern is constant. "There is not a day that passes," stated one such prisoner, "that I don't think about the electric chair and the death sentence." Others adopt a fatalistic attitude toward the death sentence. As one prisoner said:

> If it comes time for me to sit in Ole Sparky there, it's that time for me to sit in it. If I happens to escape Sparky, it was lucky, see? It's out of my hands. Nothing I can do either way.

This reaction should not be confused with the complaisant acceptance of death described by Kubler-Ross[12] as the final stage of coping with impending death. These prisoners are not complaisant: They are defeated and depressed. They tend to assume that their executions are likely and that there is little they can do to influence what they view as an essentially inexorable process. "Either way it go," stated one such prisoner,

> out the cell peaceful like, or you swing at them and hit them in the head and they bust you in the head—they gonna drag me around and strap me in the chair and go and turn on the juice.

These men display a cold realism about their circumstances. The hope is that, by directly accepting execution as a likely or even certain conclusion to their confinement, the prisoners can gain the strength to survive the various challenges and trials that lie ahead of them. The ultimate outcome of their coping efforts are unknown, awaiting a future verdict. Their pain and suffering, though, are readily apparent.

> I, frankly speaking, don't know whether I can rightly face the reality of it or not. I'm aware of the circumstances. I've got this instilled in my mind that we are all going to die. You know, we are not gonna change the fact. Now I try to take that philosophy and plant it inside of me, hoping that I can understand or meet whatever circumstances there are. It's cruel. You know, I try to prepare myself for today, hoping that I will be able to survive tomorrow.

For other prisoners, the death sentence seems less tangible and less immediate. A few deny outright the possibility of execution. Their personal safety is an article of faith, beyond question or debate. Like any article of faith, it is held sacred in the face of contradictory evidence and beliefs.

> I know every man they took to that chair had the feeling that it couldn't happen. So, I have got that same feeling. I know it will happen—ain't no doubts about it, it's going to happen—but, I still have that gusto saying that it can't happen to me.

Denial strategies—"that gusto saying it can't happen to me"—tend to emerge early in the person's confinement. Frequently denial is an outgrowth of shocked disbelief, which is then converted into a thoughtful and rational set of assertions about one's immunity from the death penalty. Some prisoners report an experience of unfettered optimism bordering on euphoria. They expect early release from their sentence. When this does not materialize, a longer confinement may be envisioned, but one that still culminates in their reprieve. This optimism—first carefree and promiscuous, then modulated—disappears as the grim reality of the situation is gradually brought home to them. There are no trumpets blaring, no walls crumbling, no ceremony marking a transition from the to-be-dead to the once-again-living.

> It doesn't sink in right away. You feel like, when I first got in, like as free as a bird about to break out of the cage. Got locked up and got death penalty, and I said, "Hey, in a couple of months I'll be out of this." Didn't get out. So I said, "Hey, in a couple of more months I'll get out of here." Shit, I'm still here and I'm gonna be here . . . When I first got here a dude told me, you know, he said, "Hey man, one point of the night you're gonna find yourself crying, and you know, you gonna wonder why, you know. You gonna cry tears in your eyes." When I first got there, you know, I said, "No, not me, I don't cry for nothing'." And all of a sudden, I saw I did. I started realizin' what I was in here for, and that I may not get out and there is a good chance of me gettin' electrocuted. Thinkin' about it, tears start runnin' down and I was cryin'. I didn't need to be crying but I was crying like a baby.

Others adopt a denial strategy that is premised on the deferral of anxiety. The death sentence is seen as a real, but distant, threat. The lengthy appeals process that must be completed for capital cases is taken as a grace period—a planned limbo during which the prisoner worries less about the prospect of execution and more about the technicalities of his case. There is, of course, some unavoidable upset associated with shouldering a death sentence. The discomfort appears minimal, however, as long as the strategy remains intact.

INTERVIEWER: Do you think much at all about the sentence you're under, the possibility of execution?

PRISONER: I never thought about being executed. I just think about how I have been sentenced unjust, because of the way they sentenced me, you know. That hurt me bad and I just think about it and wonder what went wrong and how to set it right.

INTERVIEWER: Do you worry sometimes, that you might not be able to get your case fixed in court?

PRISONER: Never crossed my mind originally, because I know how my case is and I keep telling myself not to worry about that until, you know, a lot of appeals—a whole lot of appeals—been denied.

INTERVIEWER: I see. So at this point you're putting it off, is that it?

PRISONER: Right. I'm just waiting out until next year or maybe the year after, until everything gets in appeals court, and see what happens.

INTERVIEWER: I see. So for the time being, how would you describe your situation?

PRISONER: I'm just waiting out to see that verdict when the Supreme Court do my case. Try not to worry too much.

INTERVIEWER: Is it possible to completely forget about it or does it creep into your mind?

PRISONER: Yes, it creeps in my mind. It creeps in my mind several times, you know, mostly at night, when I ain't got nothing to do. Now sometimes I got a lot of books to read. When I do, you know, I've got something to think about then, so it might ease my mind, so I can go on and sleep on it. Other times the thought stay with me—keep me a little uptight.

Religion can support a posture of denial. One prisoner claimed to be completely free of fear as a consequence of his religious beliefs. He envisioned himself as able to approach execution with the calm born of unshakable faith in Jesus. While he did not expressly class himself as a martyr, his imagined saintly demeanor in the face of death suggests a sense of righteous mission. In his words:

> Like I was tryin' to explain to some of the brothers on death row. They was talkin' about the way that I felt about execution, I said, "Well, the way I feel about it right now brothers," I said, "I know most of y'all won't believe this, but if they was to come right now and lead me to the electric chair, I could really sit in that electric chair. I could really sit in that electric chair right now. And I could smile at the people that is strappin' me down in it. And I could say, "Brothers, I don't hold nothin' against ya, because I know that y'all think that I'm guilty or y'all are just doin' your job. But I know that Jesus knows I'm not guilty and all this is just hurrying me up on home to Jesus Christ." And I could leave with a smile on my face and I could honestly in my heart not have a grudge against nobody.

Denial strategies have an obvious appeal because worry about the death sentence impedes or complicates the routine work of daily adjustment. There is also, perhaps, a certain wisdom reflected in any stance that discounts problems that are beyond one's control. Denial strategies are not without liabilities, however, and some of these are substantial. Other prisoners point out, for example, that men who deny the seriousness of their situation are apt to interfere with the adjustment efforts of their more concerned peers, who may be struggling to face and work through their fears concerning execution. These prisoners also note that denial may be a waste of time—time that may become precious indeed should executions become likely. In the words of one prisoner:

PRISONER: We can go to talking about the sentence. For instance, all right, the conversation won't last long. All right, and if we're talking serious about it, someone upstairs is making jokes. Somebody down the hall is making jokes about what we're talking about. Which is overlooked, but still, I don't believe some people have realized, not exactly, what their situation is, where they're at, and what's going to happen to them if the courts uphold this law. Now, if they realize this, and whenever they do realize this, then it's going to be too late for them to realize anything. Instead of writing their lawyers, instead of talking to their lawyers—or still trying to get them another lawyer that might do them some good or something like this—they're either playing cards, watching TV, or cracking jokes to each other. I don't believe they've really realized that, "Hey, I'm here on death row. If the law is upheld, these people are going to kill me."
INTERVIEWER: Do you think that they are trying to deny it to themselves, or you think they don't believe it?
PRISONER: I reckon you could call it is a mind block. They're just blocking it out.

INTERVIEWER: They don't want to deal with it.

PRISONER: Yeah. They don't want to deal with it by themselves, I don't guess, because they are pushing it out of their minds. I can't do that.

Persons who steadfastly deny the seriousness of their situation risk someday finding themselves deluged with remorse, recriminations, and regrets. These are the makings of crisis and breakdown. Yet the same personal difficulties may prove assimilable when handled directly or in a gradual, planned fashion. Fortunately, peer support may be available to help a person implement a newly acquired desire to accept and deal with the reality of the death sentence.

> When it starts to sinkin' in, it starts to hurt you, bad. And you be quiet, you don't talk to nobody for about a week, just layin' in the cell and think why I messed myself up. I know I did wrong. "Man, let's talk about the death penalty, let's talk about some cases, let's talk about the law or somethin' for awhile." And everybody turns the TV off, turns the radio off, and they talk in with him. We all do this, 'cause we know we all been through it so we all can talk about it. We enlighten one another about the law, you know, and talk about the death penalty. We try to keep the people in their minds that there is a possibility that they can come off of death row, that they haven't thought of before.

It is a commentary on the humanity of the prisoners that support is typically afforded these prisoners as a matter of course, even though the beneficiary only days before may have represented a problem to his benefactors. Conversely, it is a tribute to the coping competence of the prisoners that many of them survive a traumatic awakening to the reality of the death sentence and are able to avail themselves of peer support.

Most condemned prisoners achieve a strained acknowledgment of their sentence. They attempt, with varying degrees of success, to cope with chronic death anxiety as a standard feature of their lives on death row. From the interviews the following tentative sequence of adjustments has emerged: (a) shock gives way to denial; (b) denial is maintained as a consistent or recurring defense against the death anxiety associated with death row confinement; and (c) denial yields, intermittently or permanently, to depression and a fatalistic belief that the person is a pawn in a process that will coldly and impersonally result in his death.[13]

This sequence is offered as a heuristic device, of value for describing, in a preliminary manner, the attempts of condemned prisoners to understand and endure the personal implications of the death sentence. The adaptations of individual prisoners are variable, and thus the prisoners cannot be rigidly classified in terms of this scheme of adjustments. Still, the dimensions of this coping scheme can be reliably charted,[14] as in the following interview excerpt:

INTERVIEWER: Maybe you can tell me what's been the most difficult thing for you about living here on death row?

PRISONER: Trying to adjust and actually realizin' and believin' that I'm under the death sentence.

INTERVIEWER: It doesn't seem real to you?

PRISONER: It doesn't. I think about it sometimes, and it don't seem possible. When I was at the trial, it was like a dream state. And if I had to identify any of the people in the courtroom, I can only identify my lawyer, you know. And the judge, probably.

INTERVIEWER: So you weren't at all prepared for this sentence?

PRISONER: No.

INTERVIEWER: Now the fact that you can't believe it, does that cause you to be confused or upset, or to have other kinds of problems?

PRISONER: Well, it wears me down. Mentally, you know. Sometimes it upsets me, tryin' to accept it, you know. I don't believe anyone could really accept it. It's still like a dream, you know, a fucking crazy dream. I just cannot really believe this could happen to me, put me here, put me out of the world and forget me.

INTERVIEWER: You say it wears you down. Can you describe that for me? Is it that you, you get sleepy, or tired, or depressed? How does it wear you down?

PRISONER: Mostly depressed. It's (*long pause*), it's gettin' to me. I've just had it. Mind gone, broken down, cried. Stuff like that. It gets to be pretty bad sometimes. I get depressed. I get deep depressed.

INTERVIEWER: Well, you seem kind of upset right now, just even thinking about that.

PRISONER: Yeah, I am. It's a hard thing to face.

INTERVIEWER: And do you want to face it, or do you want not to face it? What do you think you want?

PRISONER: I would like not to have to face it. But I'm here, so I have to face it.

The mix of adaptations to the death sentence—more formally, the various positions on the sequence of adjustments to the death penalty represented at a given juncture—sometimes create conflict and tension. This is the case, for instance, when prisoners who loudly deny the danger posed by the death sentence impinge on others who adopt a different mode of adjustment. Prisoners who employ denial as an adaptation contribute to a climate of surface conviviality occasionally found on death row.[15] The image conveyed by such a climate is that of cold-blooded felons, impervious to the worst punishments meted out by the state. This picture is seriously misleading. Many condemned prisoners publicly advertise their freedom from despair but suffer great private anguish. Those who persistently deny they are under a sentence of death hide from reality behind gallows humor—a hollow humor known to sustain morale only until the executioner is in view, when defenses collapse:

> The row ain't serious, it's a lot of funny things happening on the row. Everybody seeing who can be the funniest, you know. So, I contribute in that there, too. I figure if I contribute in that, that will keep me going halfway. But I figure now when the things really get hard and everybody stops joking, that's when you are going to see about ten people just bug out from the jump. All of us are going to bug out sooner or later.

The electric chair was the method of execution used in Alabama and several other states when the original study reported in this book was conducted. Electrocutions have a certain visible horror. The sheer force of electricity hitting the restrained body of the condemned prisoner is awful for prisoners to contemplate,[16] let alone researchers like myself to behold.[17] There is no doubt that an electrocution is an act of violence.

Lethal injection, first used in Texas in 1982 but not used in Alabama until 2002, has a more benign exterior, suggesting a peaceful death. But from the point of view of condemned prisoners, the tableau presented by lethal injection is one of helplessness. The prisoner lies supine on a gurney, strapped firmly in place for long minutes before the administration of the chemical poisons. To make matters worse for contemporary prisoners on death row in Alabama and across the nation, the likelihood of a botched execution is higher with lethal injection than with electrocution.[18] Moreover, we now know that the analogy of the condemned prisoner being burned at the stake, intuitively obvious with electrocutions, is equally accurate with lethal injections, for a botched lethal injection is likely experienced as if one is being burned up inside.[19] It would seem there is no easy and painless way to kill a condemned prisoner, a fact well known to the condemned themselves.

Notes

1 For a vivid description of Evans' execution, see Stevenson (2014: 54).
2 See generally Johnson (2014a).
3 A similar comment was made by Gettinger (1979: 49) about the ease with which the electric chair could be viewed by death row prisoners in Florida: "Sometimes when he got into the exercise yard, he would wander over to the fence and stare at a little building across the way. That was the Death House, and the guards left the blinds up in the window so the inmates could see the electric chair. 'Old Sparky,' they call it with grim jocularity. 'You can get a pretty good look at it.' Proffitt said. 'Power control on the side. It's unnerving sometimes. Sometimes I go over there just to look at it. It's something you got to face; it's not going away. I have no desire to see it firsthand, however, right up close.'"
4 The fears occasioned in the man whose execution was at issue were not covered in any of the interviews. Possibly he was one of the two men I did not interview. Curtis Bok (1959: 178–179) may have captured the flavor of this man's predicament, however, in his novel, *Star Wormwood*: "At noon the Warden tested the reserve generators . . . Roger went cold with fear and felt as if his heart would burst with pounding. He fought his way back to some degree of stability, but he had begun to tremble and could not stop . . . There was too much else pressing in upon him . . . He sat on his bed and watched the last daylight he would ever see drain from the sky. When the window was at last dark there was nothing left to take his attention but the black door. He eyed it with increasing fright and suddenly went utterly to pieces. His legs would not support him and he fell on his bed with racking dry sobs. He would not see light again. The mean things in his cell at once became dear to him. He would live with them forever if they would let him stay and be faithful to his chair and table and bed and barred door. He would learn to live with them and love them . . . The official executioner tested the generators again. If only death might come unexpectedly. Waiting for a set hour gave the situation an air of hideous formality and deliberation that was torture."
5 History records awesomely savage executions rendered under color of law. There is no need to recount them here, however, because modern instances of barbarity in sentencing are not hard to find. The guillotine, for example, a beheading machine of seemingly humane efficiency, is said by medical observers to produce distinctly morbid effects. A medical report in Camus (1969: 183) reads: "If we may be permitted to give our opinion, such sights are frightfully painful. The blood flows from the blood vessels at the speed of the severed carotids, then it coagulates. The muscles contract and their fibrillation is stupefying; the intestines ripple and the heart moves irregularly, incompletely, fascinatingly. The mouth puckers at certain moments in a terrible pout. It is true that in that severed head the eyes are motionless with dilated pupils; fortunately they look at nothing and, if they are devoid of the cloudiness and opalescence of the corpse, they have no motion; their transparence belongs to life, but their fixity belongs to death. All this can last minutes, even hours, in sound specimens: death is not immediate . . . Thus, every vital element survives decapitation. The doctor is left with the impression of a horrible experience, of a murderous vivisection, followed by a premature burial."

Electrocution was first introduced in America in New York State as a merciful improvement to the centuries-old practice of hanging. The process by which this judgment was arrived at is instructive. "No one really knew for sure whether electricity would actually kill a human being or whether it would merely stun him into a comatose death-like state that, while having all the outward appearances of departed life, would not satisfy the legal and moral requirements of the public conscience. A cat and dog, followed by a horse, had been killed in this manner as well as an orangutan the size of a small human male (although the animal's long hair caught fire and charred his exterior) and that seemed to be enough to convince members of the New York State Legislature that electrocution would be a more humane form of execution as opposed to hanging" (Nicolai, Riley, Christensen, Stych, and Greunke, 1980: vii).

6 Washington Research Project (1975: 35).
7 Washington Research Project (1975: 36).
8 Nicolai et al. (1980: 1).
9 Washington Research Project (1975: 36).
10 An investigation cleared the officials of these charges. The Florida prisoners termed the investigation a blatant cover-up. The warden was subsequently appointed inspector general of Florida's correctional department.
11 Camus (1969: 205) The apparent numbness of the condemned may disguise frantic turmoil or internal conflict. Dostoyevsky, who himself faced a firing squad, suggests this in the following passage from *The Idiot* (1868/1914: 85): "It is strange that people very rarely faint during those final seconds. On the contrary, the brain is terribly alive and active; it must be racing, racing, racing like a machine at full speed. Imagine how many thoughts must be throbbing together, all unfinished, some of them may be irrelevant and absurd: That man staring—has a wart on his forehead, and, here, one of the executioner's buttons has rusted. And at the same time he knows everything . . . there is one point that cannot be forgotten, and he cannot faint, and everything turns around it, around that point. And to think that it must be like this up to the last quarter second, when his head is already on the block, and waits, and—knows, and suddenly he hears the iron slithering down above his head."
12 Kubler-Ross (1969).
13 This sequence has obvious parallels with the work on facing the death sentence and terminal illness reviewed in Chapter 1. Significantly, it lends some support to the speculation, recorded in that chapter, that a sense of helpless defeat may represent for the death row prisoner what growth and acceptance represent for the terminal patient: The culmination of a struggle to come to grips with the prospect of death in a particular institutional context. In Chapter 6 it will be shown that signs of deterioration, under the combined pressures of death row and the death penalty, are disturbingly common.
14 For valuable reflections on different coping strategies in extreme confinement settings like solitary confinement, see O'Donnell (2014).
15 Prior to the execution of John Spenkelink, death row prisoners in Florida had been described in similar terms. See Lewis (1979: 200).
16 Hinton (2018: 98–99) reports a fear of electrocution that closely parallels the fears covered in this chapter. On arrival on death row, he tells us, "I didn't know when they would come for me. Could them come kill me even thought I was on appeal?" Like the prisoners interviewed in this chapter, some of whose time on death row overlapped with Hinton's, he reports panic when simply contemplating execution.
17 In the years following the publication of the first edition of this book, I went on to study an execution team and observe firsthand several executions, reporting on the distinctive horror of electrocutions (Johnson, 1989, 1990, 1998).
18 Sarat (2014).
19 Johnson (2014b: 109). I have tried to describe the horror of a lethal injection in a short story entitled "Lethal Rejection," Johnson (2008).

References

Bok, C. (1959). *Star Wormwood*. New York: Knopf.

Camus, A. (1969). *Resistance, rebellion and death: Essays*. New York: Knopf.

Dostoyevsky, F. (1868/1914). *The idiot*. London: Dent.

Gettinger, S. H. (1979). *Sentenced to die*. New York: Macmillan.

Hinton, A. R. (with Hardin, L. L.). (2018). *The sun does shine: How I found life and freedom on death row*. New York: St. Martin's Press.

Johnson, R. (1989). "This man has expired": Witness to an execution. *Commonweal, 116*(1), 9–15.

Johnson, R. (1990). *Death work: A study of the modern execution process*. Pacific Grove, CA: Brooks-Cole.

Johnson, R. (1998). *Death work: A study of the modern execution process* (2nd ed.). Belmont, CA: Wadsworth.

Johnson, R. (2008). Lethal rejection. *Crime Media Culture: An International Journal, 4*(2), 279–283.

Johnson, R. (2014a). Reflections on the death penalty: Human rights, human dignity, and dehumanization in the death house. *Seattle Journal of Social Justice, 13*(2), 582–598.

Johnson, R. (2014b). Time on the cross: A meditation on lethal injection. *Seattle Journal for Social Justice*, *13*(1), 103–111.

Kubler-Ross, E. (1969). *On death and dying.* New York: Macmillan.

Lewis, P. (1979). Killing the killers: A post-Furman profile of Florida's condemned. *Crime and Delinquency*, *25*(2), 200–211.

Nicolai, S., Riley, K., Christensen, R., Stych, P., & Greunke, L. (1980). *The question of capital punishment.* Lincoln, NE: Contact.

O'Donnell, I. (2014). *Prisoners, solitude, and time.* Oxford: Oxford University Press.

Sarat, A. (2014). *Gruesome spectacles: Botched executions and America's death penalty.* Palo Alto, CA: Stanford University Press.

Stevenson, B. (2014). *Just mercy: A story of justice and redemption.* New York: Spiegel & Grau.

The Washington Research Project. (1971). *The case against capital punishment.* Washington, DC: The Project.

6

A LIVING DEATH

Thus far, the physical and social characteristics, custodial fixations, loneliness, violence, danger, and fear found on death row have been surveyed. Death row confinement, however, is experienced as a totality, and this totality of human suffering must also be examined.

Seeds of Decay

A range of insoluble problems emerge on death row to torment the prisoners. Their families, their keepers, and their peers are each implicated as sources of stress. The prisoners have few constructive options open to them and must strive, ultimately, to withstand the forces that point to deterioration—physical, mental, spiritual, or some combination thereof—as their common fate.

In the struggle for psychological survival, the help the men can give each other is limited by their constrained environment. Still, condemned prisoners may work well together to resolve shared problems, at times operating as a team to find humor in their situation and to share limited commodities, such as information and material goods. The prisoners seem particularly successful in their efforts to keep tempers under control and to relate to the guards in a manner befitting their power and authority. The controlled deportment of the prisoners, which is documented in low rates of disciplinary infractions on death row, belies the staff's portrait of them as desperate and promiscuously violent men.

> Well, we constantly talk to people, you know, about self-control, personal conduct, and attitude. And say, well, instead of saying that you want something done, ask for it to be done, you know. Because we realize that we are not in the demanding position and that we have to make the proper approach—in order to get something done. So, we try to conduct ourselves according to the rules and regulations during personal discussions with any individual that works for the staff . . . We are not out to be violent. You know, we don't want to confront violence with violence because it don't solve anything. It only makes a bad situation worse. This is not what we are out to do. We are out to make a bad situation good. And this is why we are trying, harder every day, to develop

and establish some kind of communicational relationship between the men on death row and the prison administrational personnel. We are desperate for survival, but not from the aspect of committing a violent act.

The prisoners are also quick to aid a man whose execution date approaches. The man confronting death by execution is not shunned or avoided; his impending death does not make him a pariah because he reminds his fellow-condemned of the slender thread on which their lives hang. Instead, the prisoner approaching execution receives the concerted support of his peers. As one man stated,

> His execution date was really getting close. He was within two days, and the courts were denying him another stay. I mean, the man's really getting nervous, which I can understand. You know, "I'm going to die Friday. This is hell." And they kept firing this chair up every day. You can hear it; it vibrates the floors upstairs, and it was really getting to him, you know. So we were all trying to make it easy as possible on him. You know, trying to keep his spirits up. Mainly the only thing we felt was, "Hey, we've got to take care of this guy," because, you know, it was getting awful close, and it was really doing a number on his head.

Some prisoners remain aloof from their peers. A few prefer solitude to the companionship and support of their fellow prisoners. Two of the condemned were ostracized and were alternately harassed and ignored by the other men.[1] Isolates and outcasts, however, were very much in the minority. Most condemned prisoners seek and obtain peer support. They echo the sentiments of the man who exclaimed that, at the social level, "We all get along great." Another prisoner said, "We don't never lock ourselves off from the other guy." This man described death row as a setting in which a man can count on his peers for help when pressing problems mount. Help involves small talk to distract the person in stress, or what may be described as simply "a human response."

> They can feel free to come to me, I don't care what time it is, we can come to one another. I can holler down the floor. "What did they say on the news today." You know, just talk about anything. Or, "What kind of papers did you get from court today," you know. Just go to talking like that, you know. You are always free—there is never a time when you will call one of us and he will say, "I don't feel like being bothered" . . . We all be needing a human response, and here we give it to each other.

Even "Dear John" letters can be the subject of public discussion and peer advice—as long as the problem is handled as a matter of tactics ("How should I word this letter to get her back?"), rather than as a personal crisis ("I don't know if I can make it without her"). The assumption is that a man should always try to keep his woman. "I even had papers on her," bemoaned one man, indicating his right to fight for a dying marriage. "Dear John" letters merit an appeal to the loved one who wants to end the relationship. If the appeal is granted, there is cause for celebration; if denied, there is the consolation of knowing that one has put up a dignified defense.

> One of us might get a letter from home where his girlfriend is quitting him, you know? Well, if he makes this known to somebody, we will all get together and say, "Well, OK, in my opinion, write

this letter here" . . . I will voice my opinion on how he should approach one specific problem. "Just explain yourself in this way here." . . . Another person might have another idea. Well, we combine all of our dealings and let him give it his best shot in his own way. As long as he exercises the idea. We might be able to get his girlfriend back for him; then we might not. We are not always successful with this letter thing, you know. But we do give it our best shot. And when he gets a reply back, it will be something that will ease his mind. There will be some relief for him.

The picture is less encouraging when personal problems or mental anguish are at issue. Despair remains a private matter, to be handled by the individual himself. When personal concerns are involved—doubts, regrets, recriminations—the prisoner is on his own. "Everybody is closed," stated one man, "every man on the row is to himself." Concentration camp inmates, in a similar manner, provided each other help or advice, but retreated from sentiment. "Help, yes; compassion, no," recorded one Holocaust survivor,[2] a declaration of ethics equally fitting for many prisoners on death row.[3]

Condemned prisoners are burdened with many personal problems for which peer support is unavailable or irrelevant. Some harbor what they view as shameful dependency needs, needs that cannot even be revealed to trusted intimates. One man said:

> I'd like to write my mom and say, "Mom, I'm scared. They might walk me to that chair any day." You know, really let her know I'm facing a death sentence. But I can't, 'cause I've leaned on her enough already.

Others agonize over the irremediable harm they may have caused their loved ones. "I have two kids and I love them to death," stated one such prisoner, "and what worries me most is that whatever happens to me here is really going to affect them, I think, for the rest of their lives." Yet others nurture open emotional wounds, the "deep and private hurt" that results when a family spurns one of its own as "an outcast, something they wouldn't care to even wipe their feet on."

Finally, virtually all of the men experience (or fear) the gradual decaying of ties to loved ones. Letters to and from significant others grow shorter, less hopeful, and less intimate. One prisoner, for example, described the sense of futility that inhibited his correspondence with his wife.

> When I first got here I used to write my wife a 15- to 20-page letter. Sometimes I'd have to put them in two envelopes and send them to her. But then it comes to a point where you can express your feelings, but when you come out of your emotional feelings, reality always stares you in your face.

Another prisoner retraced, with some bitterness, the decline of the support provided by his family as the finality of his sentence became increasingly apparent.

> When I came here, you know, I was loved. It helped me. It's just having somebody who will say good things to you. Seem like my people, they was sad but it only last so long. They realize, well, this person on death row, he's not getting out. They slowly cut you off. As time go by, things get old, you know? Whereas my wife was writing me 14 pages, now she write me one paragraph.

So you know, that's real cold. That turns me off . . . Quite frankly, I'd say about 90 percent of the time if you got a relationship—say if you knew somebody before you even got here, you know somebody five, ten years—well in six months, that relationship is through.

The men on death row often prop up flagging egos through recourse to the prison's image of manliness, a fiction that requires men in adversity to appear proud, impervious, and self-sufficient.[4] From this perspective, the support of others is suspect, even superfluous. "You can't get no comfort talking to nobody." Another prisoner observed, "Visitors come and visitors go, but I got to do the time—I got to face the chair." Speaking for many prisoners on death row, one man observed: "This is my life and I got to live my life. And I ain't depending on other peoples and things to live it for me. I can't depend on them to help me because I'm a grown man." For some, the "unmanly" inmates are those who advertise problems and inadequacies. They are seen as the morally weak, the manipulators who connive and whine to achieve their selfish ends. Prison manliness myths do not allow displays of human suffering or provide incentives for empathy, support, or concern. Consequently, prisoners must keep personal problems to themselves, however difficult and painful this may be, or run the risk of being ignored, scapegoated, or exploited.

When you're down in the dumps and you don't know what to do, maybe you might be able to call somebody [on the row] and you all shoot the bull and blow it off. You may call somebody and start up an argument and blow it off in that way . . . You try to, you know, get them to try to start somethin' to get your mind off the problems. But you know, in a situation like what we're in, you don't ever put too much trust in another man, because everybody gets used to beatin' and gettin' beat, you know? And so you have to watch out for the beatin', you know? You can't leave yourself open. You can't give no trust. If a brother has a gun, you ain't gonna give him no bullet to shoot you with.

Death row is often described in terms that bring to mind the image of a pressure cooker or vacuum. Many inmates respond to the immediate pressure of this environment with depression and lifelessness. Persistent feelings of powerlessness and despair breed suppressed, directionless anger. Periodic emotional outbursts give vent to anger and may provide a temporary relief from the tension that builds up within the prisoners.

You've got some people, like myself, that just get up here and things get so bad that they just holler out. You can't cry—you can't cry—so, you just let out and holler, you know, turn your radio up real loud and start hollering and jumping up and after about 15 minutes you will be alright. I know what it is. I have to get my tension off. So, I hear a man up the hall a few minutes later do the same thing and then late at night I hear a man jump up and just holler and start laughing, so I know he is getting his tension off right there.

Although outbursts of impotent anger are ostensibly symptoms of defeat, they may actually represent the principal signs of emotional life on death row. As prisoners resist their preordained fate, their anger can grow into the rage of men struggling to nurture life in an environment devoted to its extinction.

The widespread sources of rage on death row, and the battle to preserve self-control and emotional autonomy waged by condemned prisoners, are traced in the following interview excerpt:

> Bein' here, knowin' what you got to look forward to is that thing [the electric chair] next door, you know? Well, now that's a big enough problem in itself, tryin' to deal with that. Okay, then when you add other problems on, such as someone hushing you, somebody always pickin' at you. Maybe somebody only kiddin' with you, keepin' up too much noise, somethin' like that, you know. But everything adds up here. You can't get no mail. You can't get no phone calls. You want to tell somebody somethin' but you can't get to 'em and you can't tell 'em nothin' and you ain't got no way to get word out to 'em and it just all beat down on you, man, and you don't know what to do. You don't know which way to go or how to straighten out the mess that you're in, and it just seem like a big bomb inside of you that's got to explode and it ain't got nowhere to explode at. . . . So far I've been able to deal with it. But, you know, I feel that maybe someday it might even make me do somethin', or either maybe push me over the edge.

So many pressures bear down on the prisoners that they can feel alternately comfortable and depressed without reason, as though problems emerged from nowhere to disrupt their equilibrium and threaten their adjustment. For example:

> Some days you go "bang" and you're down. Sometimes you might be able to go two or three days; then you might be able to go all week. And nothin' botherin' you, you feel like ain't nothin' botherin' you, you know? And then again, all at once in the middle of a good mood, all these things fall down on you like a ton of bricks.

Death row prisoners are chronically angry, with few outlets for their suppressed resentments. Strong emotions, denied regular, meaningful, and constructive outlets, can lead to deterioration. For some men, deterioration is felt to be inevitable. "I don't know how long I can last," worried one prisoner. "I feel like every day I'm losing part of my mind." Other prisoners speak of slowing down mentally, feeling confused, forgetful, lethargic, listless, and drowsy. Their experience may have an analog in senility. Letters ramble; material objects get lost from one moment to the next, even within the limited confines of the cell; thoughts wander aimlessly, ending abruptly, only to start up again, uninvited.

> It's depression, that's what it is. I write a letter and I try to, I think of myself as having a heavy game for a woman, right? OK, I write a woman, it takes me two days to write a 20-page letter, and I used to, could do that just as fast as I could get it on the paper. I could do it. But now I have to sit and think. When I think of something to tell a woman, I forget it. Ok, I get up from my table, I turn my radio on and come back and my pencil is gone and I can just stand there looking and I won't say nothing—I'm in a cell by myself—I won't say nothing to nobody, because I don't want people to think that I'm losing out. So, I just stand there and say, "I know my pencil was here." Ok, I find my pencil on my bed and I pick it up and I laugh to myself—I say, "I'm just losing out a little bit." Constantly, I find myself losing things in my cell. Things I should keep up with.

Deliberate efforts, such as exercise, may be made to break out of a stupor, or the prisoner may lose himself in fantasy or sleep. The results, however, may not prove effective in neutralizing the effects of depression.

> I put more hours in the bed than I do anywhere else in the cell, you know? I don't be asleep; I just be laying down, be fantasizing, get up, turn the radio on, and plan to do some exercises. I get on the floor, I do about five push-ups. And I get up and I say, "Joe Blow, I can't do them." I get back in the bed. Then when I get in the bed, I say, "Man, you cold going down. You are losing out on yourself." So, I get up and I say I'm going to do it. And I try again. I end up getting back in the bed without even thinking about I'm getting in the bed, and that's when—after I get in the bed that time I think about—"Here you is in the bed and you didn't know what you were doing."

Having others comment on one's erratic behavior undermines the efforts of prisoners struggling to resist the advances of deterioration.[5] When a consistent portrait of decay is provided, it may shake a man's already eroded sense of competence.

> My brother wrote me a letter. Now, I dig my brother. He told me—he say, "When you write your letters, man, you be skipping." Like I be on one subject and I bounce from this subject to something else. I bounce back on the other subject. And he told me about it. He said, "You've got to try to control yourself and talk about one thing." I find that hard to do now . . . Ok, me and my partner—we came down here together—that dude ain't changed none. And everybody on the row say that they have seen some change in me since I have been here. And he say that he has seen a hell of a big change. He say he know I'm going crazy. I say, now, they are trying to drive me crazy. I try to use that there as a crutch to keep going. I think I can make it. I'm going to make it.

Men in the throes of deterioration diagnose themselves as physically weak, susceptible to disease, and emotionally drained. "The main thing," said one prisoner, "is the mental pressure: you're always depressed. But I think another main thing is the physical deterioration of the body. You sit up there and you just feel yourself getting weaker, you know? Your back hurts, ya know? You're sick a lot—colds and low blood. You lose all your energy." The prospect of deterioration is real to many prisoners. They sense that their adjustments to confinement are fragile, subject to collapse at any time under the weight of the pressures that surround them. "I'm already walking on a hairline of being sane and insane; I could fall either way at any time," one prisoner concluded, a poignant observation that has been made by many other prisoners on solitary confinement death rows.[6]

There are few sources of variety on death row—of novelty, stimulation, or surprise—to break the deadening routine. For this reason, even the very brief respite from the rigors of close confinement afforded by the interview represented a rare and refreshing encounter for some of the men.

> Like in a way, I can, you know, just start comin' more and more into myself, you know. I can go to talk, you know, the way, the way I used to. Well, it make me, you know, feel better to come

down here and conversate with you. 'Cause conversation with outside people, things that they talk about seem to make more sense to me than everyday things that, you know, us up on death row talk about.

In one tragic case, death row had transformed the prisoner into a psychiatric casualty, a man who had, in the words of one of his peers, "done cold left himself." Commenting on this prisoner's deterioration, a neighboring inmate related the following brief synopsis of his past and current condition:

PRISONER: When I first come down here, he talked good, he could carry on a good conversation, he could talk real good. We used to talk to each other, you know. But it's got to where now sometimes at night he would be sitting down there in his cell and he'd tear up pieces of cloth all night long, tear his mattress all night long, get at the bar and yell out "Mama, Mama," continuously at the top of his lungs. And you can't sleep with that there going on. Yell out other people's names and so forth. I think, I think he needs help, a lot more than what he's getting up there.
INTERVIEWER: Do you think it's a psychiatric condition now?
PRISONER: I think it's worked into that, yeah. Because every time somebody mentions the chair—every time someone mentions this thing in here, walking around it or anything, he flies off the handle.

Few inmates were sympathetic to this unfortunate man. Some contended that he was faking mental illness to escape execution. Others were given to "revving him up" with threats and taunts, at least until it became obvious that he was deeply and perhaps permanently disturbed.

INTERVIEWER: Anytime someone mentions the electric chair, he gets real up tight.
PRISONER: Yeah, he gets up tight. One of the inmates will joke with him about it, or say something to him in a way, I call it smart cracking, just to see if he's going to do it again. Which isn't right, but they do it. They yell at him; they say something like, "Hey, *Smith* is the first one to go" and a bunch of other stuff that they make up and say to him. This'll trigger him off. I mean, it would trigger me off.
INTERVIEWER: Do you think they want to trigger him off?
PRISONER: They do sometimes. But they got to where, I don't know, that's been about a year or something ago, and he hasn't got out of it yet. They've quit joking as far as, you know, revving him up. But he hasn't got better. It's just with him, it's just a thing that's with him and he does, he needs, he needs help, I mean, you know, a doctor's help.

This prisoner was abused because men too dependent or fearful to stand up for themselves are rejected out of hand. In the cold logic of the penitentiary, weak (unmanly) inmates are "punks" who deserve the humiliation and abuse heaped upon them.

See, they [staff] beat his ass in, they're breaking him, see what I mean? Now come a time when someone had to speak for him, he wouldn't accept it. They had a lawyer to come in to speak for him about that ass-whipping, he wouldn't accept it, go out and tell him what happened. You see what I mean? So a person like that man, I got no time for him, because I'm not gonna let him drag me down to the same category he in. I'm gonna stand on my own two feet. We all on death row offered to help the dude, file writs for the dude. He won't respond back. He done his own self in.

There was only a shell of a person left by the time I interviewed him. By chance, the interview took place during one of his more lucid days. He had been transferred to his home county jail to participate in court proceedings bearing on his case. The change of environment produced dramatic improvements in his mental health. Though the changes in behavior and attitude proved short-lived, the liberating impact of normal confinement highlights the destructive forces at work on death row.

PRISONER: Lately I've been transferred a couple of times back to _____ County and I've been to court over in _____ County. And man it seemed like I been free, ya know, and my mind just turned all the way around. Every day now, since then, ya know, it's been on a steady up beat, ya know what I mean?

INTERVIEWER: How come being transferred and going to court has helped so much?

PRISONER: I feel like it was nice because the way my mind changed, ya know? It made me feel better, ya know, mentally and physically, too. Ya know what I mean? So I say it's because I got to change environments for a while. So I got to see different things . . . I had a little more room and I was able to meet with people. Like in the jail, ya know, they got a dayroom and y'all be up there all day . . . This place here just caves in on you. The same thing everyday, that just stacks up on top of you, ya know what I mean? So I got out from under it, ya know what I mean? Like a brand new life, man. Like I just came in yesterday. I feel relaxed a lot more now, ya know, and I can hold a better conversation with you because of the time I spent in court, ya know. But before I started going to court and things, my mind just flips out on me. But now, ya know, I'm back.

The interview focused on the pains of confinement on death row. We spoke of macings that came unannounced, seemingly without cause or justification. (Significantly, a fellow prisoner observed, "They gassed that son-of-a-bitch so much 'til I don't see how he got enough fucking sense even to come out of his cell.") We also spoke of the man's occasional rampages of destructiveness in his cell, which were undertaken in perceived self-defense: "I figured they'd fuck less with me if I hit 'em with the sink." But mostly we spoke of the lengthy intervals of confinement marked by episodes of mental illness and the private traumas of his psychotic world.

PRISONER: I done flipped out three or four times in different tiers, you know? My mind just right up and leave me. I didn't expect the thing to happen. And everything just, you know, how you just go. I can't explain it and everything that's taken place, but I just flipped out.

INTERVIEWER: This happens from out of nowhere?

PRISONER: Just out of nowhere. Just flipped out. For a week or two I stayed up for weeks at a time. I don't know why, I just couldn't go to sleep, ya know?

INTERVIEWER: Do you have any memories of what it's like when you're flipped out?

PRISONER: Yeah. I have memories, I remember a lot of it. It's weird, man, ya know what I mean? To explain it would take all day.

INTERVIEWER: Can you just give me a little bit of feeling for what it is?

PRISONER: Well, yeah. Like once I flipped out there and I slept on the floor to the bed and I watered the cell down and everything and I set some fires to the cell. I burned my mattress up on 9 unit, and I set fire to a mattress on 10 unit.

INTERVIEWER: We're you trying to hurt yourself do you think?

PRISONER: I wasn't trying to hurt myself, just something told me, it said, "Set the fire," ya know?

INTERVIEWER: Is that like voices inside your head?

PRISONER: Yeah. It's just like I'm trying to light it. I done did it. Something bring me the sheet and I'm lighting it up there, and before you know it, it's like to kill me before they done get me out of there, ya know? And a day or two later after I realized what had happened, ya know, I learned to accept it, ya know? I realized it was me. Something told me in my mind to do it.

INTERVIEWER: Does it sound like a voice almost in your mind?

PRISONER: Yeah. I don't know, like just like somebody tell ya, ya know, "Do it, do it." Ya know what I mean?

INTERVIEWER: Yeah.

PRISONER: It's, I just went off man, ya know. I'd stay woke up and never go to sleep and day to day I'd stop eating and everything, ya know and just messing up.

INTERVIEWER: How were you feeling emotionally during this time? Would you be very sad, or very depressed, or very tense? How would you feel?

PRISONER: I'd be depressed and lost. Like the officers would come by and they'd talk to me, some of them, and say I was lost, man, say, "It was like you was in another world, man," ya know? I say, "Yeah, that's the way I felt, like I was in another world." I felt sometimes for weeks at a time that I wasn't even here.

The moral of this extreme response to the pressures of life under sentence of death is transparent to the men of death row. According to one prisoner, "We all know we can do just like him—go crazy." Such fears are plausible on death row, where the line separating the manly from the unmanly can easily blur and disappear. Each condemned prisoner, of course, confronts enormous stresses, and each must marshal his resources as best he can. Most men yield, gradually and almost imperceptibly, to the pressures of death row. Those adjudged weak and unmanly are doubly penalized; they are singled out for special abuse and denied the sympathy and support they desperately need to survive. They stand naked and defenseless—stark testaments to the human experience of death row confinement.

A Living Death

Some death row inmates, attuned to the bitter irony of their predicament, characterize their existence as a living death and themselves as the living dead. They are speaking symbolically, of course, but their imagery is an appropriate description of the human experience in a world where life is ruled by death. It takes into account the condemned prisoners' massive deprivation of personal autonomy and command over resources critical to psychological survival; their suspension in a stark, empty, tomb-like setting, marked by indifference to basic human needs and desires; and their enforced isolation from the living, with the resulting emotional emptiness and death.

At best, condemned prisoners can expect life imprisonment. Capital offenders are rarely pardoned, and none of the Alabama men expected a pardon. A reprieve to a life sentence—in effect, life without parole—is a possibility, but many of the prisoners consider a life sentence intolerable. "Why should I want to be a state vegetable?" asked one man. "Personal, physical freedom means different things to different people," said another. "Mine means enough to me that if I can't have it, I'd rather be dead." At least one prisoner claimed he would seek execution rather than submit to a life in prison.

> Life without parole, to me that means spend the rest of your life in a penitentiary. Now, that I know I wouldn't do. I'd say, "Burn me." If it's either living in prison or dying in that chair, I'm going to go ahead and be exterminated. There ain't no way I'm going to die in a penitentiary, unless they execute me.

A few prisoners envision the possibility of release from prison many years hence, when they are considerably older and past their prime. The futures they foresee are lonely and bleak. Said one prisoner: "Due to my age, I don't want no child when I get out of here. I don't want no wife. Just, you know, be with my mother and father 'til they pass, if they pass before I pass." Others view suicide as preferable to the marginal lives they expect to eke out after years of confinement.

PRISONER: Before a lot of people get out, they'd be 50 years old, you know, or 60 years old after they get out. I think like that 50 or 60 years old, don't make no sense to get out then. What you gonna be able to do to make a livin'? Might want to kill myself then anyway.

INTERVIEWER: Oh, so you figure your life would be over anyway?

PRISONER: Yes. If you get out at 50 or 60 years old, what can you do, really? Like I don't got no skills to go into an office and be some kind of big executive secretary or somethin'. I don't know how to type or nothin' like this. The only think that I could do is work on cars.

■ ■ ■

> Why spend the better part of your life in a penitentiary and then go out at an old age and burn your people? It's better off all the way around to go ahead and get it over with than it is to go out there. What are you going to do? You're going to get a job in a filling station, making $75 or $80 a week, and then depending on your people to pay the rest of your bills for you. That's no deal.

Death row inmates, of course, hunger for freedom now, when they are young, robust, and capable of rebuilding their lives. But escape from prison, the only remaining path to immediate freedom, is dismissed as futile. "I don't care if you grab the warden and his mother," quipped one prisoner, "You're not gonna walk out of here alive." A number of prisoners emphasized that, even in the unlikely event of a successful escape, they would be constantly on the run and unable to achieve peace of mind. One prisoner observed, "You've got the whole world looking for you! You are not going to know any peace or any happiness. It's not worth it to escape. I couldn't live like that." Lengthy confinement on death row is therefore likely, which some prisoners find unacceptable. They speak of suicide as a means of escape from death row. They also consider dropping their appeals as a means to terminate their death row confinement, which would be tantamount to committing state-assisted suicide. In their words:

I probably think about suicide more than a lot of guys up there. Like I say, I want out. Where the rest of these guys, they say, "While you live there's hope." Well, that's true. I'm not gonna be so stupid as to say it's not. But they're willing to wait five or ten years to get off death row. I'm not. And I've made this statement on several occasions, that if something's not done pretty soon, there's no doubt, I'll punch out. I'll punch my own ticket if I have to.

■ ■ ■

I'd rather be dead then be treated like this. It is a long period of time. Like, I've read cases where guys have been on death row for 12 years. I'm not going to be here that long. By their choosing or by my own choosing, I plan to end it long before it gets to that length of time.

■ ■ ■

I've been wantin' to tell them like to just drop the appeal and everything. Just let them do what they're gonna do. I would tell 'em, "Go ahead on, put me in the chair." . . . I just want to be alone. Sometimes it seem like a hopeless cause. I mean, death row ain't no kinda living.

Other prisoners seem more pragmatic and calculating about life on death row. They place survival above all else, and are agreed that, "You here and you might as well make it one day at a time, the best way you can." All that remains is the boredom of death row. "I'm not going anywhere," stated one man. "None of us are going anywhere . . . I look at it being just like this room, without the door—boxed in. Like I said, the living dead, man."

Emotional death lies at the core of the experience of living death. Men feel deeply abandoned. "A million thoughts go through your mind," said one prisoner, "but in the end, you wind up in the same condition: empty, needing somebody to comfort you, to understand you, and to accept you as you are." The condemned feel out of touch with life and the living, suspended in a kind of limbo from which they fear there is no reprieve.

We sitting up here and we are getting lost in the world. We are behind, man. And I figure we are cavemen. We can't hold no conversation with nobody out there on the street, because they are in a different world . . . My Daddy always told me, "Nothing good ever comes to a sleeper." So, I said, "He is damn sure right about that." And that's what all of us are doing up there—if we know it or not—we are sleeping. And ain't nothing we can do about it.

Gradually, many prisoners lose hope. "You need love and it just ain't there," stated one prisoner. "It leaves you empty inside, dead inside. Really, you just stop caring." Emotional death produces a psychic numbness that appears comparable to "ontological insecurity." This condition was labeled by R. D. Laing to describe the experience of people who fear they are petrifying and becoming frozen in place as lifeless objects or things, alive as organisms but dead as persons.[7] Laing, however, studied psychotics. This book deals principally with non-psychotics responding to abnormal conditions.

The image of living death is reinforced by the priorities of death row. The medical, psychological, and spiritual needs of inmates routinely take a backseat to the impersonal requirements of custody. In fact, these human needs are often discounted entirely.

Medical care, according to the inmates, is inordinately difficult to obtain on death row. Doctors are rarely seen, and even more rarely make cell calls to inmates with medical problems arising during the evening or at night. Inmates believe the doctors write off their symptoms, classifying them as hypochondriacs or malingerers.[8] In general, medical doctors are perceived as hostile or unconcerned. Complaints about chronic pain, rashes, and nerves, whatever their psychosomatic components, do not evoke a gentle bedside manner. Instead, the doctors, in the words of one inmate, act as though "an aspirin is too good for prisoners sentenced to die."

Psychological treatment may be equally unavailable, but the inmates view this as less important than the relative absence of medical care. The inmates seem to have lower expectations of psychological treatment, as though they do not believe psychologists or psychiatrists can offer them very much. The treatment staff may contribute to the reduced demand for their services on death row. They keep a low profile, excusing themselves from death row duty by pointing to the fact that the condemned prisoner is, in the main, a "model citizen" of the prison, securely harnessed to his sentence and requiring less treatment than other prisoners. Moreover, prisoners apparently receive little help in their encounters with treatment staff. The inmates speak of counselors as persons who promise help but then refuse to provide help, claiming that prisoners' problems lie beyond their professional purview. "I wish we had [legal] appeals for y'all so it could be over, but we ain't got them," one counselor allegedly said to a prisoner, abruptly terminating their therapeutic encounter. Psychiatrists are described as out of touch with the day-to-day life of the prison. There are also allegations that psychiatrists reveal confidential information to staff, betraying their trust and adding to the already substantial adjustment pressures confronting the prisoners. For example:

> I told the psychiatrist my problems, so he say, "How do you think you can stop these problems?" And so, I—we have been writing writs and going to court and so forth—so, I told him I thought I could stop these problems if they would take these handcuffs off me, I could get out there and physically fight them, heads up. One on one. What he did, he went and told the officers that I wanted to jump on them—I would beat them all at one time. Like what I say, I don't trust nobody, because the officers been fucking with me ever since then.

The prison ministry may be of even less service to inmates than are the medical and psychological professionals. It is true that some prisoners experience an upsurge or rebirth of religiosity on death row. A few inmates describe themselves as born-again Christians.[9] Most converts, however, trace their religious experiences to personal conviction or to correspondence with religious persons affiliated with outside organizations. Religious outlets provided by the prison are seen as inadequate. When mentioned at all, the ministers affiliated with the prison are described as appendages to the prison staff who treat prisoners in the same perfunctory manner as the guards.[10]

According to the inmates, the need for a secure prison takes priority over all else. "There is no way," stated one prisoner,

> to get the kind of care you need. You ain't going to get no help from none of them [staff] other than what they have to do. That's it. As far as doing anything individually for you, forget it. That's out of the question.

Another prisoner conveyed an even more disturbing picture:

> They're not gonna do anything for you. They're gonna let you sit here and one day they gonna kill you, rather than let you sit here, or you turn into an old man right here in one of these cells.

When abandonment by the prison goes hand-in-hand with abandonment by other figures of authority, condemned prisoners may feel desperately vulnerable and alone. Speaking of his failure to gain a response from his attorney, one inmate observed, "I don't know if he's dead or livin'. He don't know if I'm dead or livin'. That's what I'm worried about. I'm worried about stayin' up here til they're ready to electrocute me."

The priorities on death row—a curious mix of security and concern for appearances—seem almost unforgivable in regard to visits. The routine surrounding visits might be compared with the preparations for a funeral. Noncontact visits, in particular, seem peculiarly reminiscent of the viewing at a wake. As I observed firsthand, the inmate sits alone in an enclosed chamber, neatly dressed and carefully groomed, almost as if on display for his loved ones. The need to shout across the barrier separating the inmate and his visitors precludes intimate conversation and results in awkward interludes of silence. Visitors speak as much among themselves as with their prisoner; they appear nervous and out of place. The prisoners, too, seem ill at ease. In one revealing case, I learned, an inmate was denied dental care but was forced to shave for his noncontact visit. The public image of the prison was clearly at issue. After all, a stubbled chin would suggest slovenly prison conditions more readily than would his dental cavities. The prisoner treated in this manner is rendered cosmetically acceptable but denied his status as a full-blooded living person deserving of human solace.

Regular prison inmates suffer as well from distortions wrought by the surreal scenarios of prison. Hans Toch has described prison as "impersonal enough to help a man suspect that others want him dead."[11] Such suspicions become self-evident truths on death row, where prison policy uniformly "reflects that [we] prisoners are already doomed and forgotten."

A living death is what death row offers its inhabitants. It is a world purposefully divested of normal social functions and rewards. Condemned men are allowed only the barest existence—enough to sustain the physical organism while its emotional and spiritual counterparts threaten to wither and die. "The living dead is actually what it adds up to," observed one man. "What does a maggot do? A maggot eats and defecates. That's what we do: eat and defecate. Nothing else. They don't allow us to do nothing else."

Despite these confined and bleak conditions, there is still, as we have seen, some semblance of humanity and connection. That a living death is not the sole reality on death row is a testament to human resilience and adaptability. Prisoners persist in showing signs of life. Through words, actions, and resistance, they demand recognition of their humanity, and of their rights as human beings and prisoners. In the words of one of the more militant prisoners:

> People that are on death row are not forgotten people. You know, we still have family, friends, relatives, and associates who love and care for us dearly; being on death row doesn't mean that we are already dead—that we are not entitled to what we are seeking, you know—that we don't have any rights. We still have feelings, too. So, what we are trying to do is mostly get the system

to recognize these qualities . . . We are not doomed yet. Because we haven't been strapped in the chair, yet. And even being strapped in it don't mean that we are doomed because of last-minute changes that could be made. So, what we are seeking from them is to be treated like human beings, to be respected like human beings, and be given the same equal opportunities as the other human beings that are in confinement here in the state of Alabama.

The refusal to die in environments in which death may be the easy way out contributes to the notion that hope can remain alive in the most unlikely contexts.[12] At bottom, the hope for life among death row prisoners rests on a belief in themselves and in their ability to relate to one another as human beings, even where the obstacles to empathy and support are substantial. The prisoners repeatedly spoke of fighting to retain the capacity to care for others, to recognize and respond to the needs of others for attention, concern, help. "I try to say I still love people, I still understand people," said one man, "but I find it harder every day to believe myself saying that." They were deeply troubled by their own increasing callousness after extended exposure to the death row milieu, not that they pretended to have been especially warm persons before their confinement, but because they knew that if they completely lost the capacity to care, they would lose an essential component of their individuality and humanity. The plight of death row prisoners can be compared with that of persons in the concentration camp, the POW camp, the totalitarian regime: They must learn, as do survivors everywhere, that the challenge of survival entails more than merely staying alive in the face of hardship and misfortune. To survive, one must be decent, civil, concerned—in a word, human.[13]

By and large, the prisoners have not succumbed to the pressures of the death row environment, pressures that would have the condemned die slowly, by degrees, in anticipation of death by legal sanction. This conclusion is supported by subsequent research on death row. As Kupers has noted, drawing on an extensive body of fieldwork, "many inhabitants of death row inside solitary confinement units sustain their sanity." This, he notes, "is an extraordinary accomplishment."[14] Still, Kupers continues, echoing themes in this chapter, "Too many other inhabitants of death row are driven to mental illness, despair, and incompetence."[15] Death row prisoners are alive, then, but their lives are in jeopardy. They maintain a precarious existence in a world circumscribed by death—the living death of death row confinement and the ritual death of execution. It is a testament to the power of the imagery of living death, and by implication the resilience of the prisoners that survive this ordeal, that the notion of death row as a living death is now memorialized in a body of research that spans decades, countries, and academic disciplines.[16]

Notes

1 One man, a former police officer, was rejected because of his presumed status as an informer. He envisioned a particularly bleak future for himself: "Even if I get a commuted sentence to life, I will never ever be able to get in the population—be out amongst the other people—because they'll kill me. They don't play around about it; they tell you they'll kill you; they will; they'll kill you. And anybody, if they see you talking to one of these guards or whispering to them, or anything like that, they'll just make a real big thing out of it, that you're a rat, and you're telling the guards everything that's going on and all this, and that, and the other stuff. Okay? So then they plan to get you any way they can." The other prisoner was spurned as "mentally weak" (that is, mentally ill), and therefore as not deserving of respect or support. This man suffered greatly on death row but seemed largely oblivious of his low social status among the men.

2 Donat (1965: 237).
3 Hinton (2018: 115) reminds us that compassion is a choice. He chose to show compassion, and some prisoners reciprocated with generosity and care, especially when prisoners suffered the death of a loved one.
4 Johnson (1979: 1).
5 This may be an example of a phenomenon identified by O'Donnell (2018: 292): "What prisoners on death row describe as a fear of mental deterioration may alternatively be conceptualized as a fear of being unable to revive their pre-prison identities," which are "overwritten" by the power of situation. What is left might be seen as barely visible traces of one's former identity.
6 In the words of one Texas death row inmate, describing the same phenomenon: "In the past few years, something strange has started to happen to me: I sometimes see or hear things that aren't there ... I no longer know what is real or if I'm real. I try my best to shake these episodes and feelings off because I know too well from watching other inmates that once a person loses his sense of reality entirely, it's a slippery slope to hitting a breaking point, medication, and sedation. Men who go that route become living zombies." (Death row prisoner quoted in Kupers 2018: 50–51).
7 Laing (1965: 39–61). A similar process may be at work in other settings of extreme stress. Concentration camps produced their own "walking dead" (Bettelheim, 1969). A prisoner in Serge's (1970: 11) account of life in a French penal colony makes the following observation concerning the slow death often attendant to such confinement:

> "My intellect ... has not faltered; but it has grown dim. I have never resigned myself; but resignation has entered me, has bent me down to the ground and told me: 'Rest.' To tell the truth, I'm not sure that it didn't tell me: 'Die slowly.'"

8 Diffuse medical complaints become more common the longer the prisoner remains on death row and are often ascribed by staff to situational pressures or hypochondria (Murton, 1969: 94; Gallemore and Panton, 1972: 167). The assumption that such complaints are either bids for attention or efforts to break the routine of confinement causes them to be treated in a perfunctory manner. The underlying anxiety is not explored, nor is attention given to the need for support that may prompt the complaints.
9 One prisoner, interviewed in 2017, long after the original study ended, reports having a flock of followers among the condemned who follow his ministry.
10 One prisoner, whose experience with the official prison ministry had moved him to atheism, noted: "The chaplain, he'll bring you some gift cards, but he doesn't have time to stop and talk."
11 Toch (1992: 129).
12 The power of hope to support adaptation in extreme situations is insightfully examined in O'Donnell (2014).
13 Des Pres (1977). For philosophical considerations of the roots of personhood that emphasize the role of caring, see Camus (1948); Reiman (1976: 26).
14 O'Donnell (2018: 202) seconds this point. "The prison system's attempts to quash resistance," even in extreme confinement settings, "are never complete." This is the case because "a measure of negotiation is always possible between an individual (however tightly controlled in time and space) and their environment (however stimulus deprived and heavily guarded). Even when stripped, unarmed, and outnumbered, prisoners can use their body products offensively." O'Donnell concludes, "Desperate situations evoke desperate acts of resistance." See generally O'Donnell (2014).
15 Kupers (2018: 59).
16 These works include Hector (1984); Vogelman (1989); Guenther (2013); Peel (2013); Johnson (2016).

References

Bettelheim, B. (1969). *The informed heart*. New York: Free Press.
Camus, A. (1948). *The plague*. New York: Knopf.
Des Pres, R. (1977). *The survivor: An anatomy of life in the death camps*. New York: Oxford University Press.
Donat, A. (1965). *The Holocaust kingdom*. New York: Holt, Rinehart, & Winston.
Gallemore, J., & Panton, J. (1972). Inmate responses to lengthy death row confinement. *American Journal of Psychiatry*, *129*(2), 167–172.

Guenther, L. (2013). *Social death and its afterlives: A critical phenomenology of solitary confinement*. St. Paul, MN: University of Minnesota Press.

Hector, M. (1984). *Death row: Jamaican prison diary*. London: Zed Books.

Hinton, A. R. (with Hardin, L. L.). (2018). *The sun does shine: How I found life and freedom on death row*. New York: St. Martin's Press.

Johnson, R. (1979). Manliness myths: The high price of prison survival. *Southern Journal of Criminal Justice, 4*(1), 1–15.

Johnson, R. (2016). Solitary confinement until death by state-sponsored homicide: An Eighth Amendment assessment of the modern execution process. *Washington & Lee Law Review, 73*(3), 1213–1242.

Kupers, T. A. (2018). Waiting alone to die. In H. Toch, J. R. Acker, & V. M. Bonventure (Eds.), *Living on death row: The psychology of waiting to die* (pp. 47–69). Washington, DC: American Press Association.

Laing, R. D. (1965). *The divided self*. London: Penguin Books.

Murton, T. (1969). Treatment of condemned prisoners. *Crime and Delinquency, 15*(1), 94–111.

O'Donnell, I. (2014). *Prisoners, solitude, and time*. Oxford: Oxford University Press.

O'Donnell, I. (2018). Psychological survival in isolation: Tussling with time on death row. In H. Tock, J. R. Acker, & V. M. Bonventre (Eds.), *Living on death row: The psychology of waiting to die* (pp. 193–211). Washington, DC: American Psychological Association.

Peel, D. (2013). Clutching at life, waiting to die: The experience of death row incarceration. *Western Criminology Review, 14*(3), 61–72.

Reiman, J. H. (1976). Privacy, intimacy, and personhood. *Philosophy and Public Affairs, 6*(1), 26–44.

Serge, V. (1970). *Men in prison*. London: Gollancz.

Toch, H. (1992). *Mosaic of despair: Human breakdowns in prison* (Rev. ed.). Washington, DC: American Psychological Association.

Vogelman, L. (1989). The living dead: Living on death row. *South African Journal of Human Rights, 5*, 183–195.

PART III

Reflections on Life Under Sentence of Death and the Limits of Death Penalty Reform

I know it's cruel what I had done, but I don't consider it right, and I don't justify what I done. I regret it, and I would not do it again as long as I could help and think as a human being . . . [But] no matter what I done, I live and breathe, I'm human, just like anyone else. Ain't that right?

(Death row prisoner, Holman Prison, Alabama)

We know what the end of the road look like because we are sitting at the end of the road now. And if we go any further, we are going around into that chair. This is the way we put it. We may be going around into that chair, so ain't no sense in keep stepping deeper. So each step, and each day, we make a step forward.

(Death row prisoner, Holman Prison, Alabama)

Sometimes you need to make family where you find it, and I knew that to survive I had to make a family of these men and they had to make a family of me. It didn't matter who was black and who was white—all that kind of fell away when you lived a few feet away from an electric chair. Right now, we had more in common than not. We all faced execution. We all were scrambling to survive. Not monsters. Not the worst thing we had ever done. We were so much more than what we had been reduced to—so much more than could be contained in one small cage.

(Anthony Hinton, former Holman death row prisoner, Alabama, exonerated April 3, 2015)

7

CAPITAL PUNISHMENT

The View from Death Row

Death row epitomizes a prison system that traffics in coercion and dehumanization, leaving a trail of destruction in its wake. The essential nature of death row confinement—holding prisoners slated for state-sponsored homicide[1]—is seen most clearly in jurisdictions in which executions occur with regularity, which is to say, where death rows hold condemned prisoners under a credible threat of execution.[2] This is the case for many death rows today, including Alabama's death row, which serves as the centerpiece of this book.[3]

Death row confinement in service of executions is arguably the most total of total institutions, the penitentiary most demanding of penitence, the prison most debilitating and disabling in its confinement. On death row, the allegorical pound of flesh is just the beginning. Here, the whole person is consumed. The spirit is captured and gradually worn down; then the body is disposed of. Centuries ago, prisoners were subjected to the discipline of silence. Today on death row, this silence may prove endless. This unique regimen of dehumanizing confinement, I will argue in this chapter, is a case of torture in violation of the Eighth Amendment to the U.S. Constitution.

Death Row: Historical Perspective

The historical record, at least from the Middle Ages on, suggests that the vast majority of condemned offenders lived in oppressive, isolated, and often squalid conditions prior to their execution. They faced public executions marked by a level of torture and brutality inconceivable today. Psychological paralysis born of sheer terror was the most common reaction among the condemned. Prisoners routinely approached the scaffold numb with fear—shaking, soiling themselves, rendered mute, likely in a state of shock.[4] Some offenders would break down completely and have to be carried to their deaths; a few would attempt to escape the scaffold, only to be caught and put to an ignoble death. Even would-be suicides received no special consideration; they would be dragged to the gallows, fresh wounds recently mended (by the executioner, no less) or bleeding freely, then strapped to a chair or pole and summarily hanged so that they could be executed before they died from their own efforts.[5] The vast majority of those sentenced to public execution, however, were incapable of any kind of resistance. Defeated and demoralized, they would meekly submit to the executioner.[6]

Much of the information on public executions and the demeanor of convicts exposed to such tortures is based upon European sources. Such evidence as exists on the deportment of the condemned in America bears out these observations. An observer of mid-nineteenth-century executions in America provides evidence that suggests that offenders would first deny the import of impending execution, then be overwhelmed by the threat of death as the event approached. Nine out of ten condemned, we are told, would forsake religious advice in their cells and instead delude themselves with "vain hopes of pardon," distracting visits, and pointless posturing (maintaining a "determined carriage")—until "the eve of the fatal morning," at which point, "fatigued, weak, and worn out with his efforts, the mind becomes suddenly depressed with disappointment, corresponding to the condition of the body." The condemned man "then falls into a state of stupor and insensibility" that persists until

> the next morning, when brought out of his cell to be pinioned, you behold a man already half dead; his countenance has fallen, his eyes are fixed, his lips are deadly pale and quivering, while his whole aspect, in anticipation of the reality, gives you the personification of death's counterpart.[7]

Today's condemned prisoners, like those in centuries past, typically give us "the personification of death's counterpart" and go to the executioner "already half dead" and effectively beyond resistance.[8] Variants on a theme of dehumanization—of being alive physically but dead or dying psychologically—characterize confinement under sentence of death; this is the case, it would seem, whatever may be the particulars of the penal regime, the execution process or, indeed, the prisoner population.[9]

Until the middle of the twentieth century, American death rows were a high-turnover institution whose human inventory was routinely depleted by executions, successful appeals, and reprieves. In fact, condemned prisoners were often executed or resentenced within a matter of months after their arrival on death row.[10] Things are different today. Concern for the rights of criminal defendants—especially those facing severe sentences—has spawned a complicated, lengthy, and essentially mandatory system of appeals following conviction of a capital crime. Long-term confinement of condemned prisoners is now the norm; some men today serve as long as 20 or more years under sentence of death. Paradoxically, life-saving legal appeals, undertaken routinely by condemned prisoners, contribute to the massive human suffering and decay catalogued in this book. Nevertheless, the prisoners must fight for their lives through the exercise of their legal rights, and it is reprehensible that their legal rights are asserted at the expense of their emotional and psychological well-being. It is indefensible, in other words, that the condemned must endure a death-in-life if, through the law, they are to secure the chance to live again.

Warehousing for death, as we have seen in this book, is the grim reality of American justice for the prisoners of death row. It is hard to comprehend the enormity of this situation. In explaining why such atrocities are routinely disbelieved, Arthur Koestler observed, "Statistics don't bleed; it is the detail which counts. We are unable to embrace the total process with our awareness; we can only focus on little lumps of reality."[11] Death row confinement is much the same. We in the larger society fail to comprehend the despair of death row prisoners because the condemned are hidden behind prison walls. Moreover, the private despair of 3,000 persons is difficult to envisage. The very size of the group may render anonymous the private lives whose pain might otherwise result in a movement for reform.

In describing and analyzing the experiences of death row prisoners, I have attempted both to retain the human drama of their experience and to provide information that is often missing from discussions and decisions about the care and confinement of capital offenders. The stress suffered by condemned prisoners is manifested in feelings of powerlessness, fear, and emotional emptiness. Deterioration is a constant and formidable enemy of the condemned. Death row prisoners see themselves among the abandoned, the unloved and unlovable who must be locked away in the deepest recesses of maximum security prisons, marooned and voiceless.[12] Some prisoners, to be sure, are able to grow amidst this adversity.[13] But they are a small minority. Without support and assistance, many condemned prisoners—perhaps most—may eventually succumb to the pressures of death row confinement.

Death Row: Reducing the Harm

Enormous suffering is almost certainly an unavoidable result of death row confinement as it currently operates within our legal and correctional systems, in which dehumanization of criminals is a central and driving force.[14] The trend on death rows today is toward increased isolation and control in those states where executions occur with any regularity.[15] Texas, Florida, Virginia, Alabama, and Oklahoma are among the top execution states as of this writing.[16] Together, they account for over two-thirds of all executions carried out since the executions commenced in 1977.[17] The death rows in these states are especially repressive, featuring undiluted regimes of solitary confinement.[18] Texas accounts for over 500 executions since the return of the death penalty in 1976, the most of any state. Texas' death row offers "the most cell time and the fewest amenities" of any death row in the nation: "23 hours a day in the cell, no TV, solitary exercise, no work, and no programs."[19]

It is sobering but worth noting that, while the deleterious effects of death row confinement are most salient and pernicious on solitary confinement death rows, such as the one we have reviewed, harms emerge in vary degrees on all death rows, including reformed death rows, where milder variants of the themes uncovered in this study have been described.[20] The destructive impact of confinement under sentence of death raises serious questions about the human costs of capital punishment that are examined later in this chapter. But while significant harm may be an inevitable consequence of death row confinement, particularly solitary death row confinement, the extent of the harm reviewed in this book may not be fixed or immutable.

Action can be taken to reduce the stress of death row confinement. Custody could be maintained in a less rigid manner, although relinquishing blind reliance on custody requires hard work and sensitivity on the part of staff, for whom security is a preeminent value. Staff training should be provided to assist correctional officers in their attempts to implement more flexible custodial procedures. Rest and recuperation assignments might help staff to better handle the pressures of their job, pressures that now too often translate into harassment and even abuse of prisoners. Most of the prisoners could be managed under conditions less stringent and harsh than those currently existing on most death rows. At present, some guards informally classify and manage prisoners, scrutinizing a few with great care and subjecting others to more routine surveillance and supervision. Classification leading to differential assignment of inmates within death row would open the way for development of a more varied and humane living environment.

Several specific reforms might be implemented to reduce the rigors of death row confinement. Special programs of work or study could be developed to reduce the loneliness and boredom of isolation. For example, hobby work and self-study programs might be offered as a pastime for men confined to their cells for the greater part of each day. Such programs offer constructive ways for prisoners to focus on the moment (a useful survival strategy in adversity) and may also help prisoners "craft" resilient selves that are embodied, as it were, in their art and writing.[21] Visits, particularly contact visits, could be made more readily available, thereby facilitating the prisoners' efforts to sustain their emotional ties with family and friends. Recreational opportunities could be expanded to include supervised small-group activities. Solitary confinement need not, and should not, comprise the extent of the correctional effort on death row.[22]

Self-help may be a useful method of stress management on death row. The prisoners, in a sense, are continuously engaged in self-help. There is nowhere to go but up from death row, and there is no one to move them forward but themselves. As one prisoner observed:

> We know what the end of the road look like because we are sitting at the end of the road now. And if we go any further, we are going around into that chair. This is the way we put it. We may be going around into that chair, so ain't no sense in keep stepping deeper. So each step, and each day, we make a step forward.

The condemned prisoners studied in this book have no shortage of innovative ideas concerning self-help projects they might undertake. They believe that their survival as human beings depends on this, for the key ingredient in any genuine self-help program is that it recognizes and enhances the humanity of the participants.

PRISONER: There are all kinds of ways that we can help ourselves. If you could get together with a fellow, you could easily work on projects together as far as crafts, playing cards, Bible study, or just talking, whatever, you know. At least you feel more human than like a caged animal, but they don't allow this.

INTERVIEWER: In other words, you see lots of outlets for people in helping each other that could make you feel more like people.

PRISONER: Human, right. More so than cutting us off like they are doing to us . . . Like I said, the aspect of us helping each other could be a big asset, because I believe that when men are thrown together with one prime purpose in mind, which is to survive, they could more or less come up with some method or some way to help themselves. The world itself is built on that: when people are in trouble, they usually get together and come up with something that works.

Still, it is hard to improve oneself on death row. The condemned prisoner is, for the most part, alone and unaided. Solitary cells are not conducive to growth. The prisoner in the next cell is not always equipped or motivated to meet one's needs. Prison officials sometimes reject self-help proposals out of hand, on the ground that letting prisoners out of their cells is too risky. Some men therefore seek stimulation and support from the outside world.

Communication with religious groups and enrollment in correspondence courses figure prominently among self-help activities involving free-world groups or programs. Some prisoners discover that there are citizens who wish to express their concern for the condemned through personal letters. Such support, solicited and unsolicited, proves uplifting. It reaffirms for the prisoners that they are human and that there are people who care for them.[23]

> Most people that I write to now I never touched. I never seen 'em, I just write 'em. They write me. They write, they read about it in the paper and write me and say, "I want to be friends and help you the best way I can." So I don't like the death thing myself. I don't want to die. I just want to get a friend to keep me.

■ ■ ■

> Yesterday I got a letter from a woman that I'd never heard from before, which cheered me up. I was very thankful to receive the letter. The type of letter it was—it wasn't a criticizing letter, it wasn't a loving letter. It was a letter just letting one human being know that there was another human being that cared for a human being regardless who he was or where he was.

Death row prisoners frequently help one another with day-to-day problems of adjustment, as we have noted. With guidance, some of the prisoners might assist others with the deeper and more painful personal concerns rooted in their experience of powerlessness, fear, and emotional emptiness. A few condemned prisoners appear to possess a real talent for helping their peers with difficult and sensitive problems. These men depart sharply from the manliness myths of prison. Because of their genuine concern, they reach out to men in despair and their interventions appear frequently to be effective.

Two therapeutic encounters reveal the insightful perspectives and activities of death row's resident counselors. At issue in the first instance were delicate marital problems, which were met with empathy, and with gentle and persistent interest. The concerns of the prisoner with problems were allowed to surface and were addressed on a schedule of the prisoner's choosing. A kind of meeting of minds took place, aided by the immediacy of death.

PRISONER: A guy come to me recently, got a problem with his wife, you know, and I can see why. One day, he's gonna kill her and the next day he want to love her, you know. I can understand where he's comin' from, 'cause I was married and did the same thing. So we talks about it, you know. He leads, and I follow where he's headed. We get to where his problem's at, if he really wants to get it out on the table. Sometime I just smile to myself, 'cause I know we'd be that close to it, you know, what's eating at him. Then we drift off, and then you can sense where you been hitting it, his problem. Come so close to breakin' into the man's mind, you know, you realize what the true problem is . . . a lot of things came to the light on death row. A lot of things, you know.

INTERVIEWER: So people are learning about themselves.

PRISONER: Yeah, and you know bein' this close to that chair make you think. You can't help one thing here: if you don't find somethin's wrong somewhere with you, you got some kind of mental problem. Bein' this close to death, you got to level with yourself.

The second case involved an extended "group therapy" session, undertaken by neighboring inmates, with a man suffering pronounced mental health problems that were discussed in Chapter 6. In sharp contrast to the harsh treatment described there (which covers most of his confinement), this group of prisoners saw him as a challenge to their therapeutic skills. Rather than receiving abuse for outbursts, his symptoms and complaints elicited patient and tactful inquiries from these prisoners. Volatile subjects were avoided; no one gave the inmate condescending lectures or unsolicited advice. The prisoner was encouraged to explore his motivations and to seek help on his own terms, when he was ready to accept support. Eventually he responded, and some progress was recorded.

PRISONER: Take the case of _____, for example, he has the worse mental problem on death row. And we dealt with him for about six, maybe seven months, as a unit, as a body that is dealing with one man and his problem and were able to bring him back further into reality than we had anticipated we could, but we did it.

INTERVIEWER: How did you do it? What is it that you did?

PRISONER: To constantly talk to him about what he wants to talk about and to criticize him if he was wrong, but do it calmly, you know, in a nice way. Okay, his baddest habit was setting fire to his cell, destroying his personal property, and talking about other people's relatives. So, what we would do—we wouldn't talk to him on these subjects. We would find out, "Well, why did you burn up your clothes?" "Why did you set your bed on fire?" And whatever answer he gave us, we would continue to question him about it and ask him, "Now do you think that that was right? Do you think that benefitted you? Did that satisfy you in any way." And we would just go right on with him and whenever he would tell us that he didn't want to talk about it anymore, we didn't press him. We would leave him alone and finally he would call somebody else. Somebody else could talk to him about his problem and ask him questions and talk right along with him. And finally, he started coming back. But he hasn't come all the way back because he still goes—sometimes days, maybe two weeks—without saying anything to anybody, without accepting anything from anybody other than his tray if they brought it to him, or to take a shower and stuff like that. We just try to deal with people, just say, on their level, but at the same time trying to raise them back up to the level that they were at before their problem occurred.

Throughout these encounters and others like them, prisoners who specialize in helping troubled peers are shown to be concerned, rational, and responsive persons who make themselves available to men in trouble. But they are an embattled minority on death row. The helpers are few and the persons in need of help are many. Prisoners who strive to help others find, to their frustration, that many of their peers distrust them and therefore turn down offers of assistance. They also find themselves limited in what they can do for those willing to accept help. Many personal problems found on death row are simply beyond any prisoner's control. Marriages break up, irrevocably. Children grow up and away from confined men. Illness and death deplete families. The cumulative impact of stress on death row leaves the prisoner who wants to help feeling impotent and overwhelmed. In the words of one of these men:

> Now I think a lot of times about the relatives in families that have died since I have been in here. The ones that have been sick and they wasn't able to help them or be there. The families who

forget about them. That's pressure and sometimes it gets to a point where it's hard to cope with it, because you don't have the answer to the problem and you are not able to assist them solve their problem, you know. So, it's personal problems like these that really get to us the most . . . It's a relief to know that you are being helpful, you know. But it's not to the extent of where it's a relief that you can see results from daily, because some days go by up there and it is like a madhouse—everybody has problems and don't nobody have an answer.

There are precedents for these interventions in the rare but poignant self-help activities organized among concentration camp inmates, which occasionally occurred with the consent and cooperation of guards.[24] For decades now, self-help programs have been designed to assist terminally ill patients to live out their lives in a productive and meaningful fashion.[25] When faced directly and maturely, stress may lead to personal growth. Death row prisoners must be encouraged to respond in a mature fashion to the pressures of their confinement, which include the prospect of impending death. Currently, most prisoners endure their ordeal in stoic silence. This pose is impressive but unrewarding. Only a few condemned prisoners, it would seem, achieve growth on death row, though that growth, when it occurs, is immensely impressive.[26] Expanded opportunities for self-help may make it possible for more prisoners to grow and find meaning and dignity in their suffering. By allowing inmates to face issues of stress and suffering, self-help efforts may create bases for cooperative problem-solving and establish helping roles as a medium for responsible membership within the death row community. The experience of helping others encourages personal maturation and growth. This growth, in turn, may prove critical in assuring the welfare of the prisoners and those associated with them in other settings, should they one day be released into the prison community or the free community.[27]

Capital Punishment: A Modern Form of Torture

The suffering of prisoners under sentence of death must be recognized as a major and enduring human cost of capital punishment as it is administered today. This research suggests that the cost is extraordinarily high. The fact that prisoners are capital offenders does not abrogate their claim to humane confinement. Humane confinement, however, may be impossible to achieve on death row. The suffering reviewed in this book appears largely inevitable under present circumstances, which involve lengthy warehousing of prisoners awaiting execution under conditions that amount to torture.

Death rows, I contend, even the best of them, are human warehouses that impose a regime of confinement that amounts to torture. The majority of death rows—90 percent by a recent count—store condemned prisoners in cramped solitary cells for up to 22 or more hours a day as they await execution, much like the regime in Alabama reviewed in this book.[28] A few reformed death rows offer what amounts to congregate solitary confinement: condemned prisoners are allowed out of their cells, sometimes for many hours during the day, but are contained in small groups in dayrooms on the pod or tier in which they are housed, in isolation from the larger prison.[29] Life on congregate death rows (like life in many prisons) offers prisoners more time out of the cell but little or nothing of substance to do with that time that might prepare them for the ordeal of execution that looms over them. The result is a numbing regimen of cards, board games, and sometimes television viewing, empty exercises that create an environment marked by human interaction but no escape from others, either officers or fellow condemned prisoners, or from the hopelessness that comes with the weight of the death sentence. In the vivid and telling imagery reported by one prisoner of a congregate solitary confinement death row, "time crawls by like a hearse on four flat tires."[30] As best we can tell from existing research, the congregate death row, much like its solitary counterpart, is "a psychological nightmare that very few survive."[31]

Congregate death rows, like any prison unit that allows interaction, can also be dangerous. Though there is limited evidence about the quality of life on congregate death rows, there is reason to believe that these more relaxed environments can allow a predatory culture to evolve among the prisoners, making these settings unsafe for vulnerable inmates. Kerry Max Cook, a death row exoneree featured in the play, *The Exonerated*, reports being repeatedly raped and even mutilated by gang members during his tenure on death row in Texas when it was a congregate regime. "I had three guys pull a train on me . . . and they raped me, and sodomized me, and they carved 'good p-u-s-s-y' on my behind." This abuse was a daily event. "I'm fighting with fear for my life with these inmates every day."[32] Certainly the impression one gains from Cook's testimony is that violence was widespread on this death row.[33]

In a remarkable departure from the norm, condemned prisoners in Missouri are mainstreamed into the general prison population in Potosi Correctional Center, a maximum security prison reserved for long-term prisoners, rather than housed on a separate death row.[34] Misconducts are comparatively rare among these condemned prisoners as a group; some have even made their way to honors units within the prison. From a security point of view, mainstreaming would seem to be a viable alternative to traditional death rows. The psychological effects of this confinement have not been studied, however, so we do not know how much the general prison experience of mainstreamed condemned prisoners affects the experience of living under sentence of death. We do know, of course, that maximum-security prisons offer more options for living than can be found on death rows, but some prisons (and, apparently, some loosely run death rows) are racked by gang violence, sexual predation, and other pernicious problems in prison living. Even in the best-case scenario—a well-run and arguably decent institution—prisons, like death rows, offer no meaningful preparation for the threat of execution under which condemned prisoners live. Most maximum-security prisons, not unlike death rows, are human warehouses in their own right, though less repressive and dehumanizing human warehouses than those typically found on death row.[35]

In making the case that death row confinement is a form of torture, I will focus on solitary confinement death rows, the more common form and the form studied in this book. It is crucial to note, however, that all death rows offer prisoners a species of dead time: The death row confinement regime, whatever its details, offers no life to speak of, only an isolated world largely devoid of purpose or meaning other than waiting for the executioner. My research has led me to conclude that death rows may differ in the details of their administration, but no death row, solitary or congregate, offers its inmates a round of activity that might in any way prepare them for the ordeal they must face.[36] In this basic and profound sense, all condemned prisoners are warehoused for death under conditions that are objectively dehumanizing. Moreover, as executions approach, condemned prisoners are moved from death row to the death house, where they undergo especially close custody during a process called the death watch, which occurs during the final days and hours before a prisoner is put to death.[37] A rigid, solitary confinement regimen marked by constant and unremitting surveillance is universally imposed during the death watch.[38] Thus it can be said that condemned prisoners live—metaphorically if not literally, in solitary cells or in solitary pods, and finally in the death house—in the shadow of executions.[39]

An execution is a state-sponsored homicide—"a killing of one human being"—the condemned prisoner—"by another"—the executioner or, more typically these days, the correctional officers who make up the execution team.[40] No death row is or has ever been organized to prepare prisoners for the traumatic experience of living under the threat of death by homicide and then submitting to that killing at the hands of a team of prison officers. Instead, the regime of confinement for prisoners under sentence of death is dehumanizing, treating the condemned like so many animals or objects. Dehumanization, discussed next, is an essential element of torture.

Dehumanization

Death row confinement as defined here—solitary confinement in service of death by state-sponsored homicide—is dehumanizing because the conditions of this confinement violate essential elements of human nature and therefore are violations of the human dignity shared by all human beings by virtue of their status as human beings. The essence of human dignity, in my view, is a sense of identity or self that conveys the capacity and confers the moral right to make choices and hence be self-determining.[41] To be sure, self-determination is not an absolute; full self-determination is probably impossible in this world, but some degree of self-determination is required for the person to live as a human being. It has been my contention that self-determination, in whatever degree and form it exists in a given environment, is achieved in the world of other human beings through a process of self-defining social interactions.[42] These interactions, in my assessment, require some degree of autonomy, security, and relatedness to others to be self-affirming.

In making these assertions, I understand autonomy to mean the capacity to influence one's environment and hence exert some modicum of control over the conditions of one's existence. I understand security to mean shelter from harm, which entails some element of social stability; secure and safe, one is defined in some measure by one's choices rather than by the vagaries of one's environment. Relatedness or connectedness to others entails the ability to feel for oneself and others and hence to have caring and constructive relationships in which other human beings are seen as persons in their own right. Autonomy, security, and relatedness to others develop in interaction with one another as individuals become persons. The process of becoming a person is never fully finished, however, as "man's nature is a self-surpassing and a self-transcending one."[43] We are, then, emergent persons. The element of growth is thus a part of our nature and must be respected, even in the context of punishment.[44]

It has been my contention that

> our understanding of what it means to be a human being—to appreciate our own humanity and that of others—creates a bright line distinction: while punishments can legitimately deprive persons of their liberty, they cannot degrade them by ignoring or violating their essential human dignity.[45]

With even the worst criminals, it must be recognized that they, like all human beings, "feel and think as we do" and, further, that "our inner feelings are alike in some fundamental fashion" that marks us, criminal and non-criminal alike, as fellow human beings.[46] This line of reasoning has led a colleague and me to conclude that "Like us, other human beings, even criminals, must be seen as autonomous entities, 'separate and protected in [their] separation from others,' as we know ourselves to be separate and protected in our separation from others."[47]

The notion that human beings are "separate and protected in [their] separation from others" goes to the integrity of the human self or identity. By definition, some degree of separation from the social world—of self and society—is required for the formation of an individual human identity. It is no accident that all known societies honor "the social institution of privacy"[48] or its functional equivalent, which is to say, some social practice that offers separation or insulation of the person from the surrounding environment, such that actions can be, at least in some measure, self-generated rather than externally determined.[49] Insulation from the world, I have argued, confers and confirms selfhood and permits individual selves to become persons—that is, to negotiate their lives with some degree of autonomy, security, and relatedness to others.[50] Condemned prisoners cannot insulate themselves from an environment in which they are denied privacy and subjected to total control.[51] Death row confinement, as a profoundly isolating human warehouse, renders prisoners powerless, vulnerable, and alone, as we have seen in the testimony offered in this book by Alabama's condemned prisoners. This confinement violates each and every element of human dignity as I have defined it and is, by its very nature, profoundly and objectively dehumanizing.

Torture

It is my contention that (1) death row confinement brings in its wake an objective dehumanization of the person that is the hallmark of torture, and (2) that this torture is cruel in a way that violates the Eighth Amendment. I will consider each contention in turn.

In Darius Rejali's masterful work on torture, *Torture and Democracy*, the essence of torture is boiled down to this proposition:

> In each case one must inquire whether physical torment is involved, whether the individual is helpless and detained, whether the agents who practice it are state or quasi-state officials, and whether it is put toward public purposes. If the answer in each case is yes, then it is torture, regardless of what it is called.[52]

This definition is clear and concise, but needlessly limits suffering to physical torment. In the United Nations Declaration Against Torture, torture "means any act by which severe pain or suffering, whether physical or mental" is inflicted.[53] More importantly, the distinction between physical and psychological torment is arbitrary. Any experience of torment will necessarily merge physical and psychological elements: emotional pain (sometimes called "social" or "psychological" pain), such as occurs in the wake of social isolation (the core condition of solitary confinement), or less obviously but importantly with social exclusion or personal rejection, "activates the same brain regions as physical pain."[54] Physical pain brings with it a psychological component and indeed the reverse is true as well: psychological pain brings with it a physical component.

An instructive case in point is the experience of dread—continuing and substantial fear and anxiety. Dread is the overarching personal experience of condemned prisoners as revealed in this book, particularly as their executions draw near. Note the dread, fear, and anxiety in the account of two typical Alabama death row prisoners when merely "thinking about the death penalty":

> When that sentence comes across my mind, that brings a quite a bit of fear. It brings quite a bit of fear and worry, you know . . . causes the person to pace back and forth, become nervous, you know. Can't sit down. It's hard for such a person to sleep. This happens to me at times. The fact that my sentence might not get commuted or the death penalty might not be thrown out. This causes me to grow nervous. Can't sleep. You are full of anxiety and really it's insanity.

***

> I go to sleep and I dream of me sitting down in that chair. I mean it's such a fearful thought. Me walking down the tier, sitting down in it, them hooking it up and turning it on . . . I don't know. I can wake up, my heart's beating fast, I'm sweating like hell, just like I rinsed my head in water . . . I feel I'm gonna have a heart attack.

Fear and anxiety are experienced as mental or psychological in origin, but it is apparent in the statements of these condemned prisoners that these emotions have bodily consequences: disrupted sleep, drained energy, and physical exhaustion.[55]

On death row, the daily regime highlights one's vulnerability, which reinforces fears and anxieties. Some of the elements of life on death row that highlight one's vulnerability are physical. Prisoners are alone in a cage, physically constrained and, like the proverbial sitting duck, defenseless against insult or attack in an environment in which they are under the total control of officers, some of whom, in the words of one condemned prisoner cited earlier in this book, "take it upon themselves to be your judge and your jury and your executioner." When moved from that cage, prisoners are typically stripped and searched, then heavily (and often painfully) restrained in handcuffs and leg irons, which chaff and bruise and cut the skin in varying degrees. Even medical care can be a painful and degrading routine for condemned prisoners, as we saw in earlier chapters of this book.

Some prisoners may become inured to the degrading and often painful treatment that is common in close confinement, but these abuses almost certainly live on in their awareness as reminders of their helplessness and vulnerability at the hands of their keepers. In a frightening sense, death row is sufficiently isolated that it is experienced by prisoners as a law unto itself. The vulnerability this image of lawlessness implies is very much on the minds of condemned prisoners interviewed in this book. Life in solitary confinement under a sentence of death is a torment, pure and simple.

The remaining elements of torture in Rejali's definition are self-evidently true in the case of death row. Given the conditions of confinement on death row as examined in this book, condemned prisoners are "helpless and detained," which is the essential reality of death row confinement; the correctional officers who supervise condemned prisoners, as well as the officers that carry out their executions, are "state or quasi-state officials." The confinement regime ultimately serves "public purposes": the facilitation of executions by the imposition of a regime that dehumanizes the prisoners, rendering them, virtually without exception, passive participants in the execution process.[56]

Rejali's definition of torture is consistent in its essentials with that offered by the United Nations. In the United Nations Declaration Against Torture, torture

> means any act by which severe pain or suffering, whether physical or mental, is intentionally inflicted by or at the instigation of a public official on a person for such purposes as obtaining from him or a third person information or confession, punishing him for an act he has committed, or intimidating him or other persons.[57]

Here, intimidation would be the link to dehumanization and its usefulness on death row. The intimidating, dread-producing death row regimen is the leading edge of the dehumanization process.

The UN definition of torture excludes "pain or suffering arising only from, inherent in, or incidental to lawful sanctions."[58] This would seem to mean that death row cannot be a form of torture because it is undertaken pursuant to a lawful punishment—the death penalty. This is a logical fallacy: Any punishment that involves torturous conditions in its administration is no longer a lawful punishment. As Rejali notes acerbically, "the fact that a practice is legally authorized does not magically transform the practice into 'not torture' any more than magic words uttered over an ass change it into a Ferrari."[59] Torture must be defined independently of law. To hold otherwise is to contend that anything can be done to persons under color of law.

Suffering on death row stems primarily from what psychologists would call "psychological maltreatment" (defined as "emotional abuse or emotional neglect") rather than overt physical abuse.[60] Here it is wise to remember that the emotional traumas associated with emotional abuse can be as harmful, and sometimes more harmful, than physical abuse: neglect, which yields depression and anxiety stemming from "unseen wounds," arguably tears at the foundation of the self in a uniquely pernicious way.[61] The very authenticity of one's suffering is cast into doubt in the wake of neglect, since the source of suffering and indeed the damage it produces are hidden from view.[62] It is likely that the suffering attendant to emotional abuse and neglect on death row is not inflicted expressly because its effects are intended or useful, as one finds in much torture and as seen in the UN definition of torture.[63] Nevertheless, this suffering is known to exist, and is exploited because its effects are useful in facilitating executions that go off smoothly, without resistance from condemned prisoners.[64]

Whatever the precise origin of the suffering on death row, execution team officers recognize the dehumanization process at work, watch it unfold, and knowingly benefit from it.[65] Execution team officers provide firsthand accounts of the dehumanization of the prisoners when they get to the death house, describing prisoners on the threshold of execution as defeated, demoralized, and compliant figures in the killing process:

> His mind goes first . . . All resistance disappears, they're exhausted. I think he makes it up in his mind then, you know, that he's ready to go. He blocks everything out, you know, as far as where I'm gonna be tomorrow, what I'm gonna do, you know. I know what I've got to do. There's no more pain, no more sorrow. I'm going. And that's it, gonna get it over with. I don't have to fight the lawyers and the judges and the courts no more.

***

They work it out in their minds and they accept it . . . A lot of 'em die in their minds . . . I've never known of one or heard of one putting up a fight . . . By the time they [take that last] walk . . . they've completely faced it. Such a reality most people can't understand. 'Cause they don't fight it. They don't seem to have anything to say. It's just something like "Get it over with." They may be, they may be numb, sort of.

***

They go through stages. And at this stage, they're real humble. Humblest bunch of people I ever seen. Most all of 'em is real, real weak. Most of the time, you'd only need one or two people to carry out an execution, as weak and as humble as they are. They're really a humble bunch of people.[66]

It is telling that observations by execution team officers about the passivity of the prisoners they encounter in the death house dovetail with the observations of the French existentialist Albert Camus. Decades earlier, and in reference to an execution process that culminated in beheading at the guillotine, Camus described the condemned as "no longer a man but a thing waiting to be handled by the executioners."[67] Persons engaged in death work, confronted with "a thing waiting to be handled" are strongly predisposed to treat the condemned as already dead or dying—as the living death suffered by death row prisoners so vividly attests.

Torture in violation of the Eighth Amendment

It is customary in Eighth Amendment jurisprudence to separate the conditions of confinement from the punishment, whether that punishment is a prison term or a death sentence.[68] This separation confuses essential matters, we learn from Dolovich. Incarceration is a central element of modern punishment. The experience of incarceration as a punishment is directly related to the conditions of confinement under which the sentence is served.[69] A reasonable person would stipulate that a life sentence in a brutal prison is a more punishing experience than a life term in a safe prison that is replete with programs and services that offer the possibility of personal growth and rehabilitation. Likewise, a reasonable person would stipulate that a sentence of death preceded by years of solitary confinement on death row, with the threat of degradation and deterioration, is more punishing than a sentence of death served in a more accommodating prison setting where programs and opportunities for personal development are central to the confinement regime, offering at least the possibility, in principle, of a death that unfolds in some measure on the terms of the individual prisoner who has lived, at least prior to the death watch, as a human being.

Each of these sentences—imprisonment or execution—may be cruel in themselves, but that cruelty, in the eyes of the prisoners, hinges in some measure on the conditions of confinement under which they are served. If one reflects on the interviews analyzed in this book, the notion that death row confinement is not in itself a punishment is psychologically inconceivable. Failure to connect conditions of confinement to the punishment of imprisonment or of execution results in an inability to come to a meaningful understanding of the term cruel as it applies to the experience of prison sentences or death sentences as undergone by their recipients.

The Eighth Amendment, as Dolovich has noted, "prohibits cruel and *unusual* punishment, but its normative force derives chiefly from its use of the word *cruel*."[70] Since "incarceration is the primary mode of criminal punishment"—prisons are implicated in all harsh sanctions, including the death penalty—"it is necessary to determine when prison conditions are cruel."[71] Remarkably, as Dolovich reports, "the Supreme Court has thus far avoided this question."[72] In the key case on this matter, *Farmer v. Brennan*, the Court held that "unless some prison official actually knew of and disregarded a substantial risk of serious harm to prisoners, prison conditions are not 'punishment' within the meaning of the Eighth Amendment."[73] This analysis, Dolovich argues, is flawed. When the state puts people in prison, it puts them in a dangerous and degrading setting "while depriving them of the capacity to provide for their own care and protection."[74] (Note that individual as well as congregate solitary confinement on death row deprives prisoners of the "capacity to provide for their own care and protection," following Dolovich's line of argument.) As a result, "the state has an affirmative obligation to protect prisoners from serious physical and psychological harm."[75] This obligation, which amounts to an ongoing duty to provide for prisoners' basic human needs, may be understood as "the state's carceral burden."[76] The standard in *Farmer* undermines the state's capacity to understand and honor its carceral burden:

> It holds officers liable only for those risks they happen to notice—and thereby creates incentives for officers *not* to notice—despite the fact that when prison officials do not pay attention, prisoners may be exposed to the worst forms of suffering and abuse.[77]

Building on Dolovich's work, I contend that in capital cases, the death penalty as a punishment includes state-created conditions of confinement on death row and in the death house, not simply the method of execution by which death is administered. (Whether the method of execution, per se, is cruel is another matter entirely, beyond the scope of this book). In capital cases, the state typically puts people on death row, an isolated and restrictive prison environment in which daily life unfolds under the implicit threat of execution; prisoners on death row are unable "to provide for their own care and protection"[78] in relation to the threats and insults of daily life on death row, let alone the overarching threat of execution. Recall that an execution is a carefully choreographed homicide and, by any reckoning, an event that is horrifying to contemplate from the profound vulnerability of one's solitary cell. In the context of the death penalty, Dolovich's carceral burden includes the obligation to provide for prisoners' basic needs as human beings on death row and throughout the execution process.[79] When the carceral burden is not honored by the state, this "causes serious harm to prisoners"; the resulting "prison conditions may be said to be cruel."[80] This logic applies readily to death row confinement and execution: failure to honor the state's carceral burden results in punishment that is cruel.

Dolovich argues that

> the state will be unable to meet its carceral burden—which requires that prison officials meet prisoners' basic human needs—unless prison officials are able to acknowledge and are willing to affirm the humanity and capacity for suffering of the people in their custody.[81]

Death row confinement is typically a species of solitary confinement that fails to meet basic human needs other than food and shelter from the elements; the need for social interaction, basic to establishing autonomy, security, and connectedness to others (core human attributes), is flagrantly violated.[82] An execution is framed as an impersonal bureaucratic undertaking in which an unwillingness or inability to "affirm the humanity" of the condemned prisoner or to appreciate the "capacity for suffering" of these prisoners is central to the process.[83] Thus, the failure to honor the carceral burden on death row and during the execution process is the norm, not the exception, as documented in studies of the dehumanizing effects of death row confinement and the modern execution process.[84]

The Eighth Amendment, as Dolovich has made clear, "is concerned with a very particular form of punishment: that imposed by the state as penalty for crime."[85] The key consideration for our purposes is this: "[W]hatever conditions a prisoner is subjected to while incarcerated, whatever treatment he receives from the officials charged with administering his sentence, *is* the punishment the state has imposed."[86] As a result, "all the conditions to which an offender is subjected at the hands of state officials over the course of his incarceration are appropriately open to Eighth Amendment scrutiny."[87] It follows that when offenders are condemned to death, the conditions of confinement under which they live and under which they are executed are central elements of the punishment for Eight Amendment purposes.

A key feature of the carceral burden as enunciated by Dolovich is protection from fear. "To force prisoners to live in constant fear," she states, "is to inflict a form of physical and psychological suffering akin to torture."[88] Prisoners on death row are, without question, forced to live in a state of constant fear, not only from the hazards of life on all death rows (themselves the culmination of hazards posed by the death penalty system from charging through trial, conviction, and sentencing),[89] but from the threat of execution by officials of the prison system, which can prove traumatic.[90] To live daily in what can be called a state of dread, again following Dolovich, suggests that prisoners on death row "exist in a permanently traumatized state, bereft of any peace of mind and constantly terrorized."[91] Anticipating some of the arguments in this book, Dolovich concludes, "[t]here is something deeply dehumanizing about being forced to endure such conditions, which could leave victims desperate to protect themselves at all costs and rob them of the ability to function in any reasoned or self-possessed way."[92] Or, indeed, in the terms of my line of reasoning, to possess a self or identity from which to maintain their humanity.

Some prisoners, including some death row prisoners, escape into a state of denial, sometimes marked by intense mental fantasies,[93] but this does not alter the cruelty of the conditions of confinement. It simply shows that human beings cope, well or badly, with extreme, even tortuous conditions of confinement. Such coping in extremity has been well documented in studies of death camps, perhaps the most extreme setting of torture and death known to modern man.[94] That people can psychologically survive cruelty of great magnitude does not make the conditions to which they are exposed less cruel. Conditions are objectively cruel or not, independent of the person's reaction. As Dolovich notes, "psychological suffering need not leave its victims in a state of heightened desperation for its infliction to be cruel."[95] As a corollary of this observation, conditions are cruel even if they are the usual fare of life in confinement for those serving prison terms or death sentences.

The state's carceral duty

> may be understood as that of ensuring the minimum conditions for maintaining prisoners' physical and psychological integrity and well-being—those basic necessities of human life, including protection from assault, without which human beings cannot function and that people in prison need just by virtue of being human.[96]

The carceral duty thus "offers a standard for assessing claims of cruel prison conditions as they arise."[97] That standard can be readily applied to treatment of condemned prisoners. On death row and in the death house,

> individual officers responsible for designing and running the prison must be ever-conscious that prisoners are human beings with the same capacity for suffering as anyone else. Otherwise, those officers will be incapable of meeting prisoners' basic needs or of recognizing dangers to their well-being.[98]

No such humane consciousness is apparent on death row, and there is no evidence that "prisoners' basic needs" or "well-being" are met on death row, particularly if one adds social interaction to the list of protected basic needs of prisoners as fellow human beings.

Dolovich's carceral duty is universally violated in the solitary confinement in service of death by state-sponsored homicide that is typically imposed on condemned prisoners. Research reviewed here shows unequivocally that death rows are human warehouses. Human beings cannot be stored like so many commodities without violating their human dignity. Warehousing condemned prisoners denies that "prisoners are human beings with the same capacity for suffering as anyone else,"[99] a key element of Dolovich's carceral burden. These regimes embody the notion that "officers will be incapable of meeting prisoners' basic needs or of recognizing dangers to their well-being,"[100] another key element of Dolovich's carceral burden. It is clear that the carceral burden owed condemned prisoners is not met on death row, and likely can never be met under the conditions of death row confinement as they exist today. We as a society are left with a punishment that, in its present and likely future form, is an instance of torture that is cruel as that term is understood in an Eighth Amendment context.

Institutional Dynamics of Torture

Torture is normally thought to comprise extreme physical or psychological brutality, the object of which is to produce a range of harmful effects: suffering for its own sake; conversion to an ideology, religion, or cause; confession of guilt or inadequacy; the betrayal of trust. To inflict torture is therefore conceived as an intended event; torture also implies active harm rather than passive indifference or neglect. Yet torture, as we have seen, need not be restricted to situations in which physical or psychological brutality is consciously employed to achieve an end. Standard instances of torture and death row confinement have in common an assault on the person that both causes him intense suffering and violates his integrity as a human being by treating him as if he were a mere animal or object. That either or both of these conditions is not intended as torture is irrelevant. The palpable fear and ever-present threat of deterioration and decay stands as proof that they have suffered real harm far in excess of that required by sentence and have been victims of real brutality. Thus, for all intents and purposes, a death sentence amounts to death with torture in a society that has explicitly renounced torture as a remnant of barbarism.

Moreover, death row prisoners are exposed to conditions that will typically, if not inevitably, produce a torturous regime. Research on institutionalized violence suggests that moral restraints against brutality are removed or seriously weakened when officials are authorized to harm in the service of a belief to which they subscribe (such as justice or law and order or ethnic cleansing) and hence are committed followers of directives; when procedures to impose harm are made routine and hence become shared personal habits undertaken without much reflection on their deeper meaning; and when prospective victims are dehumanized and, as damaged or deficient creatures, seen as morally deserving of harm both as members of a defiled group and as sullied individuals. Several execution team officers with whom I have spoken over the years emphasized that the condemned prisoner, by his flawed choices and brutal actions, placed himself among the worst murderers and earned a berth in the death house. "He put himself in the death house" is a common refrain among execution team members.[101]

Conditions that foster institutional violence operate with particular salience and impact on death row. Correctional personnel responsible for death row are explicitly and unambiguously *authorized* by laws and policies they respect to warehouse prisoners awaiting execution as a punishment for serious crimes. Guards and their superiors can readily view themselves as impersonal instruments of an authority, in this case, the law, to which they are committed agents; as such, they bear no individual moral responsibility for the actions necessary to maintain an orderly death row or for the executions that may take place under their auspices. These actions, in the eyes of the officers, are virtuous because they are just and deserved, given the enormity of capital crimes. As many officers contend, the condemned prisoner condemned himself by his actions; the officers thus are passive players in the deadly process of execution. And since *routine* is almost blindly relied upon to structure each day, and especially each execution day, correctional personnel come to normalize the daily round of life on death row, and hence are further removed from the human consequences of the policies they implement. Indeed, this preoccupation with routine stimulates enthusiasm to achieve technical proficiency at the various tasks attendant to death work and discourages more thoughtful examination of the nature and import of these activities. Finally, death row inmates are effectively isolated from one another and the larger world, and hence are denied the personal and group support necessary to retain their autonomy in the face of overwhelming authority, a suffocating routine, and a degrading existence. Thus, their *dehumanization* emerges as the culmination of instruments of authority acting within stipulated routines on condemned prisoners rendered as dehumanized entities to be stored and ultimately dispatched in the execution chamber in service of law and, no doubt, justice.[102]

Persons engaged in executions are strongly disposed to treat the condemned as dead or dying—as the living death suffered by death row prisoners so vividly attests. Albert Camus may thus have been correct when he maintained that capital punishment killed the offender twice: once on death row while awaiting execution and once again in the death chamber. This punishment is excessive, even by the hard reckoning of the person who demands the life of the murderer in return for the life of the victim. Quoting Camus on this point:

> As a general rule, a man is undone by waiting for capital punishment well before he dies. Two deaths are inflicted on him, the first being worse than the second, whereas he killed but once. Compared to such torture, the penalty of retaliation seems like a civilized law. It never claimed that the man who gouged out one of his brother's eyes should be totally blinded.[103]

It could be argued, of course, that some murderers cold-bloodedly claim multiple victims or torture their victims, and thus deserve the additional suffering inflicted by death row confinement. Experience with capital punishment laws indicates that it would be impossible to reliably identify such persons; terms like "heinous" or "atrocious" are liberally construed by judges and juries, and hardened offenders are frequently wise enough to plea bargain and thus obtain prison terms instead of death sentences. Moreover, the closer one gets to murderers whose acts approach the unemotional calculation of state-sanctioned killing, the more likely it is that serious mental health problems are indicated. Capital punishment is then inapplicable because the subject of punishment must freely choose his crime and hence deserve his punishment, and the mentally impaired offender cannot rightly be said to exercise free choice. It is doubtful, in any event, that the state should seek to imitate the cruelty of some criminals in order to afford them justice.

The suffering of prisoners on death row has significant implications for the justice of the death penalty. As a practical matter, the administration of capital punishment involves torture; any justification of capital punishment must therefore include a justification for torturing capital offenders, not simply taking their lives. It is difficult to envision any such justification. Certainly none is provided in the voluminous philosophical or legal literatures on punishment or in the U.S. Constitution, which expressly forbids the use of torture under the Eighth Amendment ban against cruel and unusual punishments. Even the philosopher Immanuel Kant, for whom *only* capital punishment would "satisfy the requirements of legal justice" in the case of murder, acknowledged that, to be just, "the death of the criminal must be kept entirely free of any maltreatment that would make an abomination of the humanity residing in the person suffering it."[104] The abomination of the prisoner's humanity, we now know, is part and parcel of the culture of harm that flowers with special vigor in isolated prison housing units like death row and is central to the dread evoked by the threat of execution; an execution that, as a seen by condemned prisoners, amounts to an impersonal state-sanctioned homicide.[105] The destructive personal impact of death row confinement in service of executions provides the basis for a complete moral argument in opposition to capital punishment.

It is my contention that no reform—however well intended, from housing condemned prisoners in regular maximum-security prisons (which often feature their own distinctive brutality) to reducing the rigors of death row in ways we have discussed in this book—can change the fundamental realities of the confining-and-killing process as they unfold in our prisons. Reforms matter, particularly to the condemned prisoners, but cruelty endures. Jamie Fellner, noted human rights authority, captured this point well:

> Even if those condemned to die have the same conditions of confinement as other prisoners (conditions that can be appalling in any event) or even if they are confined in "kinder, gentler" death rows, the cruelty of awaiting execution would remain. I see no way around the conundrum—being condemned by a court to die means being condemned to a painful period of waiting. From a human rights perspective, both are intolerable. [106]

The key and enduring point, Fellner argues, is this: "from a human rights perspective" both the penalty of death *and* the waiting in confinement under the threat of death are "intolerable."[107] Is solitary confinement under sentence of death uniquely cruel? Yes. Extensive social science research proves this point, a point developed at length in this book.[108] Is regular prison confinement generally less cruel than solitary confinement? Yes, but regular confinement, given all we know about the warehousing dynamics of prisons, is cruel as well. Is a "kinder, gentler" death row, such as embodied in the reform suggestions made in this book, likely to be less cruel than solitary confinement under sentence of death? Yes, but reformed death rows, given all we know about the distinctive dynamics of life under sentence of death—with the feelings of abandonment, vulnerability, and emotional emptiness that ensue—are still cruel.[109] With the death penalty, cruelty endures. Degrees of cruelty matter greatly to condemned prisoners, I want to reiterate. But from a moral and legal perspective, the essential point made by Fellner is that, even in the best of conditions available in the real world of modern prisons, "the cruelty of awaiting execution would remain."[110]

Imperfect Justice

Other aspects of the condemned prisoners' experience with the administration of capital punishment, particularly in the courts, suggest a related moral argument against the death penalty. The essence of this position is that an imperfect justice system operating in an imperfect world is not morally qualified to exact the ultimate punishment of death, which requires absolute guilt on the part of the offender and absolute innocence on the part of the society that stands in judgment of one of its own. Imperfections in the justice system, let alone in the larger society, were obvious to the condemned prisoners and served to underscore their beliefs about the injustice of both death row confinement and the death penalty.

The frailty of human beings and their judgments seems painfully apparent to condemned prisoners. Absolute judgments, they know, terminate lives that might be rehabilitated and allowed to make partial reparations for the harms they have caused. Though none of the prisoners spoke of having read Camus on the crucial link between the moral status of judges and the morality of their judgments, the intuitive validity of Camus' arguments would be apparent to them. They stand squarely on the moral terrain of which he writes.

> There are no just people—merely hearts more or less lacking in justice. Living at least allows us to discover this and to add to the sum of our actions a little of the good that will make up in part for the evil we have added to the world. Such a right to live, which allows a chance to make amends, is the natural right of every man, even the worst man. The lowest of criminals and the most upright of judges meet side by side, equally wretched in their solidarity. Without that right, moral life is utterly impossible. None among us is authorized to despair of a single man, except after his death, which transforms his life into destiny and then permits a definitive judgment. But pronouncing the definitive judgment before his death, decreeing the closing of accounts when the creditor is still alive, is no man's right. On this limit, at least, whoever judges absolutely condemns himself absolutely.[111]

Compare Camus' observations with those of a condemned prisoner recorded in the following interview excerpt. Once again there is a recognition of human fallibility—of the capacity to make mistakes, including lethal mistakes. There is also a faith in the possibility for change and reform inherent in every man—if only his fellow man would show tolerance and mercy. There is, finally, the belief that absolute judgments reflect man's arrogance and folly, and defile the judge more than the object of judgment.

I think about the execution. I question myself. I say, "Now are you that corrupt that you should be killed?" "You don't believe that you could go back out there into society and make some contribution? Do you feel that you are a wild man?" You know you are going to be killed. And the people say that you should be executed to death for the crime that you did, that to kill a man you have got to be stoned corrupt. You have got to go ahead and get rid of him because he ain't no good to himself and he ain't no good to nobody else . . . You think about it—I think about it all the time. I know I'm not that corrupt. I ain't crazy, you know. I say I know I ain't that corrupt to whereas I can't go around nobody unless I'm going to kill them, you know. As for me to say "Kill you," you have got to be mighty corrupt, you know. Because everybody can change. There's a chance to change for everybody, you know . . . I feel within the depths of our hearts that you can't show a court—a real court—where a man is that corrupt. I feel that court that sentences us to death is corrupt.

The collective wisdom of the condemned concerning the justice of the death penalty might be summarized as follows: absolute judgments require absolute guilt of the offender and absolute innocence of the society. To render a sentence of death—a cool, calculated, and irrevocable social judgment—demands no less than this.[112] The implication of a death sentence is that the offender deserves death because he is irredeemably corrupt and that society has the right to reach this verdict because it bears no responsibility for the offender's moral corruption or immoral actions. Society assumes a mantle of innocence; the capital offender, personifying evil, forfeits his humanity. Executions proceed with impunity. When would such conditions be met? Probably never, and surely not with today's capital offenders, who are invariably drawn from the ranks of the underprivileged and inadequate. Each and every one of these persons can point to mitigating circumstances that relieve them of full culpability for their crimes and partially implicate society in their actions.

To be sure, serious crime cannot be excused or minimized. To speak of mitigating circumstances is not to deny guilt, and to strive for a justice system based on mutual restitution and service is not to dismiss punishment as a response to crime. As a practical matter, justice systems must attempt to dispense justice, even though they may do so imperfectly, punitively, and sometimes inaccurately in the context of unjust societies. The defense for these anomalies may lie in balancing matters of equity, redress, and obligation. Fair procedures must be sought to minimize the likelihood of arbitrary harm at the hands of the law. Final judgments must be withheld so that room remains to correct errors or compensate losses. Some effort must be made to assess a person's overall debt to society in terms that reflect material benefits bestowed by the society (like wealth and education), rather than solely in terms of obligations incurred as a consequence of crime. The condemned prisoners' experiences, however, have indicated that the justice system too readily accepts guilt when street crime and criminals are involved; that it is biased against the poor, and especially poor people of color; and that it is susceptible to pressure for convictions in order to allay community fears. The total indebtedness of capital offenders to the society is taken for granted, even in the face of evidence that these men typically received little guidance, support, or even sustenance from the society that now stands in absolute judgment over them (see Chapter 2).

Condemned prisoners have few illusions about human nature or human institutions. They believe that the rubric of legal punishment does nothing to alter the inhumanity of the death sentence. A number of them contemplate suicide as their final response to the justice system, and indeed the suicide rate on death row is high.[113] In so doing, they reflect sentiments shared by every prisoner on death row.

> What we're up against is legalized killing. I mean, they give it a name, but I don't feel they have a right to do this. And judging from the attitudes of the people around here, they are more than anxious to strap somebody in that chair. So I feel that if I can deprive them of this, then in a way I've struck back . . . Suicide is just my way of depriving them of something that they lust for.

The tragedy is that these bitter sentiments reflect basic truths about capital punishment. What is capital punishment if not legal homicide? What is death row if it is not a repository for victims of state-sanctioned violence? Is this not a macabre and chilling enterprise, an affront to humanity sufficient to make suicide a rational rejoinder to one's keepers?

Some would respond that condemned prisoners deserve to die, that those who murder innocent men and women lose the right to live. Any added punishments undergone in the process of carrying out executions, such as those inflicted on death row, are considered unfortunate corollaries of the sometimes ugly and arduous task of doing justice. Now some murderers may in fact forfeit their right to live, though the pathways to death row we have reviewed in this book suggest that they would be few and far between. Arguments about the right to life, sometimes clear in principle, are inevitably murky and complex when one considers individual cases in the real world. In any event, no definitive account of this matter is sought in this book. *For even if some murderers do forfeit their right to live, they need not be put to death.*[114] There is no duty to take the lives thus forfeited in consequence of crime, particularly in light of the egregious failures of social and legal justice that occur regularly in our society. Indeed, the sparing of life in this context may constitute both a recognition of the awesome violence in which death row confinement and the death penalty implicate us all, and a modest refusal to seek perfect justice in an imperfect world.

Notes

1 Portions of this chapter are reprinted with permission, in modified form, from Johnson (2016).
2 On congregate solitary confinement death rows, executions rates are low. It would appear that prisoners on these death rows "no longer viewed death row as a place where they were going to die" (Yale Law School Report, 2018: 346).
3 As Jackson and Christian (2018: 218) note, it is telling that "Texas and Oklahoma have accounted for nearly half (45%) of all U.S. executions between 1977 and 2016 . . . Death row conditions in both prisons are similar. Texas and Oklahoma prisoners wait out their days under conditions that by comparison make the daily routine of a medieval monk festive." This observation applies to death rows in all high-execution states, with the exception of Missouri, which will be discussed later in this chapter.
4 Gatrell (1996); Harrington (2013).
5 See, for example, Spear (1845/1994); Harrington (2013).
6 Rare exceptions to this observation have received much attention from historians and criminologists. They make up a mythology of the "brave condemned" (Gatrell, 1996).
7 Spear (1845/1994: 50).
8 Johnson (1998); Christianson (2000).
9 Johnson and Davies (2014).
10 See generally, Johnson (1998).
11 Koestler (1945: 94).

12 It is likely they suffer something approximating "ethical loneliness," described by Stauffer (2015) as "the experience of having been abandoned by humanity compounded by the experience of not being heard."

13 Kohn (2009). Note that the subjects of Kohn's original and important work lived on death rows in states in which executions had not been carried out in years, in one case, decades.

14 Bastian, Denson, and Haslam (2013).

15 Johnson and Davies (2014: 668–669).

16 Death Penalty Information Center (2018).

17 Johnson and Davies (2014: 668).

18 Johnson and Davies (2014). See this source for severe examples of solitary confinement in death rows in the United States. States with less active death penalties, in which years or even decades may pass between executions, typically have confinement regimes that are less repressive. Noting, however, that some of these states still retain repressive regimes mimicking solitary confinement. Some offer what I have termed congregate solitary confinement, allowing condemned prisoners more time out of the cell and more human contact with other condemned prisoners but no contact with the larger prison, from which they are strictly isolated (examples at the time of this writing would include North Carolina, and Utah). See generally McGunigall-Smith (2004).

19 Johnson and Davies (2014: 669). See also Mann (2010) for a discussion on the negative effects of prolonged isolation on death row inmates and also the Human Rights Clinic (2017).

20 Aldape, Cooper, Haas, Hu, Hunter, and Shimizu (2016).

21 These strategies are used by condemned prisoners who grow in adversity on death row. See Kohn (2009) and (2012) for further discussion. Note that the subjects of Kohn's original and important work lived on death rows in states in which executions had not been carried out in years, in one case, decades. Growth may occur and follow these dynamics on high-execution state death rows, but I am not aware of research on the topic. I have maintained a somewhat abbreviated correspondence with two prisoners on Alabama's death row who appear to show signs of growth in adversity in ways consistent with Kohn's observations.

22 On February 22, 1980, the United States District Court for the Southern District of Alabama formally approved settlement of *Jacobs v. Bennett*, Civ. No. 78-309-H, the litigation for which this research was undertaken. The settlement provided, in part, for the following:

    1 The placement of a desk, stool, and shelf in death row cell.
    2 A handbook of regulations detailing the rules under which death row inmates will live as they await the outcome of appeals.
    3 A law library solely for use by death row inmates.
    4 Abolition of past restrictions on who may visit the inmates.
    5 An exercise period in which inmates will be allowed to exercise with one or more of the other death row inmates. The warden of the prison will determine any restrictions necessary to ensure safety under this new procedure.

    Additionally, death row inmates will receive a thorough physical examination upon entering death row, and they will be entitled to the same health care rights as those granted to the general prison population under a 1976 federal court order. The settlement agreement affords inmates greater access to items in the prison store, and allows them one two-hour "contact visit" each week, as opposed to past procedures allowing one "contact visit" each month. Correspondence with some of the prisoners subsequent to the settlement indicated that there was much official resistance to implementing these changes. In particular, as I learned during a visit to Holman prison in the summer of 2018, group exercise periods were difficult to obtain. Group exercise periods are still difficult to obtain due to chronic staff shortages.

23 The prison administrators might be reminded that these persons may represent a supply of volunteers for programs involving condemned prisoners.

24 Frankl (1977).

25 One such program, entitled "Living Until Death: A Program of Service and Research for the Terminally III," might be adaptable to death row. See Carey (1975).

26 Kohn (2009: 218–227); Kohn (2012: 71–83).

27 Some condemned prisoners have had their cases overturned and have subsequently adjusted to life in the prison or the free world without resort to crime. We do not know much about the conditions of confinement

they endured, or how they coped or failed to cope with them, though the stays on death row in such cases tended to be short; nor do we know the ways these prisoners adjusted to the transition from death row to other settings. See generally Marquart and Sorensen (1989).

28 American Civil Liberties Union (ACLU) (2013: 6–7). It is worth reiterating the basic conditions of life on solitary death row regimes: Death row prisoners are housed alone in tiny cells, ranging from just 36 square feet to little more than 100 square feet. Most are the size of an average bathroom. Most cells generally contain a steel bed or concrete slab, steel toilet, and small utility table. The majority of death row prisoners eat alone in their cell, fed on trays inserted through a slot in the door. They also receive the majority of their medical and mental health care through these slots.

   "Face-to-face contact with another human being," the ACLU report concludes, "is rare." See also Hammer, Cody, Gerson, Greene and Mushlin (2002).

29 Johnson and Davies (2014).

30 May (2016).

31 Johnson and Davies (2014).

32 Blank and Jensen (2004: 51).

33 That impression is reinforced by the fact that there was a virtually unprecedented escape from Texas' congregate death row featuring a group of prisoners; that escape, which resulted in the installation of a solitary death row regime, is itself an indicator of the sort of failure of security that would allow predation of the sort described by Cook to thrive. Likewise, a group escape from Virginia's death row in 1984, then housed in a new facility considered escape-proof, was the product of failures of basic security. "An investigation determined that sloppiness among the prison staff had made the escape possible. The prison reviewed its practices and tightened up security" (Bovsun, 2015). Here, I know from interviews conducted years later on Virginia's death row, lax procedures made for a dangerous death row environment for vulnerable prisoners.

34 See Cunningham and Reidy (2018). As Cohen (2018: 94) has observed: "Death-sentenced inmates appear to be no more dangerous as a class than others. Accordingly, the conditions of their confinement should be dictated by their reception classification and subsequent conduct, subject to generally applicable constitutional limits on procedure, conditions, and duration."

35 For further discussion of the confinement of condemned prisoners in Missouri and also North Carolina and Colorado, which offer a similar congregate regime, see Aldape et al. (2016) and Yale Law School Report (2018). See also Cunningham, Reidy and Sorensen (2016: 185). For further discussion of the limits of maximum-security prisons as living environments, see Johnson, Rocheleau and Martin (2017). Robert Bohm, a noted death penalty authority, sees the Missouri's mainstreaming model as a viable alternative to death row that "fully integrates most death-sentenced inmates with non-death sentenced-inmates in the general prison population" (Robert Bohm, personal communication, June 2018).

36 Johnson (1998).

37 Johnson and Davies (2014: 669); see also Yale Law School Report (2018).

38 Ingle (2012). As an example, prisoners housed on North Carolina's comparatively congenial congregate death row, who are allowed in pod dayrooms from 7 am to 11 pm, are sharply restricted during the death watch. Once an execution date is set, a correctional administrator explained, "death-sentenced prisoners would be moved 3 to 7 days prior to the scheduled execution to the 'death watch' area of Central Prison. The single cells in the death-watch area each had a bed, lavatory, commode, and writing table. The prisoner, who spent the entire day in the cell except 15 minutes for a shower, had no contact with other prisoners" (Yale Law School Report, 2018: 334).

39 Ingle (2012).

40 For a discussion on modern execution teams, see Johnson (1998: 123–141).

41 Johnson and Miller (2012). It is significant that human "reason is an adaptation to the hyper-social niche humans have evolved for themselves" over the course of evolution (Mercier and Sperber quoted in Kolbert, 2017). For more detail, see Mercier and Sperber (2017).

42 Johnson (2014: 585). The notion that we are fundamentally social persons has been thoughtfully developed by Liberman (2013) and O'Donnell (2014).

43 Lewis Mumford (1944) cited in Johnson (1998: 205): "Man's nature is a self-surpassing and a self-transcending one . . . Hence, growth is part of our nature as a species."

44 For a discussion on an incentive structure based on the recognition of the innate human need for personal growth, see Ferguson (2014: 222–224). In Ferry (2011: 112–114): "[N]o essence predetermines it, no programme

can ever succeed in entirely hemming it in; no system can imprison it so absolutely that it cannot emancipate itself ... The human individual is free: endlessly improvable, and in no sense programmed by characteristics supposedly linked to race or gender." Prisons limit or impede growth, even under the best conditions. "At a fundamental level," observes O'Donnell (2018: 200), "prisons will always be dehumanizing, no matter how good the physical conditions or the relationships between prisoners and staff, because they curtail the individual's capacity to look ahead, to plan, to wonder, to project themselves into novel scenarios."

45 Johnson and Miller (2012: 112).
46 Johnson and Miller (2012: 113).
47 Johnson and Miller (2012: 113).
48 Mumford (1944); Reiman (1976). See generally Mumford (1944).
49 See generally Mumford (1944) quoted in Johnson (1998: 205).
50 Johnson (1998: 206).
51 Johnson (1998).
52 Rejali (2009: 554).
53 United Nations (1984).
54 Bergland (2014). See also Lieberman (2013). I am indebted to Fred Cohen (2018: 97), who reminds us that solid research across several disciplines establishes that "we are profoundly social beings" and, further, that "the importance of social connection is so strong that when rejected we feel pain in the same way we feel physical pain."
55 The experience of condemned prisoners seems to parallel that of persons who suffer from general anxiety disorder, with the difference being that their anxieties are triggered by widely shared perceptions of the environment (Bergland, 2014: 116). In the death row context, the essentially accurate perception that prisoners "are already doomed and forgotten," in the words of the Alabama death row prisoner interviewed for this book, translates into a life on the knife edge of dread. For further discussion, see Ingle (2012).
56 There are, to my knowledge, one or perhaps two prisoners who have physically resisted the execution process since the return of the modern death penalty with the 1977 execution of Gary Gilmore. Gilmore dropped his appeals and, in effect, volunteered to be executed. See *Gilmore v. Utah* (1977) for a description of Gilmore's opposition of others trying to intervene on his behalf). Over 10 percent of executions involve volunteers (Blume, 2005: 939–940). Oppressive death row conditions and the dreary prospect of a life sentence in the event that one's death penalty is overturned are factors that influence some, perhaps many of these decisions, as alluded to by Justice Breyer in *Glossip v Gross* (2015) when he observed: "given the negative effects of confinement and uncertainty, it is not surprising that many inmates volunteer to be executed, abandoning further appeals ... Nor is it surprising that many inmates consider, or commit, suicide." For further discussion, see Johnson (2014).
57 United Nations (1984).
58 United Nations (1984).
59 Rejali (2009: 554).
60 From Tracy (2016: n.p.): "Emotional abuse can happen to anyone at any time in their lives," which "can have devastating consequences on relationships and all those involved. Just because there is no physical mark doesn't mean the abuse isn't real and isn't a problem or even a crime in some countries."
61 Tracy (2016).
62 A report from the APA (2014: n.p.) states that, "Children who are emotionally abused and neglected face similar and sometimes worse mental health problems as children who are physically or sexually abused." The same holds for adults. Similarly, Tracy (2016: n.p.) contends: "Make no mistake about it; the effects of emotional abuse can be just as severe as those from physical abuse."
63 United Nations (1984).
64 Johnson (1998). As noted by the philosopher, Emmanuel Kant (2000: 368), persons should never be used as a means to and end but rather as ends in themselves who are possessed of intrinsic moral value: "For one man ought never to be dealt with merely as a means subservient to the purpose of another. He has a right to be protected from such ill-use by his in-born personality though he may be condemned to lose his civil personality."
65 Johnson (1998: 156).
66 Johnson (1998: 156).
67 Johnson (1998: 156). See generally Camus (1969).

68 Dolovich (2009: 890): "As the *Farmer* Court put it, '[t]he Eighth Amendment does not outlaw cruel and unusual "conditions"; it outlaws cruel and unusual "punishments."' And, the Court found, prison conditions not explicitly authorized by the statute or the sentencing judge qualify as punishment only if some prison official actually knew of and disregarded the risk of harm."

69 Dolovich (2009: 885–886): Noting how different factors must be considered when the prison conditions are challenged as being cruel and unusual, as opposed to challenging the death sentence itself.

70 Dolovich (2009: 881).

71 Dolovich (2009: 881).

72 Dolovich (2009: 881).

73 Dolovich (2009: 881).

74 Dolovich (2009: 881).

75 Dolovich (2009: 881).

76 Dolovich (2009: 882).

77 Dolovich (2009: 882).

78 Dolovich (2009: 881).

79 Dolovich (2009: 881): "[T]he state has an affirmative obligation to protect prisoners from serious physical and psychological harm."

80 Dolovich (2009: 892).

81 Dolovich (2009: 893).

82 As Cohen (2018: 97) has noted, "The basic human needs identified thus far by the Supreme Court are food, clothing, shelter, medical care, and reasonable safety." Missing among these needs is the profound human need for social interaction. Thus, "If we accept socialization as a basic human need, then its enforced deprivation should take its place in the Court's panoply of previously listed enforceable human needs."

83 Johnson (1998).

84 Johnson (1998); Jackson and Christian (2012).

85 Dolovich (2009: 898).

86 Dolovich (2009: 899). Emphasis added.

87 Dolovich (2009: 899).

88 Dolovich (2009: 915).

89 These hazards are noted by condemned prisoners at several junctures of this book and are subjected to careful analysis in Bohm (2015).

90 Ingle (2012: 25) reports a vivid case of trauma on the threshold of execution. The prisoner lived in constant anxiety evidenced in physical and psychological suffering described by a psychological professional as "complex post-traumatic stress disorder."

91 Dolovich (2009: 916).

92 Dolovich (2009: 916).

93 For further discussion, see McGunigall-Smith and Johnson (2008). Hinton (2018: 125) developed mental fantasies into an art form that allowed him hours, even days, of mental escape from the rigors of death row confinement. Hinton's travels did not appear to have a downside, but that may not be universally true. See O'Donnell (2014: 236) for a consideration of the limits of reverie as a coping strategy: "If it is allowed to wander too freely in reverie the mind may prove difficult to bring back on track."

94 For further discussion, see Des Pres (1977).

95 Dolovich (2009: 916).

96 Dolovich (2009: 921).

97 Dolovich (2009: 921).

98 Dolovich (2009: 931).

99 Dolovich (2009: 931).

100 Dolovich (2009: 931).

101 See generally Johnson (1998).

102 In making these assertions, I am drawing on a large body of research and theory. For a general review of these materials, see Johnson (1986) and Haritos-Fatouros (2003). There are lively debates in the area of institutional violence. Broadly speaking, one school of thought focuses on how one's conscience must be neutralized in order to carry out violence against a person who poses no immediate threat to one's welfare. Moral disengagement

and objectification of others are key considerations. This view, perhaps best exemplified in the work of Milgram (1963); Bandura, Ross, and Ross (1961); and Haney and Zimbardo (1998), separates objectification from dehumanization. See Bandura (1999) for a comprehensive review. Other scholars, like Haslam (2006), Bastian and Haslam (2010), and Haslam and Loughnan (2014), think of objectification as a species of dehumanization, which includes seeing the person as an object, or animal, or morally degraded creature outside the normal moral discourse or social community. Rafter (2016: 2215), in her seminal research on genocide, exemplifies the view that one's conscience must be neutralized to allow for the atrocities that are part and parcel of genocide:

> My answer to the "How could they do it?" question runs as follows: psychological mechanisms involved in moral disengagement lead to a temporary and selective shutdown in empathy and identification with others; and that shutdown leads to the objectification that enables individuals to commit genocide. This is the splitting process. First comes moral disengagement, then neutralization of empathy, and finally the objectification that makes victims seem like objects, things we can get rid of rather than individuals like ourselves.

Other scholars, like Fiske and Rai (2015) focus on institutional violence as an example of virtuous violence, which it to say, violence of which one should be proud, not ashamed. The challenge here is to neutralize repugnance to the often gory physical act of violence; the motivation to engage in violence is a largely settled matter. In the case of virtuous violence, persons believe they are doing good and feel obligated to carry out acts of violence. The agents of virtuous violence are committed followers of beliefs that justify the violence in which they engage. This does not mean that virtuous violence is easy. It isn't. Agents who inflict virtuous violence will likely be repelled by the acts of violence themselves, which often involve victims who beg, plead, collapse, or react with eerie stolidity or unseemly emotion when brutal pain is inflicted upon them. These reactions can be construed to validate the degraded status of the victims, but reactions to violence among victims are tangibly visible human reactions. It is one thing to embrace and, in one's work, validate an abstract belief and another to carry out a concrete act in violation of a flesh-and-blood individual. We are socialized to abhor violence and most of us do. Paradoxically, rising to the occasion to inflict virtuous violence can be one measure of commitment of the person carrying out such violence. Fiske and Rai (2015: 515) write: "Now, for the most part, people hate hurting others. It is extremely distressing to directly kill or injure another person face-to-face, no matter how socioculturally justified or legally obligatory it is . . . Like many other moral acts, killing or hurting others can be difficult, requiring training, social support and modeling, effort, practice, and experience before it becomes second nature. Few people become unambivalently dedicated to moral violence or do it easily, but that is true of many difficult moral practices other than violence—people often resist or fail to do what is morally required of them, even when they have no doubt about whether they should do it."

There is overlap in these perspectives. Whether one is a passively or reluctantly obedient participant or an actively engaged agent of violence, support for one's violence is helpful. This support may come from peers or authority figures or organizational structures. Authorizations from organizations to engage in violence, especially when embraced by one's peers, give permission and hence a degree of reassurance that one is in the right when one is called upon to use violence. Training and institutional routines can make violence more palatable, whether one thinks of the violence as virtuous or as a repugnant but necessary evil. Dehumanization—socialization or training that allows actors to see the target of violence as an object, animal, or morally degraded creature—can create a motive for violence (protection from dangerous, animal-like others) or can smooth the way to work in service of what one takes to be virtuous beliefs (cleansing the world of others who would contaminate it or make others unsafe). Persons who are ridding the world of dangerous and unregenerate criminals in service of legal and other institutions they trust presumably need less to mute their conscience than they would under other circumstances. None of the execution team officers I interviewed expressed guilt, remorse, or regret, at least before, during, or after the executions they conducted and that I studied firsthand (Johnson, 1998). Socialization and training of persons engaged in institutional violence is meant to indoctrinate them in the value of what they do. To the degree persons have doubts about the virtue of the enterprise, some degree of neutralization of conscience may be sought by the individual or promoted by the organization.

103 Camus (1969: 205).
104 Kant (1973: 36). Pushing this point to its limits, Kupers (2018: 48) maintains that even the worst of the worst—for example, an unrepentant multiple murderer who says he will kill again—"has the right to be confined in decent surroundings and be permitted meaningful social contacts and activities." People can do monstrous things but they remain human beings.

105 Haney (2003).
106 Fellner (2018: xvii).
107 Fellner (2018: xxi).
108 Kupers (2018: 47), who has conducted seminal research on solitary confinement, makes this point succinctly: "Execution is the ultimate cruel punishment. But then there is solitary confinement. Adding a long stint in solitary confinement before execution certainly makes life significantly more miserable for the condemned."
109 Tellingly, a prisoner living on a comparatively congenial congregate solitary confinement death row described his life under sentence of death as "an endless sorrow and hurt that's refused to heal," leaving him feeling "like a dog about to be euthanized" (May, 2017).
110 Fellner (2018: xvii)
111 Camus (1969: 221): The human basis of social institutions is intentionally distorted by some, who argue that their very imperfections must be shielded by a cloak of false majesty. Perversely, the death penalty is advanced as a means of securing popular support for the fiction that law and government are grounded in an immutable moral order. For example, "Capital punishment . . . serves to remind us of the majesty of the moral order that is embodied in our law and of the terrible consequence of its breach. The law must not be understood to be merely statute that we enact or repeal at our will and obey or disobey at our convenience, especially not the criminal law. Wherever law is regarded as merely statutory, men will soon enough disobey it, and they will learn how to do so without any inconvenience to themselves. The criminal law must possess a dignity far beyond that possessed by mere statutory enactment or utilitarian and self-interested calculation; the most powerful means we have to give it that dignity is to authorize it to impose the ultimate penalty." Thankfully, "only a relatively few executions are required to enhance the dignity of the criminal law" (Berns, 1979: 183).
112 Life and death decisions necessarily made in the heat of the moment, such as by police officers effecting an arrest of an armed and dangerous suspect or by soldiers or citizens engaged in wartime combat, do not fall into this category when the elements of deliberation and choice are absent, or when the exercise of deliberation or choice would be unduly dangerous. Policemen sometimes have no choice but to fire their weapons in self-defense. Soldiers, similarly, must defend themselves when under attack, and sometimes must launch attacks and counterattacks if they are to carry out their mandate as soldiers. Citizens in time of war sometimes must look to their own lives, even if this requires them to kill invading enemies. None of these extenuating circumstances applies in the case of sentencing criminals. There is always a safe alternative to the death penalty in our perennial war against crime and criminals, namely, a natural life sentence.
113 Tartaro and Lester (2016) found that between 1978 and 2010, with the exception of two years, the suicide rate on death row was higher than the general population and higher every year when compared to the national average.
114 Bedau (1980: 149).

References

Aldape, C., Cooper, R., Haas, K., Hu, A., Hunter, J., & Shimizu, S. (2016). *Rethinking "death row": Variations in the housing of individuals sentenced to death*. New Haven, CT: The Arthur Liman Public Interest Program: Yale Law School. Retrieved from https://law.yale.edu/system/files/documents/pdf/Liman/deathrow_reportfinal.pdf.

American Civil Liberties Union. (2013). *A death before dying: Solitary confinement on death row*. New York. Retrieved from www.aclu.org/sites/default/files/field_document/deathbeforedying-report.pdf.

American Psychological Association. (2014, October 8). *Childhood psychological abuse as harmful as sexual or physical abuse*. Washington, DC. Retrieved from www.apa.org/news/press/releases/2014/10/psychological-abuse.aspx.

Bandura, A. (1999). Moral disengagement in the perpetuation of inhumanities. *Personality and Social Psychology Review*, *3*, 193–209.

Bandura, A., Ross, D., & Ross, S. A. (1961). Transmission of aggression through imitation of aggressive models. *Journal of Abnormal and Social Psychology*, *63*, 575–582.

Bastian, B., Denson, T. F., & Haslam, N. (2013). The roles of dehumanization and moral outrage in retributive justice. *PLoS ONE*, *8*(4), 1–10.

Bastian, B., & Haslam, N. (2010). Excluded from humanity: The dehumanizing effects of social ostracism. *Journal of Experimental Social Psychology*, *46*(1), 107–113.

Bedau, H. (1980). Capital punishment. In T. Regan (Ed.), *Matters of life and death*. New York: Random House.

Bergland, C. (2014, March 3). The neuroscience of social pain. *Psychology Today*. Retrieved from www.psychologytoday.com/blog/the-athletes-way/201403/the-neuroscience-social-pain.

Berns, W. (1979). *For capital punishment: Crime and the morality of the death penalty*. New York: Basic Books.

Blank, J., & Jensen, E. (2004). *The exonerated: A play* (1st ed.). New York: Farrar, Straus, & Giroux.

Blume, J. H. (2005). Killing the willing: "Volunteers," suicide, and competency. *Michigan Law Review, 103*, 939–1009.

Bohm, R. (2015). *DeathQuest: An introduction to the theory and practice of capital punishment in the United States* (4th ed.). New York: Routledge.

Bovsun, M. (2015, June 14). Mecklenburg six: How death row inmates busted out of prison that was considered "escape-proof." *New York Daily News*. Retrieved from www.nydailynews.com/news/crime/prison-serving-time-hell-article-1.2256866.

Camus, A. (1969). *Resistance, rebellion and death: Essays*. New York: Knopf.

Carey, R. (1975). Living until death: A program of service and research for the terminally ill. In E. Kubler-Ross (Ed.), *Death: The final stage of growth* (pp. 75–86). Englewood Cliffs, NJ: Prentice-Hall.

Christianson, S. (2000). *Condemned: Inside the Sing Sing death house*. New York: New York University Press.

Cohen, F. (2018). Death row solitary confinement and constitutional considerations. In H. Toch, J. R. Acker, & V. M. Bonventre (Eds.), *Living on death row: The psychology of waiting to die* (pp. 93–128). Washington, DC: American Psychological Association.

Cunningham, M. D., Reidy, T. J., & Sorensen, J. R. (2016). Wasted resources and gratuitous suffering: The failure of a security rationale for death row. *Psychology, Public Policy, and Law, 22*(2), 185–199.

Cunningham, M. D., & Reidy, T. (2018). The failure of a security rationale for death row. In H. Toch, J. R. Acker, & V. M. Bonventre (Eds.), *Living on death row: The psychology of waiting to die* (pp. 129–159). Washington, DC: American Psychological Association.

Death Penalty Information Center. (2018, April 20). *Number of executions by state and region since 1976*. Retrieved from www.deathpenaltyinfo.org/number-executions-state-and-region-1976.

Des Pres, R. (1977). *The survivor: An anatomy of life in the death camps*. New York: Oxford University Press.

Dolovich, S. (2009). Cruelty, prison conditions, and the Eighth Amendment. *New York University Law Review, 84*(4), 881–979.

Fellner, J. (2018). Foreword. In H. Toch, J. R. Acker, & V. M. Bonventre (Eds.), *Living on death row: The psychology of waiting to die* (pp. xvii–xxii). Washington, DC: American Psychological Association.

Ferguson, R. A. (2014). *Inferno: An anatomy of American punishment*. Cambridge, MA: Harvard University Press.

Ferry, L. (2011). *A brief history of thought: A philosophical guide to living*. New York: Harper Perennial.

Fiske, A., & Rai, T. S. (2015). *Virtuous violence: Hurting and killing to create, sustain, end, and honor social relationships*. Cambridge, UK: Cambridge University Press.

Frankl, V. (1977). *Man's search for meaning*. New York: Pocket Book.

Gatrell, V. A. C. (1996). *The hanging tree: Execution and the English people 1770–1868*. Oxford: Oxford University Press.

Gilmore v. Utah, 429 U.S. 1012, 1013–1014 (1977). (Burger, C. J., concurring).

Glossip v. Gross, 135 S. Ct. 2726, 2766 (2015). (Breyer, J., dissenting).

Hammer, D. S. Cody, A. C., Gerson, R. B., Greene, N. L., & Mushlin, M. B. (2002). Dying twice: Conditions on New York's death row. *Pace Law Review, 22*(2), 347–383.

Haney, C. (2003). Mental health issues in long-term solitary and "supermax" confinement. *Crime & Delinquency, 49*(1), 124–156.

Haney, C., & Zimbardo, P. (1998). The past and future of US prison policy: Twenty-five years after the Stanford Prison experiment. *American Psychologist, 53*(7), 709–727.

Haritos-Fatouros, M. (2003). *The psychological origins of institutionalized violence*. New York: Routledge.

Harrington, J. F. (2013). *The faithful executioner: Life and death, honor and shame in the turbulent sixteenth century*. New York: Farrar, Straus, & Giroux.

Haslam, N. (2006). Dehumanization: An integrative review. *Personality and Social Psychology Review*, *10*(3), 252–264.

Haslam, N., & Loughnan, S. (2014). Dehumanization and infrahumanization. *Annual Review of Psychology*, *65*, 399–423.

Hinton, A. R. (with Hardin, L. L.) (2018). *The sun does shine: How I found life and freedom on death row*. New York: St. Martin's Press.

Human Rights Clinic at the University of Texas School of Law. (2017). *Designed to break you: Human rights violations on Texas' death row*. Austin, TX: University of Texas School of Law. Retrieved from https://law.utexas.edu/wp-content/uploads/sites/11/2017/04/2017-HRC-DesignedToBreakYou-Report.pdf.

Ingle, J. B. (2012). *The inferno: A southern morality tale*. Nashville, TN: Westview Press.

Jackson, B., & Christian, D. (2012). *In this timeless time: Living and dying on death row in America*. Chapel Hill, NC: University of North Carolina Press.

Jackson, B., & Christian, D. (2018). Time on death row. In H. Toch, J. R. Acker, & V. M. Bonventre (Eds.), *Living on death row: The psychology of waiting to die* (pp. 213–225). Washington, DC: American Psychological Association.

Johnson, R. (1986). Institutions and the promotion of violence. In A. Campbell & J. J. Gibbs (Eds.), *Violent transactions: The limits of personality* (pp. 181–205). Oxford: Blackwell.

Johnson, R. (1998). *Death work: A study of the modern execution process* (2nd ed.). Belmont, CA: Wadsworth.

Johnson, R. (2014). Reflections on the death penalty: Human rights, human dignity, and dehumanization in the death house. *Seattle Journal of Social Justice*, *13*(2), 582–598.

Johnson, R. (2016). Solitary confinement until death by state-sponsored homicide: An Eighth amendment assessment of the modern execution process. *Washington & Lee Law Review*, *73*(3), 1213–1242.

Johnson, R., & Davies, H. (2014). Life under sentence of death: Historical and contemporary perspectives. In J. R. Acker, R. M. Bohm, & C. S. Lanier (Eds.), *America's experiment with capital punishment: Reflections on the past, present, and future of the ultimate penal sanction* (3rd ed., pp. 661–685). Durham, NC: Carolina Academic Press.

Johnson, R., & Miller, C. (2012). An Eighth Amendment analysis of juvenile life without parole: Extending Graham to all juvenile offenders. *University of Maryland Law Journal of Race, Religion, Gender, and Class*, *12*, 101–112.

Johnson, R., Rocheleau, A. M., & Martin, A. B. (2017). *Hard time: A fresh look at understanding and reforming the prison*. New York: Wiley.

Kant, I. (1973). The right to punish. In J. Murphy (Ed.), *Punishment and rehabilitation* (pp. 35–39). Belmont, CA: Wadsworth.

Kant, I. (2000). The philosophy of law. In L. Pojman (Ed.), *Life and death: A reader in moral problems* (2nd ed., pp. 368–370). Belmont, CA: Wadsworth.

Kolbert, E. (2017, February 27). Why facts don't change our minds. *The New Yorker*. Retrieved from www.newuorker.com/magazine/2017/02/27/why-facts-dont-change-our-minds.

Koestler, A. (1945). *The yogi and the commissar*. New York: Macmillan.

Kohn, T. (2009). Waiting on death row. In G. Hage (Ed.), *Waiting* (pp. 218–227). Melbourne, Australia: University of Melbourne Press.

Kohn, T. (2012). Crafting selves on death row. In D. Davies & C. Park (Eds.), *Emotion, identity, and death: Mortality across disciplines* (pp. 71–83). London: Ashgate.

Kupers, T. A. (2018). Waiting alone to die. In H. Toch, J. R. Acker, & V. M. Bonventure (Eds.), *Living on death row: The psychology of waiting to die* (pp. 47–69). Washington, DC: American Press Association.

Liberman, M. (2013). *Social: Why we our brains are wired to connect*. New York: Crown.

Mann, D. (2010, November 10). Solitary men. *Texas Observer*. Retrieved from www.texasobserver.org/solitary-men.

Marquart, J. W., & Sorensen, J. R. (1989). A national study of the Furman-commuted inmates: Assessing the threat to society from capital offenders. *Loyola of Los Angeles Law Review*, *23*(5), 5–28.

May, L. (2016, October 30). Prison is time. *Life Lines Collective*. Retrieved from https://lifelines.is.

May, L. (2017, April 16). Highrise, part two. *Life Lines Collective*. Retrieved from https://lifelines.is.

McGunigall-Smith, S. (2004). *Men of a thousand days: Death-sentenced inmates at Utah State Prison* (Unpublished doctoral dissertation). University of Wales, Bangor.

McGunigall-Smith, S., & Johnson, R. (2008). Escape from death row: A study of tripping as an individual adjustment strategy among death row inmates. *Pierce Law Review, 6*, 536–545.

Mercier, H., & Sperber, D. (2017). *The enigma of reason.* Cambridge, MA: Harvard University Press.

Milgram, S. (1963). Behavioral study of obedience. *Journal of Abnormal and Social Psychology, 67*, 371–378.

Mumford, L. (1944). *The condition of man.* New York: Harcourt, Brace, & Co.

O'Donnell, I. (2014). *Prisoners, solitude, and time.* Oxford: Oxford University Press.

O'Donnell, I. (2018). Psychological survival in isolation: Tussling with time on death row. In H. Tock, J. R. Acker, & V. M. Bonventre (Eds.), *Living on death row: The psychology of waiting to die* (pp. 193–211). Washington, DC: American Psychological Association.

Rafter, N. (2016). *The crime of all crimes: Toward a criminology of genocide* (Kindle ed.). New York: New York University Press.

Reiman, J. H. (1976). Privacy, intimacy, and personhood. *Philosophy and Public Affairs, 6*(1), 26–44.

Rejali, D. (2009). *Torture and democracy.* Princeton, NJ: Princeton University Press.

Spear, C. (1845/1994). *Essays on the punishment of death.* Littleton, CO: Fred B. Rothman.

Stauffer, J. (2015). *Ethical loneliness: The injustice of not being heard.* New York: Columbia University Press.

Tartaro, C., & Lester, D. (2016). Suicide on death row. *Journal of Forensic Sciences, 61*(6), 1656–1659.

Tracy, N. (2016, May 26). Emotional abuse: Definitions, signs, symptoms, examples. *Healthy Place.* Retrieved from www.healthyplace.com/abuse/emotional-psychological-abuse/emotional-abuse-definitions-signs-symptoms-examples.

United Nations. (1984, December 10). General Assembly Resolution 39/46. Convention against torture and other cruel, inhuman or degrading treatment or punishment. Retrieved from www.un.org/documents/ga/res/39/a39r046.htm.

Yale Law School Report. (2018). Appendix: Rethinking death row: Variations in the housing of individuals sentenced to death. In H. Toch, J. R. Acker, & V. M. Bonventre (Eds.), *Living on death row: The psychology of waiting to die* (pp. 331–357). Washington, DC: American Psychological Association.

AFTERWORD

Even after several decades of "tough on crime" media sensationalism, political posturing, and punitive lawmaking, much of American society remains deeply ambivalent about many forms of state-sanctioned punishment, especially capital punishment. The nation embraces punitive toughness overall, and in some quarters, citizens even seem to revel in it, but most do not much like getting close to it or even looking at it. Justice Kennedy once wrote that there is a "hidden world of punishment" that would shock most citizens who encountered it close up.[1] But, of course, they rarely do, and that is by design. In fact, our entire system of state-sanctioned punishment is geographically and architecturally engineered to prevent that from happening. Except for the relatively small number of unfortunate people who are actually incarcerated—and even in the era of mass incarceration, unless you are a person of color, only a small percent of the population in the United States is—almost no one else has direct access to the actual sites where punishment is meted out. Our system of punishment is not only a "hidden world" but a kind of abstraction, about which there are vehement debates—whether we administer "too much" or "too little"—that take place largely between people who really know nothing about it.

One might think that capital punishment would be an exception to that. After all, understanding the "pains of imprisonment" more generally requires an act of empathy. One has to actually conjure and contemplate what it might feel like to live around-the-clock, for years on end, inside a cramped and deprived prison cell, afforded few if any of the freedoms most people reflexively take for granted. But capital punishment—extinguishing the one thing we all naturally and intuitively hold sacred, our very life—is something it might seem that anyone could quickly grasp. The profound weight and magnitude of such a thing ought to give most respectable people pause. And yet it does not. It turns out that a large number of citizens (even those who intellectually oppose capital punishment) do not think much about the true nature of the process by which the state carefully orchestrates and then carries out the execution of one of its citizens. They think even less about the agonizing and bizarre existence that condemned prisoners are subjected to in the years or decades between their death sentence and ultimate execution. However, anyone who reads Robert Johnson's compelling book will be jarred into a deeper and more painfully conscious understanding of the terrible mechanics that are set in motion when someone is condemned to die in the United States.

Because Johnson does such a masterful job, and covers so many aspects of the topic so well, it is difficult to know what to add to his compelling analysis of life on death row. Indeed, in his succinct but nuanced and insightful account of "the bare essentials of life under a sentence of death," Johnson manages to touch on virtually every important dimension of this strange anomaly in American corrections—the place where our legal system keeps prisoners in a cruel kind of suspended animation, one where they are simultaneously hoping to continue to live but waiting to be killed. His writing is eloquent yet brutally honest and accessible. And, even though his direct observations and interviews were conducted decades ago, I can attest to the fact that they are grimly accurate today as they were when he originally made them. Aside from the fact that the electric chair that was in fashion when Johnson did his research on Alabama's death row has been replaced by the lethal injection gurney, in the nation's never-ending quest to make executions appear to be something other than just killing, little else has changed.

The relative stability and generic nature of conditions on death rows around the country stem largely from the fact that there is a certain insurmountable internal logic to the "machinery of death" that, as Justice Blackmun once said, admits to little more than an ultimately pointless kind of "tinkering."[2] Of course, there are all sorts of things that could and should be done to make these places somewhat more humane, and less needlessly painful. Johnson admirably outlines many of them. But few prison systems have undertaken these modest reforms. And so, despite Johnson's eminently reasonable proposals, his final judgment, that death rows, "even the best of them" represent "human warehouses that impose a regime of confinement that amounts to torture," is difficult to refute.

The insurmountable internal logic that governs the machinery of death stems in part from the irresolvable psychological tension that is at the heart of our system of capital punishment. Treating condemned prisoners more humanely, even in the limited way that non-death sentenced prisoners are treated "better," would force us to acknowledge that they are full-fledged human beings. But this in turn would lay bare the true nature of the task at hand—eventually putting actual persons to death. If the state is going to methodically undertake actions that violate our society's most basic and widely agreed upon ethical, moral, and religious norm—against taking the life of another—then certain cruel deceptions must follow. One of them is that the place where condemned prisoners are housed before they are put to death must be designed to keep prisoners "alive" but not really "living." Dehumanization, in the fullest sense of the term, is not an unfortunate by-product of some other, overarching penological purpose, it is the purpose. So death rows in the United States do not vary much, over time or between places. As grotesque as capital punishment is—so grotesque that most civilized nations no longer engage in it—many people have observed that it is made all the more inhumane by the horribly deprived conditions under which condemned prisoners are forced to live, many of them for decades on end. Johnson's thick descriptions of the Alabama condemned row certainly buttress this conclusion.

Among the many moving themes that Johnson has so effectively weaved together throughout his book, there are several that I want to underscore. The first is one that I have already alluded to—the moving way that Johnson depicts the depth of the abject isolation and deprivation to which death row prisoners are subjected. Condemned prisoners in the United States now spend on average more than a decade confined on death row, as they and their lawyers pursue all remaining avenues of appeal and await sometimes long-delayed rulings from the courts. Here, too, the nation's ambivalence about capital punishment plays a role. State officials and citizens in general no longer clamor as loudly or vehemently for a pound of flesh as they did just a few decades ago. In my home state, California, the electorate was unwilling to completely abandon capital punishment in several recent statewide referenda but few citizens express much urgency about or appetite for having executions actually resumed. The state has not executed anyone in a dozen years and the number of prisoners on San Quentin's death row exceeds 750. Californians, at least, seem content to have the death penalty but not really use it.

In addition to the agony of such long and uncertain periods of waiting to be killed, death rows throughout the country subject prisoners to exceedingly harsh forms of social and material deprivation. Alabama's death row where Johnson's study was conducted is located inside a large administrative segregation building on the grounds of the notorious Holman Prison. The entire building is still operated as an extraordinarily dehumanizing and deprived isolation unit, where condemned prisoners are locked in their cells nearly around-the-clock. The day-to-day routine to which they are subjected is, as Johnson accurately describes it, is "something close to unadulterated solitary confinement." When I recently toured the larger segregation unit, in conjunction with a statewide lawsuit over unconstitutional conditions of confinement generally, I described it as resembling nothing so much as bedlam and unlike anything I had seen in many, many years of doing such work. The death row unit is a smaller section situated inside this one. It is literally a prison within a prison within a prison.

This setting is evocatively described in Johnson's narrative—condemned prisoners live in cells that "are narrow, dark, and close, and without amenities." Because death row prisoners are kept in isolation, they live in these cells, where they eat, sleep, and defecate. As masterful a writer as Johnson is, even he cannot quite recreate the heavy smell and dank atmosphere of a small cell in which someone is forced to live for virtually all of their life. There is a heaviness to it that feels—unscientifically, I readily admit— part biochemical and part spiritual, as though there is physical substance in the air that is produced by the suffering that accumulates there.

The fact that death row prisoners in many states are kept in solitary confinement is not only needlessly cruel, and dangerous to their mental health, but also reflects the state's investment in maintaining their despised and degraded status. Because these men are not "worthy of living" they are not worthy of being afforded a humane existence. To be sure, there is no actual penological justification for the blanket isolation of condemned prisoners; as a rule, they maintain much better disciplinary records than prisoners in general. As I suggested above, this practice is motivated by something more psychologically sinister than merely imposing extra deprivation, as a kind of extra punishment for those who have committed the worst crimes. Instead, I believe that prison systems deny death-sentenced prisoners meaningful contact with others because this is the only hope that the prisoners have of maintaining a remotely meaningful life. It is as though the cruel prison policies that are applied to death-sentenced prisoners are explicitly designed to prevent them from truly living in order to facilitate the final act of taking what remains of their life away.

Thus, in addition to the solitary confinement regimes that are internally imposed, these environments are structured and operated in such a way that they impede even minimal contact with the outside world. Visitation routines are made so inhospitable for visitors that, even if they do not complain, prisoners are aware of the inconvenience, the implied disrespect, the bureaucratic and security-related measures (that not infrequently can turn into what feels like harassment). So, there may come a time when death-sentenced prisoners begin to discourage family members and friends from coming. And when even this vicarious connection to the outside world falters, their grip on a viable, sustaining social identity can begin to slip as well. The "living death" Johnson encountered in Alabama's condemned row is similar to the "social death" that I have documented in many long-term solitary confinement units throughout the United States. That is, the condemned prisoner's long-term isolation—"being cut off, abandoned, forgotten, even dead"—can lead to a kind of "social death," lived in, as Johnson says, a kind of "grave for the living." Indeed, when prisoners get to the point where they begin to think, "why don't I just get it all over with, you know," they have reached exactly the point that at least some members of the prison staff would like them to reach.

Johnson also very effectively depicts the daily struggle that many of the death-sentenced prisoners that he interviewed engage in to maintain their humanity and sanity in the face of the systematic dehumanization and life under the shadow of death to which they are subjected. In the course of his moving accounts, he underscores the disjuncture between the sensationalistic and demonizing public and media portrayals of persons who have been convicted of capital murder and sentenced to die, on the one hand, and the mundane, basic, undeniable humanity of the prisoners themselves, on the other. The disjuncture does not necessarily pertain to what they have done—acts that are depicted as, and typically are, truly heinous—but to the persons who have committed them. Bryan Stevenson has cautioned us against judging persons on the basis of the worst thing they have ever done, and Johnson's interviews remind us why. He is careful to put their lives "in context" and to acknowledge the traumatic paths marked by deprivation and abuse that led the men he interviewed to their terrible acts and ultimately to the terrible place where they are now confined. The "grim biographies" he recounts go a long way in explaining (albeit not excusing) the violence in which they have engaged. This is precisely the kind of social historical context that is virtually always ignored in media accounts of capital crimes that are used to terrify the public by portraying the perpetrators of capital crime as little more than monsters. But in the course of the explanatory context Johnson provides, he gives the death-sentenced prisoners voice and personhood, so we hear them and feel them as the sentient, striving beings they are, different, deeper, and far more complex than the one-dimensional fearsome figures they are typically made out to be.

Finally, there is the tension that develops among and within members of the correctional staff who must maintain an ultimately untenable psychological balance between overseeing and administering to death-sentenced prisoners, treating them as if they are not fully human (although they most certainly and unmistakably are), and ultimately participating in the process of taking their lives. After all of the political grandstanding has run its course, the media exploitation served its purpose, and the public outcry over their original crime has died down, many years after the death sentences were imposed, the time will come when a group of state employees will be required to orchestrate the unthinkable. There are many truly dirty jobs in our society, ones that people unfortunately find themselves forced to undertake, sometimes out of sheer necessity or a misguided sense of duty, but none is worse than this one. Johnson's thoughtful and nuanced narrative reminds us of the lengths to which correctional staff must go to maintain emotional distance in whatever ways they can, lest the ugly reality of what it is they have agreed to do comes crashing through. Yet it is likely that the aftermath of participating in an execution takes a terrible psychological toll. We know that even indirect involvement in the act of killing has a profound psychosocial impact on combat veterans and can inflict long-lasting "moral injuries" on them.[3] The psychic costs incurred by death row staff and execution team members, whose contact with death-sentenced prisoners is more prolonged and intimate, and the purpose of whose work is increasingly regarded as far more questionable and controversial in our society, must be at least as great.

I remain convinced that if more people in our society understood the true nature of the death-sentencing process in our society—how it actually operates and what it necessarily entails—and came to terms with, as Camus said,[4] what the death penalty "really is," as opposed to the "padded words," myth, and misinformation typically used to depict it, then the practice would have ended a long time ago. Robert Johnson's extraordinary book brings us much closer to that enlightened understanding.

Craig Haney
Distinguished Professor of Psychology
University of California Presidential Chair, 2015–2018

Notes

1 Kennedy (2003).
2 *Callins v. Collins* (1994).
3 For a review, see the Moral Injury Project (2018).
4 Camus (1995: 173).

References

Callins v. Collins, 510 U.S. 1141 (1994). (Blackmun, H., dissenting).
Camus, A. (1995). *Resistance, rebellion and death: Essays.* New York: Knopf.
Kennedy, A. M. (2003, August 9). *Speech at the American Bar Association annual meeting.* Washington, DC. Retrieved from www.supremecourt.gov/publicinfo/speeches/sp_08-09-03.html.
The Moral Injury Project. (2018). What is moral injury? Syracuse University. Retrieved from http://moralinjury project.syr.edu/about-moral-injury.

BURNT OFFERINGS*

There
in the dank basement
of the aging prison
home to the chair

death
the bitter scent
of burnt offerings
lingers in the air

a haunting brew
of mildew, flesh, and fear

the chair is gone
(the latest reform)
the smell lives on.

Robert Johnson

Note

* An earlier version of this poem, with art by Jennifer Adger, appears in the journal *Crime Media Culture* (2007) 3(1): 138.

INDEX